Bertolt Brecht

Dialectics, Poetry, Politics

Peter Brooker

Routledge REVIVALS
Routledge
Taylor & Francis Group

First published in 1988
by Croom Helm

This edition first published in 2017 by Routledge
2 Park Square, Milton Park, Abingdon, Oxon, OX14 4RN
and by Routledge
711 Third Avenue, New York, NY 10017

Routledge is an imprint of the Taylor & Francis Group, an informa business

Publisher's Note
The publisher has gone to great lengths to ensure the quality of this reprint but points out that some imperfections in the original copies may be apparent.

Disclaimer
The publisher has made every effort to trace copyright holders and welcomes correspondence from those they have been unable to contact.

A Library of Congress record exists under LC control number: 8727608

ISBN 13: 978-1-138-24512-9 (hbk)
ISBN 13: 978-1-315-27633-5 (ebk)
ISBN 13: 978-1-138-24514-3 (pbk)

Routledge Revivals

Bertolt Brecht

First published in 1988, this book argues against received accounts to reclaim Brecht's emphasis on his self-described 'dialectical theatre'. It firstly re-examines the concepts of *Gestus* and *Verfremdung*, and their realisation in Brecht's poetry, in terms of his attempt to consciously apply the methods of dialectical materialism to art and cultural practice. The author also takes issue with the customary view of Brecht's career and politics which sees him as compromising either with Communist party dogma or bourgeois aesthetics — finding developing parallels between Brecht's own political and artistic thought, and the critical dialectics of Marx, Lenin and Mao. This development is examined in later chapters via the early and late plays, *The Measures Taken* and *Days of the Commune*, as well as in relation to Brecht's changed circumstances in the years of war-time exile and, subsequently, in post-war East Germany.

BERTOLT BRECHT

Dialectics, Poetry, Politics

PETER BROOKER

CROOM HELM
London • New York • Sydney

Croom Helm Ltd, Provident House,
Burrell Row, Beckenham, Kent BR3 1AT
Croom Helm Australia, 44-50 Waterloo Road,
North Ryde, 2113, New South Wales

Published in the USA by
Croom Helm
in association with Methuen, Inc.
29 West 35th Street,
New York, NY 10001

British Library Cataloguing in Publication Data

Brooker, Peter
Bertolt Brecht: dialectics, poetry
politics.
1. Brecht, Bertolt — Poetic works
I. Title
831'.912 PT2603.R397Z/

ISBN 0-7099-5015-2

Library of Congress Cataloging-in-Publication Data

Brooker, Peter.
Bertolt Brecht: dialectics, poetry, politics.

Bibliography: p.
Includes index.
1. Brecht, Bertolt, 1898–1956 — Criticism and
interpretation. I. Title.
PT2603.R397Z58112 1987 832'.912 87-27608
ISBN 0-7099-5015-2

Printed and bound in Great Britain
by Billing & Sons Limited, Worcester.

For friends in different zones

'I drink to the incomplete'
Langevin in *Days of the Commune*

Contents

Acknowledgements

Terry Eagleton, Anthony Hosier and Peter Whitaker read parts of this book in earlier drafts, and I would like to thank them for their encouraging and very useful comments. Working on Brecht has emphasised that constructive criticism of the kind they offered is one of the many things which cannot be taken for granted.

I would like to record my thanks here also to the Leverhulme Trust, for the award of a six months fellowship in 1984-5, without which I would not have been able to begin this study, and to The British Academy for the award of a grant in the summer of 1986, which enabled me to travel to East Berlin to examine material in the Brecht Archive there. I am grateful also to those at the Archive for their generous and patient assistance.

I have quoted extensively from *Brecht on Theatre* and from *Poems. 1913-1956* and would like to thank Eyre Methuen for permission to do so. Thanks are due similarly to Surhkamp Verlag, Frankfurt am Main, for permission to quote from Brecht's works in German, to Lawrence and Wishart for permission to quote from the volume Marx, Engels, Lenin, *On Dialectical Materialism*, and to New Left Books for quotations from Walter Benjamin *Understanding Brecht*.

Abbreviations

The following abbreviations with accompanying page numbers are used throughout:

BT *Brecht on Theatre. The Development of an Aesthetic*, edited and translated by John Willett (Hill and Wang, New York; Eyre Methuen, London, 1964).

P *Bertolt Brecht. Poems. 1913–1956*, edited by John Willett and Ralph Manheim with the co-operation of Erich Fried (Eyre Methuen,London, 1976, 1979).

UB Walter Benjamin *Understanding Brecht*, translated by Anna Bostock, introduced by Stanley Mitchell (NLB, London, 1973).

Introduction: Why Should Brecht's Name be Mentioned?

Because I praised the useful, which
In my day was considered base
Because I battled against all religions
Because I fought oppression or
For another reason.

Because I was for people and
Entrusted everything to them, thereby honouring them
Because I wrote verses and enriched the language
Because I taught practical behaviour or
For some other reason.

Therefore I thought my name would still be
Mentioned; on a stone
My name would stand; from books
It would get printed into the new books.

But today
I accept that it will be forgotten.
Why
Should the baker be asked for if there is enough bread?
Why
Should the snow be praised that has melted
If new snowfalls are impending?
Why
Should there be a past if
There is a future?

Why
Should my name be mentioned? (P, pp. 264–5)

There have been any number of studies of Brecht's theatre and dramatic theory, but still very few discussions, in English certainly, even ten years after the publication of the excellent *Poems. 1913–1956* which make use of this resource to examine his ideas and work as a poet. Brecht the poet tends consequently to trail behind Brecht the playwright and theorist of 'epic theatre' like a private shadow behind the more public persona. In another way, however, in a quite distinct and heavily connotated usage, Brecht has been persistently regarded and even defended as, above all, a 'poet'. The by now notorious, but by no means only example of this, is Martin Esslin who deploys the terms 'poet' and poetry' in a familiar lexicon of artistic analysis and appreciation, to rescue the 'real' Brecht, the unconscious, natural creative talent, from Brecht the self-willed Marxist theorist. Thus Esslin writes of how 'The poet deep within him always had to hide behind the Marxist';[1] but of how Brecht was able, nevertheless,

> to follow his creative impulse and to produce plays, which based as they are on his intuitive perception of reality rather than his consciously held beliefs, constantly belie the pedantic concepts of Marxism and give the audience a genuine insight into the dilemmas of the human condition.[2]

Esslin returns to this emphasis in a later review of *Poems. 1913–1956*, to insist again, and by way of self-quotation prove the rightness of his own earlier claim, that 'Brecht was a poet, first and foremost a poet' (the plays would have gone unnoticed 'Without the stamp of greatness impressed upon them by their poetry'; his ideas in other fields 'became important only as the ideas of a major poet').[3] At one level this is how Esslin solves the 'problem' which Brecht otherwise presents of the relations between art and politics. For if Brecht was above everything a (great) poet, and this consideration governs all others, he can on these supreme 'artistic' grounds be consolingly and somewhat triumphantly separated from his objectionable political views. At a profounder level, however, Esslin's real argument has been not so much that Brecht's work and ideas were distinguished by their poetic greatness, or even that his 'poetry' was distinguishable from his political views, but that the evidence, simultaneously, of his 'poetry', creative instinct and insight into the human condition, in fact *contradicted* Brecht's expressed ideas and intentions. Esslin's theme, therefore, and the subject consequently of much agitated discussion and manoeuvring in his writing, is as much the scare of Brecht's politics, the violence, hatred, totalitarianism and evil Esslin associates equally with Nazism and Communism, as the saving grace of his poetic greatness.[4] He comes close to saying as much in a later essay. 'The value of a poem or a play', he avers in traditional vein, 'remains unaffected by the psychological background or the political attitude of its creator.'[5] Yet to recognise Brecht as a 'political poet' as Esslin then does, means that he cannot 'simply be subjected to the structural analysis of the *formal* aspects of his work.' 'Inevitably', says Esslin, 'the study and analysis of a poet such as Brecht involves an examination of the public implications of his plays, poems, and novels and, consequently, also an inquiry into the genesis and real nature of his political ideas.'[6] This study of the 'political subject matter' (rather than of 'his poetry and his aesthetic effect') 'imposes the duty to inquire into the truth, the correctness, of the facts, the soundness of the political ideology it propounds.'[7] Esslin therefore invokes an aestheticist assumption of separated artistic value, while at the same time policing the intentions and ideas this art is made out of. He appeals vaguely to a distinction between artistic 'form and effect' and political 'content', while in fact his analysis is at all points formal and political, no more so than in the way he mobilises the valorised categories 'poet' and 'poetry' to stand witness against 'the totalitarian concept of politics', and its domination of 'the private personality and the private life of the individual'.[8] What Esslin does in this 'political' argument is to set the largely unspoken, privileged ideology of humanist aesthetics which finds in 'poetry' the pre-eminent literary vehicle for authentic personal expression and universal psychological and moral truths, against the concern in Marxism for the historically specific, social basis of literary production and the tactics of social change (or, in something like Esslin's own terms, against the manifold distortions and evils Marxism is responsible for in art and society).

Effectively, Esslin reconstructs Brecht for bourgeois aesthetics and bourgeois humanism. Some of the priorities and leading assumptions in his account then reappear, as his own review pointed out, in John Willett and Ralph Manheim's edition of the collected *Poems*. Their 'Disclosure of a poet', as the introduction to the volume is titled, offers to reverse the conventional hierarchy which ranks Brecht as in turn dramatist, theorist and poet in favour of what is in fact only a more traditional order. Poetry becomes 'the primary aspect' of all his writing, and 'Anybody who fails to see that his language was that of a poet is missing the main motive force of all his work' (P, p. ix). We have, they say, approached Brecht 'from the wrong end', when in truth 'the poems led into and permeated the plays from which the theories in turn sprang.' (ibid.) Poetry, we learn, 'was private to him', 'so natural and fluent' as to count as a distraction from the 'real hard work', the 'less natural job' of writing and staging plays which therefore required 'self-denial'. (P, p. xixi) Brecht's political views demanded a further self-sacrifice, requiring him predictably 'to subordinate his imagination to the class struggle'. (P, p. xii) In this view poetry comes in Keatsian fashion as leaves to the tree and political motivation only stymies its growth. Willett and Manheim do not share Esslin's sense of political 'duty', and are not entrapped in the same contradictions. They have some difficulty in maintaining their interpretation nevertheless. Thus, in spite of the above, we are told that 'self-abnegation' was also 'natural' to Brecht (P, p. xiii); that 'his poetry was almost wholly devoted to political objectives' in the late 1920s and 30s (P, p. xvii); and that for it to have grown 'any less political' in the period of the *Svendborg Poems*, 'would have been against his nature'. (P, p. xviii)

Brecht replied in his own way of course to bourgeois aesthetics. 'I wanted', he said, invoking Marx's 11th thesis on Feuerbach, 'to take the principle that it was not just a matter of interpreting the world but of changing it, and apply that to the theatre.' (BT, p. 248) This political aim so 'permeated' his developed theory and practice that it exposes the inconsistencies and covert ideological motivations in any ranking or separation of modes of writing, or of the writer from the man, such as in the above. One of its principal effects in Brecht's work, moreover, was, I believe, to 'alienate' and so transform the bourgeois conception of the poet and of poetry. However, this was but one example of the more general claim he has on our attention as the outstanding representative this century of an attempt to politicise art and culture from an informed Marxist perspective: an aim it should immediately be said which has provoked chastisement and self-protective or encorporative readings from Marxist and bourgeois humanist criticism alike.[9] The proper emphasis and lead in this was given early on and very clearly by Brecht's musical collaborator, Hanns Eisler:

> The significant thing about Brecht is that he *consciously* applied the method of Marx and Engels to an area where it had not yet been applied, namely to the theatre and to poetry — the method in fact of dialectical materialism [10]

Eisler is careful to point out that the method Brecht applied was indeed 'dialectical materialism' and not simply 'dialectics', and adds that one still needs then to ask what *kind* of Marxist he was *(wie* Brecht Marxist war'[11]). Eisler's own view was that Brecht was more a Leninist than is commonly supposed or accepted,[12] but it is also clear that Brecht was influenced by Marx's own texts, and by Marxist thinkers, artists and 'teachers' of Marxism, such as Fritz Sternberg, Walter Benjamin and Karl Korsch, Piscator, Tretiakov, Margarete Steffin, and Eisler himself. In his last years Brecht also placed considerable value on Mao Tse Tung's *On Contradiction*, naming this as the most important book he had read in 1954.[13]

A number of questions therefore arise concerning the most influential or changing sources of Brecht's dialectical materialism, his application, quite critically, of these to artistic theory and practice, and the kind of constraints and hopes acting upon and directing this selection, its results and reception. What kind of specifically dialectical-materialist theory of theatre and poetry did Brecht develop? What new forms and techniques, and what revision of traditional forms and techniques did this imply? In short, what kind of Marxist artist was he, both 'consciously' in Eisler's word, and in a word of Brecht's own, as far as this was 'permissible' in the dramatically changing conditions between his first reading of Marx's *Capital* in the mid-1920s to the mid-1950s when he had added Mao to his 'Marxist classics'?

These are the general questions I try to tackle in what follows. Some of them naturally have been discussed by others. There is nothing new, for instance, nor in itself very useful, as Hanns Eisler points out, in saying that Brecht was a Marxist (which even Esslin cannot deny though the term is for him synonymous with 'Communist' dogma and the totalitarianism of Soviet-styled state socialism). There is also a body of literature which, with varying degrees of documentation, debates Brecht's Marxism and his reliance on a series of Marxist teachers such as those indicated above.[14] Some of these studies, written in the main in German, are also alert to the dialectical or dialectical-materialist character of Brecht's work and thinking. Inevitably, I have my own agreements and disagreements with this criticism. It is not my intention, however, to foreground these similarities or differences, or the more internal debates of Brecht studies. I prefer rather to argue with those critical texts and attitudes which are most 'visible', and even demonstrably 'popular', and can therefore be thought to have some interpretative and ideological currency in English literary culture. In this way I hope that what I have to say will connect with more general movements in literary ideology, and thence with movements for cultural change.

Martin Esslin's *Brecht. A Choice Of Evils*, reprinted five times and once revised since its first publication in 1959, is one such 'popular' text and dominant understanding of Brecht. I take issue first of all, however, in treating Brecht's theory, with John Willett's presentation of this in *Brecht on Theatre*, because his book, unrevised and in print since its publication in 1964, has supplied an English speaking readership with its knowledge of that theory. Without Willett's work and his collaboration with Ralph Manheim, the study of Brecht in English would plainly be nowhere. Here indeed, over the texts they have prepared, Brecht scholarship and academic criticism meet with the interests of the more general reader. But although Willett's *Brecht on Theatre* has proved indispensable (to myself as to others), its selections and commentary are also inadequate and misleading if we are to understand Brecht's theory as a dialectical-materialist theory. I try to show how and why this is so in the first part of this book.

Secondly, I discuss Brecht's poetry and his writings on poetry as an instance of his 'application' of dialectical materialism. Not simply because this area of Brecht's work has been relatively neglected, though it is true that it has, but because, firstly, this neglect, in this key area, leaves undisturbed those bourgeois categories of the individual and of art which Brecht meant to alter; and because, secondly, I believe that political verse and Marxist criticism, whether in its unreconstructed and 'vulgar' or more sophisticated versions, has much to learn from Brecht's example. I am led in this respect, and with an even sharper sense of deference and difference, to quarrel with Walter Benjamin's reading of certain of Brecht's poems. Though Benjamin is rightly acknowledged as a key figure in the development of a Marxist theory of art and as a leading commentator on Brecht's theatre and poetry, I believe that he misconstrues the dialectical operation and indeed the politics of Brecht's verse.

I take what I see as the risk finally of discussing Brecht's political aesthetic and political beliefs in the early 1930s and the post-war period in East Berlin. I attempt this quite simply because to separate questions of artistic theory and practice from history and politics only reinforces the divisive routines of scholarship and criticism and so helps seal off literary culture from a broader public sphere. The kinds of questions Brecht raises concerning the forms and function of socialist art and the position of the socialist intellectual in response to fascism and the advent of a type of socialist society are complex, and in a number of ways testing, but remain, I believe, pertinent. This is true in particular of Brecht's anti-Stalinism, indirect, cautious and delayed though this was, and of his adjusted debt to

Lenin. I have no doubt over-simplified some issues here and over-subtlised others. Many will think I have been too generous to Brecht. In reply, I would say, firstly, with Brecht, that 'it is not clever to make no mistake', and secondly, that the view we take of Brecht's career and politics is, as I try to show, a matter itself of critical ideology and strategy. In the end I am less concerned with Brecht's personal character, or integrity, though I mostly defend this, than with the character of his situation in the extreme conditions of this period, and with drawing some positive, but not 'disinterested', instruction from it.

These brief statements are offered in answer to the question 'Why this additional book on Brecht?' Any study at all conscious of the role of ideology and of recent changes in literary culture ought, I believe, to seek and present its own justification. In Brecht's case there is more to this precisely because of his expressly politicised aesthetic. The question 'why should Brecht be mentioned?' is of concern, that is to say, to more than writers of critical studies of Brecht. It is a question which others, interested in constructing a socialist culture, are required and keen to answer. For, aside from an inevitably mixed relationship between itself and bourgeois culture, a socialist culture in the making will seek to build upon even as it quarrels with a rediscovered or retained tradition of socialist work and thought. And in this tradition Brecht represents a contested, but for the most part positively valued, and in some ways exemplary figure. A 'critique' of Brecht's work, moreover, which from this point of view discriminates between what is presently valuable and viable and what is not, is consistent with the view in Marxism of the necessary double-handed appropriation of past knowledge and culture, and entirely in keeping with Brecht's own criterion of 'usefulness' and the 'collective creative process' he saw his work as placed within. (BT, p. 211)

To put this another way, there is no one and only, true Brecht. It is false, therefore, and as it turns out paradoxically unBrechtian, to suggest that there is a final and absolute reading of the theory, theatre or poems, and wrong to assume that their political 'value', their meaning and effect, remains the same. As Marc Zimmerman in the course of examining the realisation of the politics of Brecht's *The Good Person of Szechwan* on a American campus in 1975, puts it:

> A Brechtian theatre which represents a changing world implies that the theatre itself must change. A Brechtian production

> today which copies Brecht, or which adheres to his production models, is not Brechtian.[15]

Fidelity to a form of words or performance for their own sakes is misplaced monumentalism. The truth is that Brecht has been put to use, directly or indirectly, as a means of ideological reinforcement or subversion; not only in stage productions, but in the selective publication of his work, in the East as in the West, and in the commentaries and interpretations of critics, whether Marxist or bourgeois. Obviously this reflects upon my own disagreements with Esslin, Willett and Benjamin. I do not in these arguments set out to correct a 'critical imbalance' and so 'put the record straight', because there is *always* a critical imbalance and the record is *never* straight. The question is not how one can climb to the Eldorado of critical disinterestedness, there to survey once and for all the true plan of Brecht's work and so put this in a book or on stage, but of how the constructed and reconstructed phenomenon 'Brecht' can be most usefully, positively, and strategically presented and deployed in an acknowledged critical and cultural intervention.

These issues arise in a concrete fashion in Zimmerman's essay referred to above. They appear also in a fascinating study of the influences and uses of Brecht in relation to the new East German avant-garde by David Bathrick.[16] Bathrick concludes that a leading avant-garde playwright such as Heiner Müller, though Brecht's acknowledged heir, has needed to undermine his authority, expose his rationality, and politicise the repressed 'male fantasies' implicated in Germany's fascist past, if he is himself to perform a subversive artistic and political role in present society. Brecht has been used in such a way in East German culture, Bathrick argues, that he helps only to further inter the past and legitimise the existing 'socialist' order. This is a persuasive argument, but it is difficult all the same not to quarrel with the statement that Brecht's aesthetic disallows '*a priori* any expression which would challenge the collective peace';[17] whether this consensus reigns in East Germany, London, or New York. Elsewhere Bathrick describes 'the dialectics of the avant-garde', by which though ever prone to encorporation, it can also be transformative and disruptive 'at the level of presentation and re-presentation'.[18] In this connection he suggests that Brecht's aesthetic emphasised 'self-organisation' and called 'for self-initiative and pluralism as the constituent parts of a democratised cultural public sphere.'[19] This aspect of Brecht has been repressed, Bathrick says, in the GDR. But, unless we concede that what is once repressed is always repressed, we must 'allow' the possibility that it can be liberated there to unsettle the 'collective peace' of already existing 'socialism'. We might want to think too of course how Brecht in this aspect, with this 'progressive' political meaning and value, can be constructively deployed elsewhere. If so, we need to recognise that to be effective reflections such as these need also to be historically and politically specific. As Bathrick rightly says:

> judgements about the political integrity of any literature can be made only in relation to its function within a particular social order[20]

In Brecht's case we need to ask which Brecht we are mobilising, for what effect, and in which particular literary culture and society. It might be said that these are questions for those in the public cultural realm, for producers and directors and actors rather than for critics, to answer. In fact this is true and will remain so, unless, taking positive instruction from Brecht's theory and the scope of his own work, we are able to broaden the concept and practice of 'criticism' to include cultural production, and see dramatic and literary work as themselves properly instances of what Brecht called the 'critical attitude'.[21] This attitude ranges across art, culture and society, and, says Brecht, 'taken to its logical conclusion' entails 'ultimately revolution'. (BT, p. 146) In the poem 'On the critical attitude', he writes,

> . . . Give criticism arms
> And states can be demolished by it.
>
> Canalising a river
> Grafting a fruit tree
> Educating a person
> Transforming a state
> These are instances of fruitful criticism
> And at the same time
> Instances of art. (P, p. 309)

Elsewhere in Brecht's writing the 'critical attitude' is used interchangeably with what he terms 'interventionist thinking' and with dialectical materialism, and this strikes a particularly contemporary note. Thus Terry Eagleton in his critique of the orthodox institution of 'English Literature' and of 'literary theory' which he sees as 'no more than a branch of social ideologies', calls for a 'political criticism' of 'discursive practices' which would understand that literature is used and is of strategic use.[22] In *The Function of Criticism*, Eagleton describes the theoretician and political radical as a Brechtian actor who would persistently estrange 'and raise to self-reflexivity the very enabling conditions of a range of routinised practices.'[23] The contemporary socialist or feminist critic, he concludes, is 'defined by an engagement in the cultural politics of late capitalism', it being the task of criticism to reconnect symbolic with political discourse and so help form 'repressed needs, interests and desires . . . into a collective political force.'[24]

Edward Said, though he chastises Eagleton, and other, American Marxist critics, for a 'cloistral seclusion from the inhospitable world of real politics.'[25] calls for what is in the end a similar 'politics of interpretation', demanding

> a dialectical response from a critical consciousness worthy of its name. Instead of noninterference and specialisation, there must be *interference*, crossing of borders and obstacles, a determined attempt to generalize exactly at those points where generalisations seem impossible to make.[26]

'one of the first interferences to be ventured', says Said, involves a crossing from literature to other forms of representation, in the interests of what he describes as 'the crucial next phase: connecting these more politically vigilant forms of interpretation to an ongoing political and social praxis.'[27]

Brecht is worth mention finally because he assists us in understanding what in theory and practice this conscious use of literature and a crossing of borders has meant. I hope in what I have to say of his writing and situation and the politics of *their* interpretation, that I have helped make 'Brecht' newly available for this task; not as a fixed model, but like his own model books, as an instructive basis open to variation and improvement in altered and as Brecht would have it 'alterable' circumstances. I would like to think that this itself amounts to a minor 'intervention', but it is only that, only 'useful', or in Said's words, something more than 'the murmur of mere prose' if it connects with 'the crucial next phase'.

Notes

1. Martin Esslin, *Brecht. A Choice of Evils (Eyre Methuen, London, 1959, revised 1980),p. 213.*

2. *Ibid., p. 218.*

3. *Esslin, 'Brecht's Poetry in English — A Review of Poems 1913-1956'* (August 1976), reprinted in *Mediations* (Sphere Books, London, 1983), pp. 66-7.

4. See Esslin, *Brecht*, p. 237.

5. Esslin, 'Brecht' — the icon and the self-portrait' (December 1977), reprinted in *Mediations*, p. 51.

6. Ibid., p. 52.

7. Ibid.

8. Ibid.

9. In a still very accurate characterisation, Roland Barthes in an essay of 1956, listed four main types of Brecht criticism. Thus,

> By the extreme right, Brecht's work is totally discredited because of his political commitment: Brecht's work is mediocre *because* it is communist. By the right . . . Brecht is subjected to the usual political denaturation: the man is dissociated from the work, the former consigned to politics (emphasising successively and contradictorily his independence and his servility with regard to the Party), and the latter enlisted under the banners of an eternal theatre: Brecht's work, we are told, is great in spite of Brecht, against Brecht.

On the left Barthes identifies firstly 'a humanist reading' which, although sympathetic to Brecht 'disguises an anti-intellectualist prejudice' for 'in order to "humanise" Brecht, the theoretical part of his work is discredited or at least minimized', and secondly, the reservations of communist critics 'with regard to Brecht's opposition to the positive hero, his conception of theatre, and the "formalist" orientation of his dramaturgy.' Roland Barthes, 'The tasks of Brechtian criticism', in *Critical Essays*, translated by Richard Howard (Northwestern University Press, Evanston, 1972), pp. 72-3.

I take up further examples of Brecht criticism in a later chapter. Most, I believe, gravitate towards 'a humanist reading', including Esslin and Willett. In an early 'Marxist' example of this tendency, P. Ivanov in a review in July 1934 in *Izvestia* of Brecht's 'Epicheskie dramy' felt that,

> . . . it is essential to credit him with praiseworthy enthusiasm directed towards the revolutionary goal, but also to mention the schematism of Brecht's 'epic plays' . . . However gifted and fine his present style, this most promising writer of the German revolution must make the transition from rhetoric to a Shakespearian theatre of great passions, to a theatre of live and rounded personalities who make history.

Quoted in Marjorie L. Hoover, 'Brecht's soviet connection Tretiakov', in *Brecht Heute. Brecht Today*, 3 (1973), pp. 51-2.

10.. Hanns Eisler, 'Gespräche', in *Sinn und Form. Sonderheft Hanns Eisler* (Rütten and Loening, Berlin, 1964), p. 293.

11. Ibid., p. 294.

12. Ibid., p. 292. This view has been most vigorously pursued in Roland Jost, *Er War Unser Lehrer. Bertolt Brechts Leninrezeption am Beispiel der 'Massnahme', des 'Me-ti/Buch der Wendungen' und der 'Marxistischen Studien'* (Pahl-Rugenstein, Köln, 1981).

13. *Gesammelte Werke,* 20 (Suhrhkamp, Frankfurt am Main, 1967), p. 343.

14. Of relevant studies in German, see Hans Mayer, *Bertolt Brecht und die Tradition* (Neske, Pfullingen, 1961); Klaus Detlef Müller, *Die Funktion der Geschichte im Werk Bertolt Brechts. Studien zum Verhältnis von Marxismus und Äesthetik* (Max Niemeyer, Tübingen, 1967); Käthe Rülicke-Weiler, *Die Dramaturgie Brechts. Theater als Mittel der Veränderung* (Henschelverlag, Berlin, 1968); Helmut Jendreiek, *Bertolt Brecht. Drama der Veränderung* (August Bagel, Düsseldorf, 1969); Heinz Brüggemann, *Literarische Technik und Soziale Revolution. Versuche über das Verhältnis von Kunstproduktion, Marxismus und literarische Tradition in den theoretischen Schriften Bertolt Brechts* (Rowohlt, Hamburg, 1973); Roland Jost, *Er War Unser Lehrer* (Pahl-Rugenstein, Köln, 1981); *Brecht 1983. Brecht und Marxismus. Dokumentation* (Henschelverlag, East Berlin, 1983).

Of studies in English, see Joseph Franklin Dial, *The Contribution of Marxism to Bertolt Brecht's Theatre Theory*, unpublished doctoral thesis, University of Harvard, 1975; the essays in Betty Nance Weber and Hubert Heinen (eds), *Bertolt Brecht. Political Theory and Literary Practice* (Georgia University Press, Athens, Georgia, and Manchester University Press, 1980); Darko Suvin, *To Brecht and Beyond. Soundings in Modern Dramaturgy* (Harvester Press, Brighton, Sussex, and Barnes and Noble, Totowa, New Jersey, 1984); Eugene Lunn, *Marxism and Modernism. An Historical Study of Lukács, Brecht, Benjamin, and Adorno* (University of California Press, 1982, and Verso, London, 1985).

Of single articles, see Wolfdietrich Rasch, 'Bertolt Brechts marxistischer Lehrer', *Merkur*, 17 (1963), pp. 988–1003; T.W.H. Metscher, 'Brecht and Marxist dialectics', *Oxford German Studies*, 6 (1971–2), pp. 132–44; Helmut Dahmer, 'Bertolt Brecht and Stalinism', *Telos*, 22 (Winter 1974–5), pp. 96–105; Anthony Hosier, 'Empathy and dialectics — Brecht', *Red Letters*, 13 (Spring 1982), pp. 13–22.

15. Marc Zimmerman, 'Brecht and the dynamics of production', *Praxis*, 3 (1976), p. 125.

16. David Bathrick, 'Affirmative and negative culture: the avant-garde under "actually existing socialism" — the case of the GDR', *Social Research*, 47:1 (Spring 1980), pp. 166–87.

17. Ibid., p. 183.

18. Ibid., p. 181.

19. Ibid., p. 182.

21. Anthony Hosier, who argues, as I would, that Brecht's theory and example are now of most use to us and that we need to see 'his theatrical practice in the light of the socio-political context of our own', discusses the obstacles preventing present-day actors from adopting a 'critical attitude'. He points to significant differences in the conditions prevailing

in the commercial and subsidised theatre, and in community-based and theatre in education groups, but sees them all as finally constrained by the facts of ownership and control of the 'apparatus of production' and by 'the logic of the market-place.' 'Brecht's epic form: the actor as narrator', *Red Letters* 14 (Winter 1982–3), esp. pp. 33–8.

22. Terry Eagleton, *Literary Theory. An Introduction* (Basil Blackwell, Oxford, 1983), p. 204, and see pp. 208–11.

23. Eagleton, *The Function of Criticism* (Verso, London, 1984), p. 89.

24. Ibid., p. 123.

25. Edward Said, 'Opponents, audiences, constituencies and communities', in *Postmodern Culture*, Hal Foster (ed.), (Pluto Press, London, 1985), p. 149.

26. Ibid., p. 157.

27. Ibid., p. 158.

Part One
Dialectics and Drama

1

Dialectics in the Theatre

Discussion of Brecht's dramatic theory has centred on the triple concepts of 'epic theatre', *Verfremdung* and *Gestus*, and described the techniques of staging, acting, and the intended social function of Brecht's work in these terms. For an English-speaking reader John Willett's *Brecht on Theatre* remains the best introduction to Brecht's own theoretical statements and to his developing aesthetic. It is symptomatic of much of the commentary and criticism of Brecht, however, that Willett marginalises Brecht's use of a different theoretical vocabulary drawn from Marxist dialectics, and that in the process he narrows the provenance of the more customary terms. In the last years of his life in Berlin, for example, Brecht conceived a series of nine articles (consisting of a letter, notes and dialogues) under the general heading of 'Dialectics in the theatre'.[1] Willett prints two of these, 'The study of the first scene of Shakespeare's *Coriolanus*, and 'Conversation about being forced into empathy', although it is not immediately clear from their placing in his book that they belong together with other essays under a common heading. (BT, pp. 252–65, 270–1) The remaining essays are titled 'Relative haste' (On Ostrovsky's *Zeihtochter* produced in December 1955);'A diversion' (on a revision to *The Caucasian Chalk Circle*); 'Another case of applied dialectics' (on the playing of Frau Carrar in *Frau Carrar's Rifles*); 'Letter to the actor playing the young Hörder in *Winterschlacht*' (a play by Johannes R Becher produced by Brecht in January 1955); '*Mother Courage* performed in two ways'; 'An example of scenic invention through the perception of error' (on the Chinese agit-prop play *Hirse für die Achte*, performed by the Berliner Ensemble on 1 April 1954); and 'Concerning the presentation of character' (a note on the same play). Willett lists these essays in the 'editorial note' he chooses to write on 'Dialectics in the theatre' (this is a one and a half page section separated from the two essays he prints referred to above). Here he presents Brecht's prefatory note to the series and quotes from a set of fragmentary notes titled posthumously'Epic theatre and dialectical theatre'. Elsewhere he quotes from the same notes, from other later notes including an article titled 'Socialist realism in the theatre' and includes a translation of 'Can the present-day world be reproduced by means of theatre?' (BT, pp. 281, 269-70, 274-5)

These statements and essays are quite clearly related to Brecht's main theme and indeed have appeared in his published *Collected Works* along with several others, including pieces titled 'Notes on dialectics in the theatre' and 'Dialectical aspects' in a 73-page section given the overall title 'Dialectics in the theatre 1951 –1956'. Willett confines himself in his 'editorial note' to the nine essays referred to; he says that the *Coriolanus* discussion 'is the backbone of the whole affair', that three of these essays ('Another case of applied dialectics' and the two notes on *Hirse für die Achte*) 'are seemingly not even by Brecht' and that as a whole the collection 'is a miscellaneous one which is far from presenting a coherent argument'. 'It is' he says, 'something of a makeshift, and interim report'. (BT, p. 282) These comments are prefaced, finally, by an opening remark suggesting that the reorientation of Brecht's theory and the substitution of a 'dialectical' for an 'epic' theatre which it involved, was limited to 'the last year of his life'. (BT, p. 281)

Two points can be made quickly in response to this. It should be clear, firstly, from what has been said, that Willett's selective and separated presentation of the relevant late essays by Brecht, itself contributes to an impression of incoherence. Secondly, the dates of the nine essays alone make it quite clear that the revision of Brecht's theory, if not the title of the series, was in progress from 1951. Other essays, under other titles, but containing as a simple test a direct reference to dialectics, suggest that this revision had begun even earlier, in the late 1940s. To set these essays along with other still earlier examples of Brecht's study and use of dialectics produces a different graph of his theoretical development than the customary one which sees dialectics as appearing in the early 1930s, only to immediately fade, then disappear, before surfacing again in the very last years of Brecht's life.

I offer a reappraisal of this development in a later chapter. As it will be seen, the terms 'epic', *Verfremdung* and *Gestus* acquire a different, and I suggest, fuller meaning and function than those which Willett and others have assigned to them. Initially, however, I want to answer the limiting and negative judgements contained in

Willett's 'editorial note' and to do this by referring the essays on 'Dialectics in the theatre' to their broader and I think proper context. I mean by this the style of work and thinking established in the Berliner Ensemble, Brecht's view of the political function of this theatre, and his firm commitment to dialectical materialism.

First of all, the nine essays which Willett refers to take a similar view of the productive value of contradiction and the need for an informing historical sense, schooled in dialectical materialism. This emerges, moreover, as not only Brecht's belief, but as a common principle and approach amongst the members of the Berliner Ensemble who take part in discussions or who report on them.

To take the nine essays in sequence. In the discussion titled 'The study of the first scene of Shakespeare's *Coriolanus*', Brecht and members of the company analyse the initial conflict in Shakespeare's play between the Roman plebeians and patricians and their subsequent unity under Marcius Coriolanus in war against the Volscians. Brecht refers to Mao Tse Tung's *On Contradiction* (it is clear that a knowledge of this text is shared by the participants since one of them then presents Mao's distinction between dominant and secondary contradictions,[2] to explain that the first conflict is an example of class struggle which becomes subordinated to the new, main contradiction engendered by a national war against the Volscians, until this in turn gives way to a Rome governed by People's Tribunes. (BT, pp. 261–2) The participants agree that the military leader Coriolanus should be shown as unquestionably useful, even as a great hero, but as nevertheless tragic in his belief that he is irreplaceable. Asked if the resulting lessons on class conflict, division, and oppression are the reasons for their doing the play Brecht answers, 'We want to have and to communicate the fun of dealing with a slice of illuminated history. And to have first-hand experience of dialectics.' And to the objection that this is over-sophisticated, he replies, 'the simple people (who are so far from simple) love stories of the rise and fall of great men, of eternal change, of the ingenuity of the oppressed, of the potentialities of mankind'. (BT, pp. 264–5)

In the note titled 'Relative haste' Brecht recommends that the busy preparations for tea in a scene from Ostrovsky's *Zeihtochter* be presented as a dumb-show, as solicitous but casual. In 'A diversion' (on *The Caucasian Chalk Circle*) he points out the contradictory feeling the maidservant Grusche has towards her own interests and towards the child whose true parentage is the subject of the play's scene of judgement. In 'Another case of applied dialectics' a reported discussion on the problem of presenting the politicisation of Frau Carrar in a credible way, tells how the Ensemble arrived at a solution which they then realised had been already present in an earlier performance by Helene Weigel. Here, Weigel had shown Frau Carrar as first hardening, then collapsing under the succcessive blows of local agitation and her son's death. This prompts Brecht to comment, 'Merkwürdig . . . dass es jedesmal von neuem dieser Anstrengung bedarf, die Gesetze der Dialektik zu beachten.' ('how remarkable . . . that it requires this effort each time afresh to observe the laws of dialectic.')[3]

In 'A letter to the actor playing the young Hörder in *Winterschlact'*, Brecht offers advice on the contradictory and unheroic character of Hörder, and links this with the disease of Nazism and the health of the 'other Germany', so as to point out the need for a knowledge of history in presenting contradictory attitudes of fear and sympathy. In *'Mother Courage,* performed in two ways' he refers to a performance by Helene Weigel which prevented the audience's being drawn into empathy. Weigel had played Mother Courage's occupation as a peddler, not as if it were natural, but as belonging to an historical period, and as especially suited to a time of war. It was, Brecht says, the contradictory roles of peddler and of mother which disfigured the character. Her feelings were abrupt and irreconcilable; she damns war with as much sincerity as she praises it, and though the rebellion of her daughter stuns her she learns nothing from it. Her tragedy lies in the appalling and destructive nature of such contradictions which can only be solved through a long and dreadful struggle in society.

The first of the two pieces on *Hirse für die Achte* ('Millet for the 8th') describes how Brecht turned the errors of a young director to productive use. The director resists Brecht's advice to move a table to one side of the stage because this would create an imbalance. It appears then that it would also expose the unused space on stage of a second room. Making a virtue of necessity Brecht suggests that two women be stationed in the room, and shown as repairing a saddle to be given to the partisans of Mao's 8th army, while a collaborator is concealed in the first room. This would create a comic and instructive contrast, and point to the wide, popular support of the partisans in a scene in which just such people were shown to be beneath the notice of the collaborator. Brecht concludes 'In der Nähe der Fehler wachsen die Wirkungen' (Useful effects grow close to mistakes'.)[4]

In the note 'Concerning the presentation of character' Brecht is reported as criticising a director's wish to cast an actor suitable to the cunning displayed by the Burgermeister, who in the play is involved in a plan to outwit the Japanese and the forces of Chiang Kai-Shek. The man, says Brecht, could be simple and wise but shown as forced by circumstances and necessity into cunning. Finally in 'The conversation about being forced into empathy' Brecht confirms his long-standing belief that any attempt to compel empathy is 'barbaric'. The discussion closes with the remarks by 'W' (Manfred Wekwerth, then a young co-director at the Berliner Ensemble) that in the case of a sister mourning her brother's departure for war, 'We must be able to surrender to her sorrow and at the same time not to. Our actual emotion will come from recognising and feeling the incident's double aspect'. (BT, p. 271)

What even this cursory examination reveals is that this 'miscellaneous' collection ' which is far from presenting a coherent argument' has in fact an informing theoretical coherence. The essays show that it was a principled habit on Brecht's part, and a matter of custom and practice almost, within the Berliner Ensemble company, to seek out and foreground contradiction in the solution to a range of practical problems. These problems involve matters of interpretation. staging and acting, and their treatment confirms not only Brecht's long-standing opposition to theatrical inducements to empathy, or the need to historicise characters and narrative, for example, but demonstrates these principles in practical terms, often with reference to successful models of such practice. In this respect it is interesting that the essays refer as they do to performances by Helene Weigel since she did not theorise her acting style (at least not in writing), but is consistently praised by Brecht as the successful embodiment of his theory. While the essays are plainly not examples of theoretical argument, neither are they a set of fragments on miscellaneous practical questions. They are examples of theory *in* practice, and this is quite consistent with Brecht's conscious reorientation in the last phase of his work.[5] To adapt the title of one of the essays Willett is inclined to dismiss, the series presents 'several cases of applied dialectics'. Nor should this be taken to mean that the traffic is one way and that an established and predetermined theory is applied to practice which would languish without it. In the example 'Another case of applied dialectics' itself, theory does not organise practice in an *a priori* sense; rather the process of discussion — and it is important that it is presented as a process — confirms the merits of a dialectical procedure afresh. In the dialogue on *Coriolanus* also, where theory, in the shape of Mao's *On Contradiction*, appears to be introduced from the outside, to explain the class relations and movements in the play, this represents an addition to Brecht's canon of Marxist classics, and is in itself evidence of the extension and revision his theory was undergoing.

A further answer to the view that this set of writings was 'makeshift' of fragmentary and anonymous ('Three of its items are seemingly not even by Brecht') is that Brecht in this phase was acting, and prepared to publish, according to the principles of collaborative work established on his return to Europe in the Berliner Ensemble. 'The act of creation', he wrote in the Foreword to *Antigone* in 1948, 'had become a collective creative process, a continuum of a dialectical sort in which the original invention taken on its own, has lost much of its importance'. (BT, p, 211) From this date Brecht began to make model books of certain productions. According to Willett these were of productions 'which he wished to establish as standard'. But Brecht did not introduce models with a view to fixing an 'ideal' version of a production in the way this suggests. The use of models, as Brecht clearly saw, challenged notions of the 'original', 'incomparable' and 'unique' work of art. In the 'continuum of a dialectical sort' he mentions 'the learner becomes the teacher and the model itself changes.' He goes on

> For the model is not set up in order to fix the style of performance; quite the contrary. The emphasis is on development: changes are to be provoked and to be made perceptible; sporadic and anarchic acts of creation are to be replaced by creative processes whose changed progress by steps of leaps. The model [of *Antigone*] was worked out in a dozen and a half rehearsals at the Municipal Theatre in Chur, and must be regarded as by definition incomplete. The very fact that its shortcomings cry out for improvement should stimulate theatres to use it. (BT, p. 212)

This conception of the proper use and function of the model books consorts also with other features of Brecht's work in his last phase. The fact that he wrote only one 'original' play, the uncompleted *Turandot or the Congress of the Whitewashers* in the period 1949–56, that he produced no play of his own directly on contemporary Germany, choosing instead to re-stage earlier plays of his own, to adapt past works and to produce plays such as Erwin Strittmatter's *Katzgraben* and Becher's *Winterschlacht* — all this has been seen, by Martin Esslin for example, as evidence of Brecht's 'tiredness', his 'sterility', or simply as being 'safer' than working on new material.[6] The answer to this is that

Brecht and the Berliner Ensemble saw it as a major task in addressing a contemporary audience which had experienced life under Hitler, or under an earlier form of capitalism, to reconstitute the theatrical repertory, to bring new techniques and an historical sense to the theatrical record of the past, and so free it and the public of the 'drosses' (den Schlacken') of class society.[7] Both the model books and the plays of this last period show how Brecht was prepared to engage critically and productively with the work of the past (including his own), with the work of contemporaries, and in 'a dialectical continuum', with work of the future. In addition, the open and democratic directing style, attested to by visitors, co-directors, actors, designers and stage-hands of the Berliner Ensemble illustrates Brecht's readiness to pursue these aims in an non-hierarchical and collective working environment.[8] In this sense the frequent dialogue form and the relative anonymity of the collection 'Dialectics in the theatre' represent collective discussion in the forms most appropriate to it, just as the to and fro between question and answer, problem and solution, theory and practice in these essays demonstrate general dialectical principles.

At another level, Brecht's later essays and the collaborative ethos of this work, especially within the Berliner Ensemble, can be seen as the outcome of a pronounced anti-idealism and anti-individualism characteristic of his thinking from the late 1920s. As early as 1926 in connection with the play *Man equals Man* Brecht had stated that 'The continuity of the ego is a myth'. (BT, p. 15) As an ancestor of 'a new human type', the character Galy Gay in the play 'becomes the strongest once he has ceased to be a private person; he only becomes strong in the mass'. (BT, pp. 18, 19) Brecht's view at this time was that the individual was infintely malleable and manipulable, and would gain strength even when his absorption into the 'mass' converted him into the military machine of a destructive army. In his subsequent more openly politicised conception of the internally fraught and contradictory social 'mass', Brecht distinguished between the forces of reaction and oppression and liberation, seeing the source of 'a new human type' more in the discontented, the simple ('who are so far from simple') and in the working class. In a retrospective comment on *Man equals Man*, written in 1954, he sees Galy Gay as 'a socially negative hero' and describes the play's theme as:

> the false, bad collectivity that Hitler and his backers were even then in the process of recruiting by an exploitation of the petty bourgeoisie's vague longing for the historically, timely,

genuinely social collectivity of the workers.[9]

The Berliner Ensemble, also, from 1949 and then from 1954 when it was housed in the Theater am Schiffbauerdamm, gave Brecht the opportunity in the changed political climate of post-war Berlin, first of all to renew the co-operative working style (often initially with the same personnel) of the years before his European and American exile of 1933–46. Secondly, the work of the Ensemble, including the essays on a dialectical theatre, were explicitly conceived as contributing to social change and the making of socialism in the interests of a 'genuinely social collectivity'. Thus Brecht addressed his colleagues in a poem on the Ensemble's move from the Deutsches Theater to its new premises:

> At first you acted in the ruins. Now
> You'll act in this fine house, for something more than
> fun.
> From you and us a peaceful WE must grow
> To help this house to last, and many another one. (P, p. 446)

Subsequently, in an undated draft of a later essay on the 'Special characteristics of the Berliner Ensemble', Brecht writes of how the theatre will be in its own way implicated in the social and intellectual changes necessary for the achievement of socialism. He lists six anticipated changes: that the theatre must be realistic and its representations in accord with the collective life of people, that the theatre must communicate effective insights and aims in its representation of real life, that human nature must be shown as changeable, that theatrical representations must be dialectical-materialist in character, and that dialectical materialism must be brought to consciousness in the realm of art and made pleasurable. Finally he says that these changes should be taken up in the realm of art so as to subsume the achievements of earlier revolutions in a dialectical process. This point, which serves as a criterion and perspective upon the work of the theatre, is the most pressing one, says Brecht, for the Berliner Ensemble to consider.[10]

Often aims such as these were expressed and pursued in the face of official hostility and indifference, and in opposition to a bureaucratic insistence on Soviet-styled socialist-realism. For Brecht's commitment to dialectical materialism and to a genuine collectivism by no means meant that he was unequivocally committed to the emergent form of socialism in the GDR. In fact the

Berliner Ensemble as a model of such thinking was engaged in its own dialectical relationship with the East German regime, since both in their different ways sustained yet were critical of the other. Brecht saw his work as a contribution to socialism; as performing a 'pedagogic' or 'anticipational' function, but not as in itself the sole means to, or guarantee of, social transformation. The form in which the above tasks for the Berliner Ensemble are presented bears this out. Brecht looked forward to a time when 'collective productivity became the basis of morality'.[11] In the absence of any unequivocal signs that such an order had come into being, the Berliner Ensemble, as what one visitor termed 'an arena of collaboration', or what Keith Dickson has described as a 'private utopia' in which Brecht 'came very close to the ideal of an artistic democracy.'[12] served as itself a 'model' of the full social application of dialectical materialism.

There is a last aspect to the essays on 'Dialectics in the theatre' which is worth bringing out further. In the essays, past and present problems, or errors and achievements are acknowledged and talked through. The 18-page discussion 'Some errors on the mode of acting in the Berliner Ensemble', dated 1955, and included in the *Collected Works* section on 'Dialectics in the theatre', is a salient example of this. The co-operative work of the Berliner Ensemble, as this indicates, took the form of mutual reinforcement and self-criticism. Just as the model books had been designed in their very incompleteness and shortcomings to assist and provoke change 'by steps or leaps', so the conversations and notes of 'Dialectics in the theatre' show how the later productions and the working principles of the Ensemble were set together in a dialogic process, which tested, reaffirmed and revised them. The resulting unfinished and provisional aspect of the essays is no doubt what prompts Willett to describe the collection as 'a makeshift, an interim report'. He and Martin Esslin make similar comments also on Brecht's paragraph introducing the series. Brecht wrote:

> The works which follow relate to paragraph 45 of the 'Short Organum' and suggest that 'epic theatre' is too formal a term for the kind of theatre aimed at (and to some extent practised). Epic theatre is a prerequisite for these contributions, but it does not of itself imply that productivity and changeability of society from which they derive their main element of pleasure. The term must therefore be reckoned inadequate, although no new one can be put forward.[13]

Esslin introduces this statement by saying (it is his only comment on 'Dialectics in the theatre') that Brecht's 'last theoretical essays . . . *foreshadow*' the substitution of a 'dialectical' for an 'epic' theatre. 'his disciple Manfred Wekwerth', Esslin says, 'describes how he spoke of his theatre as a "dialectical theatre" shortly before he died. But in the introductory note to *Dialectics in the Theatre*, published after his death, Brecht *merely* says . . . ' (my italics). Brecht's introductory paragraph then follows without further comment.[14] Willett glosses Brecht's statement by saying, 'in other words the actual phrase "dialectical theatre" was still to be held in reserve'. (BT, p. 282) This is of a piece with Willett's response to a roughly contemporary and equivalent statement, in which Brecht had said the idea and practice of epic theatre 'were by no means undialectical . . . All the same we envisage a sizeable transformation.'[15] Willett's comment on this is 'Almost as interesting as the change of terminology . . . is the fact that none of these notes was published in Brecht's lifetime. He was not yet ready to go quite so far as they suggested.' (BT, p. 281)

The only real truth in these comments is that Brecht's essays were not committed to print in his lifetime (though they had been passed for publication), and that Brecht was undecided about the description ('the actual phrase') 'dialectical theatre'. Turning Willett's comment around, we might say that almost as interesting as the fact that none of these notes were published in Brecht's lifetime is the way he projects the idea and intention of a dialectical theatre back into his earlier career. To answer the general implication, however, that Brecht was here merely sketching out a change that was yet to come into being, it is quite obvious that a great deal of Brecht's work was provisional and incomplete, and in this sense 'a makeshift, an interim report', which 'foreshadowed' subsequent developments. As a result many of his most interesting and far from occasional works were unfinished, or not published in a final form in his lifetime. The work *Me-Ti* (a collection of prose passages, anecdotes and political aphorisms) is an example of this, so too was the related 'Tui novel' (on the hypocrisy of intellectuals), both works occupying Brecht at intervals from 1934 until the last years of his life. The posthumously published *Flüchtlinggespräche* and the unfinished *Messingkauf Dialogues* are further examples. In addition, numerous plays and poems or cycles of poems were projected but unrealised, or begun and not finished, or revised (sometimes several times). Or they were excluded from Brecht's repertory, or from later published editions of his works. In the realm of theory, even the important *A Short Organum*, itself a 'short condensation of the Messingkauf' and a prelude to an unwritten 'larger Organum', was extended in a set of more decidedly Marxist appendices. These in their turn, following Brecht's expanded reference to dialectical materialism, then ran into the series 'Dialectics in the theatre'. Hence the opening sentence of Brecht's introductory paragraph referring to paragraph 45 of the *Short Organum*.

Nor did Brecht's works take on this provisional unfinished and accretional appearance because he was a frenetic gadfly who was unable to commit himself, or because he kept things in reserve. As Brecht wrote in the poem 'The learner', 'only the grave will have nothing more to teach me.' (P, p. 257) His work was consciously held open to revision; sometimes, it is true, as a matter of calculated expediency, but more often as a matter of principle. The cultivated exercise of doubt and self-criticism of the kind Brecht talks of in the poem 'The doubter' and 'In praise of doubt' has to be seen therefore as an integral part of his political aesthetic. 'New experience', he writes in the second poem, 'makes the established truth open to question'. His 'doubter' is not the vacillator, who doubts 'not in order to come to a decision but/To avoid a decision', whose 'favourite phrase is: not yet ripe for discussion', but one schooled in the lessons of historical change. For those who see 'invincible armies' put to flight, and 'impregnable strongholds collapse' . . . 'Stop believing in the strength/Of their oppressors.' (P, pp. 335–6, 334) Doubt of this kind received its authority from Brecht's belief in the indisputable fact of change and fuelled his own attempts to help engender and anticipate the conditions of social and political revolution. In the words of Marx's 11th Thesis on Feuerbach which Brecht repeatedly evoked, 'The philosophers have only *interpreted* the world in various ways; the point, however, is to *change* it'.[16]

There would be little dispute amongst critics and commentators on the general fact of Brecht's debt to Marxism or his intention to apply it to the theatre. What is more often in question is the degree of his loyalty to Soviet-styled communism in its Stalinist phase, or in its East German form, and secondly the corrupting or liberating effect, as it is seen, of this political commitment upon his art. Some of these views will be taken up later. What can be said meanwhile, is that these apparently divergent opinions share an erroneous identification of Marxism with a particular form of communism. As a result Marxism is misrepresented on either side of an ideological fence as either 'dogma' or 'the final truth'. In fact

Marx, Engels, Lenin, and following them Brecht, consistently argued against any such conception. In a poem, contemporary with 'In praise of doubt', titled 'Song of the good people', Brecht identifies 'the good people' as those who 'are/changing the world' and 'are of use to us'. But these are the people who also 'invite one to improve them', who 'don't seem to be able to finish anything by themselves/All their solutions still contain problems'. (P, pp. 337–8) Changing the world, Brecht implied, meant being open to change; it meant being engaged as teacher/pupil in an unfinished dialectical process of teaching and learning, of solving and bequeathing problems. There are many echoes of this thinking in what Brecht termed 'the Marxist classics'. Much of what Engels writes in *Ludwig Feuerbach and the End of Classical German Philosophy,* for example, serves as a gloss to the poems quoted above. Speaking at one point of the 'revolutionary side' of Hegel's philosophy, Engels writes:

> Truth, the cognition of which is the business of philosophy, was in the hands of Hegel no longer an aggregate of finished dogmatic statements, which, once discovered, had merely to be learned by heart. Truth lay now in the process of cognition itself, in the long historical development of science, which mounts from lower to ever higher levels of knowledge without ever reaching, by discovering so-called absolute truth, a point at which it can proceed no further, where it would have nothing more to do than to fold its hands and gaze with wonder at the absolute truth to which it had attained. And what holds good for the realm of philosophical knowledge holds good also for that of every other kind of knowledge and also for practical action. Just as knowledge is unable to reach a complete conclusion in a perfect, ideal condition of humanity, so is history unable to do so; a perfect society, a perfect 'state', are things which can only exist in imagination. On the contrary, all successive historical systems are only transitory stages in the endless course of development of human society from the lower to the higher. Each stage is necessary, and therefore justified for the time and conditions to which it owes its origin. But in the face of new, higher conditions which gradually develop in its own womb, it loses its validity and justification. It must give way to a higher stage which will also in its turn decay and perish. Just as the bourgeoisie by large-scale industry, competition and the world market dissolves in practice all stable time-honoured institutions, so

> this dialectical philosophy dissolves all conceptions of final absolute truth and of absolute states of humanity corresponding to it. For it [dialectical philosophy] nothing is final, absolute, sacred. It reveals the transitory character of everything and in everything; nothing can endure before it except the uninterrupted process of becoming and of passing away, of endless ascendancy from the lower to the higher. And dialectical philosophy itself is nothing more than the mere reflection of this process in the thinking brain. It has, of course, also a conservative side; it recognises that definite stages of knowledge and society are justified for their time and circumstances; but only so far. The conservatism of this mode of outlook is relative; its revolutionary character is absolute — the only absolute dialectical philosophy admits.[17]

Lenin quotes approvingly from this statement in the section 'Dialectics' of his essay on Marx, and quotes elsewhere, once again from the same essay, in defending Marxism against the charge of dogmatism and Engels against the charge of 'revisionism':

> Engels says explicitly that 'with each epoch-making discovery even in the sphere of natural science [''not to speak of the history of mankind''], materialism has to change its form' . . . Hence, a revision of the 'form' of Engels' materialism, a revision of his natural-philosophical propositions is not only not 'revisionism', in the accepted meaning of the term, but, on the contrary, is an essential requirement of Marxism.[18]

Dialectical materialism is therefore committed to the idea of change, including the revision of its own form, and this, says Lenin, is a mark of its comprehensiveness and richness compared with the common idea of evolution. It is committed to a belief in the relativity of events and ideas, caught in a process of unceasing and progressive change — 'of endless ascendancy from the lower to the higher' — through the operation of contradictory forces.

It might be thought that Brecht was tempted on occasion to read the 'higher' present into the past in such a way as to 'falsify the historical record'; in his claim, for example, that the unheroic and cynical character Kragler in *Drums in the Night* was 'intended' negatively, or in the over-positive interpretation he gave of his response to the 1919 Spartacist rising before Soviet dignatories in 1955.[19] In other changes and revisions, however, such as to *The*

Threepenny Opera and *Man equals Man*, his project for an 'anti-social Baal', or in the many other changes he made to plays and poems he avoided this for the more honest and educative course of dialectical change, in keeping with a 'true', and progressive historical record.

As a last reply to Willett and Esslin on this point there are Brecht's own words in the poem, 'About the way to construct enduring works':

> How long
> Do works endure? As long
> As they are not completed.
>
> Those devised for completeness
> Show gaps
> The long-lasting
> Are always about to crumble
> Those planned on a really big scale
> Are unfinished
> Still imperfect . . .
>
> Works for endurance must
> Be built like
> A machine full of shortcomings. (P, pp. 193, 194)

Works (of theory, as of drama and poetry) were not to be judged in Brecht's eyes according to their 'completion', but according to their 'use'. And this was to be assessed, as this same poem makes clear, in relation to changing circumstances and changing needs. Brecht of course titled his published works 'Versuche' ('Experiments') from 1930 onwards. The fact then that many of these works, including the essays on a dialectical theatre, were often 'unfinished' or 'makeshift', or 'foreshadowed' a new development was only the more obvious sign of their openness to change, and of Brecht's adherence to his own materialist criterion of value.

Notes

1. *Gesammelte Werke,* 16 (Suhrkamp, Frankfurt am Main, 1967), pp. 869–900.
2. Ibid. 'Anmerkung 13' states that the members of the Berliner

Ensemble were acqainted with both Lenin's 'On the question of dialectics' and Mao's *On Contradiction*.

3. Ibid., p. 891.

4. Ibid., p. 898.

5. 'So far as theory goes', said Brecht in the notes on Strittmatter's play *Katzgraben*, 'I offend against the inflexible rule that the proof of the pudding is in the eating — which happens to be one of my own favourite principles.' *Brecht on Theatre*, p. 248. Brecht's favourite principle was at the same time perfectly consistent with the Marxist 'criterion of practice'. The question of objective truth, Marx said, 'is not a question of theory but is a practical question. man must prove the truth, ie., the reality and power, the this-worldliness of his thinking in practice.' 'Theses on Feuerbach', in *On Dialectical Materialism* (Progress Publishers, Moscow, and Lawrence and Wishart, London, 1977), p. 29. Cf. also statements by Lenin in the same volume, pp. 249, 378. Engels in fact used the phrase 'the proof of the pudding is in the eating' when arguing for the primacy of the material world over sense impressions, ibid., p. 181.

6. Martin Esslin, *Brecht. A Choice of Evils* (Eyre Methuen, London, 1959, revised edition 1980), p. 89.

7. 'Einige Irrtümer über die Spielweise des Berliner Ensembles', *Gesammelte Werke*, 16, p. 908.

8. See the accounts in *Brecht As They Knew Him*, Hubert Witt (ed.) and John Peet (trans.) (Seven Seas Books, Berlin, and International Publishers, New York, 1974, 1977; Lawrence and Wishart, London, 1974, 1980), pp. 90–1, 126–30, 152–8. In an interview in 1949, Brecht declared, 'it is high time that the theatre too evolved a method of working which fits our age, a collective method drawing on all possible experiences', *Brecht on Theatre*, p. 224.

9. Brecht *Man equals Man* John Willett and Ralph Manheim (eds), Gerhard Nellhaus (trans.) (Methuen, London, 1979), p. 108.

10. 'Eigenarten des Berliner Ensembles', *Gesammelte Werke*, 16, pp. 724, 725–6.

11. Ibid., p. 909.

12. Keith A. Dickson, *Towards Utopia. A Study of Brecht* (Clarendon Press, Oxford, 1978), p. 57.

13. *Gesammelte Werke,* 16, p. 869.

14. Esslin, *Brecht*, pp. 133–4.

15. *Gesammelte Werke*, 16, p. 923.

16. Marx, 'Theses on Feuerbach' in *On Dialectical Materialism*, p. 32. As early as 1930, Brecht spoke of one of the functions of the play *Mahagonny*, as being 'to change society'. In *The Mother*, he said, he was 'anxious to teach the spectator a quite definite practical attitude, directed towards changing the world'. In a later comment he describes the 'theatre of instruction' as 'an affair for philosophers, but only for such philosophers as wished not just to explain the world but also to change it.' Thirdly, in a posthumously published note on *Katzgraben,* Brecht spoke retrospectively of wanting to 'take the principle that it was not just a matter of interpreting the world but of changing it, and apply that to the theatre.' *Brecht on Theatre*, pp. 41, 57, 72, 248.

17. Engels, *On Dialectical Materialism*, pp. 156–7.

18. Lenin, ibid., p. 319. and cf. also pp. 373–4.

19. See Esslin's response to Brecht's alteration and 1954 foreword to *Drums in the Night* in *Brecht*, p. 139. For a more sympathetic view see Frederic Ewen, who remains unconvinced, however, on Brecht's stated early response to the Spartacus uprising, *Bertolt Brecht. His Life, His Art and His Times* (Citadel Press, New York, 1969), pp. 62, 109.

2

Dialectical Drama and a Changing World

Many commentators have recognised that in adopting the term 'dialectics' for his late essays, Brecht was in fact returning to a much earlier usage. In 1930 he had announced a series of essays under the title 'On a dialectical drama'. The title 'On a non-aristotelian drama' was in the event preferred to this, but the *Collected Works* includes a 14-page set of notes, dated 1931, titled 'The dialectical drama', whose sub-title announces 'Grundgedanke: Anwendung der Dialektik führt zu revolutionärem Marxismus' ('The fundamental theme: the application of the dialectic leads to revolutionary Marxism').[1] Some of the arguments of this essay are also very close to those developed in surrounding essays, such as 'The epic theatre and its difficulties' (1927), 'On form and subject matter' (1929) and the notes to *The Rise and Fall of the Town Mahagonny* (1930) and *The Threepenny Opera* (1931).

In 'The dialectical drama' Brecht describes how a new form has developed dialectically out of the naturalistic novel to produce a drama which is appropriate to contemporary subject matter, and which promotes an objective or 'scientific' attitude on the part of its audience. This drama (which Brecht describes as 'epic') is, however, incomplete, in that it has not been concretely realised, and remains in many respects bourgeois. It has accepted, Brecht says, that the individual is no longer to be seen as autonomous and sovereign, it has adopted an historical perspective, and it has recognised experience as a process of ceaseless change ('alles im Fluss'), but it presents only an imperfect grasp of external reality, construing real events as the meagre signs of intellectual processes (p. 219). 'Epic' in this manifestation was a formal category only; 'Man muß verstehen,' writes Brecht, 'dass es sich immer noch nur um einem *technischen Vorstoß*, keineswegs um irgendeine politische

Aktion handelte' ('One must understand that it was a matter still only of a *technical advance*, and in no way of any political action') (p. 220). In a period when typical human behaviour was subjected to contemporary methods of objective investigation which gave unquestioning assent to the existing order, the new drama joined in tracing merely 'den "Kurven menschlicher Geschicke" ' ('the "curves of human fates" ') (ibid).

Beyond this Brecht points to the development of a pedagogic element, inherent within naturalistic drama, which gave what had been a series of hollow constructivist experiments an application to the real world, 'worauf sie die Dialektik der Realität entdeckte (und sich ihrer eigenen Dialektik bewußt wurde') ('whereupon it discovered the dialectic of reality (and became conscious of its own dialectic)') (p. 217). As Brecht describes it, this development required not only a 'quantitative' change in the audience (from individuals to a collective mass) but a subsequent 'qualitative' change in political consciousness.

> Aufgefordert, eine nicht willenlose (auf Magie, Hypnose beruhende), hingegebene, sondern eine beurteilende Haltung einzunehmen, nahmen die Zuhörer sofort eine ganz bestimmte *politische* Haltung ein, nicht eine *über* den Interessen stehende, allgemeine, gemeinsame, wie die neue Dramatik gewünscht hätte.
> (Called upon to adopt a critical rather than a passive and submissive attitude (based on magic, hypnosis) the spectators adopted immediately a quite definite *political* attitude, not a general, commonly held one, standing *above* the interests, as the new drama would have wished.) (p. 223)

Educating and informing the audience in this dialectical transformation would lead in its turn, however, to a change in the function of the theatre, and standing in the way of this change, says Brecht, is the institution of the theatre itself. Brecht argues here, as he does in the notes to *Mahagonny* and *The Threepenny Opera*, that the class character and economic conditions of the theatre mean that it employs its practically inexhaustible capacity for absorbing new work to neutralise any sign of genuine innovation in the name of an evening's entertainment and the *status quo*: 'It theatres it all down' is how he puts it, adding 'Of course this priority [of the theatre's means of production over its dramatic productions] has economic reasons'.[2] In 'The dialectical drama' Brecht is suggesting that in following its own internal dialectic, especially the implications of its pedagogic aspect, the new drama will be led to challenge the ideological function of the theatre and thus to confront its economic basis. He ends the essay 'die Ökonomie führte sie zu einer höheren Stufe der Dialektik, der *bewußten* Stufe'. ('Economics led it to a higher stage of the dialectic, the *conscious* stage.') (p. 225)

As 'The dialectical drama' and other essays in the same period reveal Brecht felt it imperative to grasp and transform the ideological function of the theatre: 'It is not the play's effect on the audience' he wrote in 'The epic theatre and its difficulties', 'but its effect on the theatre that is decisive at this moment'. And later in the same essay 'it is precisely theatre, art and literature which have to form the 'ideological superstructure'' for a solid, practical rearrangement of our age's way of life'. (BT, pp. 22–3) In his slightly later discussions of radio and film he extends this priority and the related case for a socialisation of the means of production to media other than theatre. (BT, pp. 48–9, 52) The co-operative, non-profit-making film company, including Brecht, Ernst Ottwalt, Hanns Eisler and Slatan Dudow, which made *Kuhle Wampe* in 1932, was an attempt to put this thinking into practice. But the banning of this film and Brecht's mixed experience over the filming of *The Threepenny Opera* in 1929 and 1930 (his much revised film script was rejected and Brecht lost the case when it was brought to court, though he accepted a substantial money settlement), seemed to demonstrate not only the importance, even the necessity, of gaining effective control over the means of production, but also the difficulty of securing and maintaining this control.

Brecht was in fact contemplating no less than a form of revolutionary change; his argument being that a change in the theatre's audience would lead to a change in the theatre's social function and thence in its economic basis, and that this would in turn provoke a change in the entire social order. This would seem to be the movement of the dialectic as Brecht sketches it in 'The dialectical drama'. His practical experience, however, not only demonstrated that the realisation of this apparently logical sequence was beset with difficulties, but went some way to confirm his description of the problems of social change in the same essay as 'insoluble' (p. 224).

Brecht's reading of Marx, which he had begun in 1926, might have explained why this was the case. For Marxism argues that to see social change as proceeding, as in this perspective, from formal changes in drama, or from more general changes in attitude to society in general, is to misconceive the dialectical relationship by which 'social consciousness' acts upon 'social being', or the 'ideological superstructure' acts upon 'the economic base', but are both 'in the last instance' determined by these forces. There is enough evidence to suggest that Brecht had taken the point of this essential Marxist premise, and that he likewise, in his own terms, appreciated the distinction Marxism makes between the means and the relations of production. In the essay, from 1929, 'On form and subject-matter' included in *Brecht on Theatre*, for example, Brecht writes, 'The first thing therefore is to comprehend the new subject-matter; the second to shape the new relations. The reason: art follows reality.' He goes on to talk of 'the extraction and refinement of petroleum' and related 'quite new forms of human relationship' and comments, 'But it wasn't the new mode of behaviour that created this particular way of refining petrol. The petroleum complex came first and the new relationships are secondary. The new relationships represent mankind's answers to questions of "subject matter"; these are the solutions.' (BT, p. 29)

In the table of characteristics listed under 'Epic theatre' in the notes on *Mahagonny*, Brecht is even more decided. There he categorically sets the materialist 'social being determines thought' against the idealist 'thought determines being' of 'Dramatic theatre'. (BT, p. 37) But if this was indeed the case, social change on the scale Brecht was envisaging it could not proceed unchecked, unaided, or undetermined, from a beginning in artistic and intellectual work. Brecht's 'The dialectical drama' does address social change from *within* a discussion of artistic change, but it also takes this argument to its possible limits — that an audience will be enjoined to adopt 'a quite definite *political* attitude' — while simultaneously exposing its limitations as a means to social transformation. A 'dialectical' drama, that is to say, is said to arrive at (no more, nor less than) 'consciousness', not itself to perform social and economic change, and Brecht sees it thwarted in the full prospect of its political objectives by the institution of the theatre, and by the prevailing economic order. As a *Marxist* intellectual and writer he was therefore brought in this essay to recognise the specific but limited kind of change art could of itself hope to effect. All the same one feels that this discovery was more adventitious than calculated, and that the essay is an expression as much of Brecht's frustration as it is of his political realism.

In the opening to 'On form and subject matter', Brecht draws a distinction which adds to our picture of his thinking on these issues:

> Difficulties are not mastered by keeping silent about them. Practice demands that one step should follow another; theory has to embrace the entire sequence. The new subject-matter constitutes the first stage; the sequence however goes further. The difficulty is that it is hard to work on the first stage (new subjects) when one is already thinking about the second (humanity's new mutual relationships). Establishing the function of helium is not much use in helping one to establish a vast picture of the world; yet there is no hope of establishing it if one has anything other than (or more than) helium in one's mind. The proper way to explore humanity's new mutual relationships is via the exploration of the new subject-matter. (Marriage, disease, money, war, etc.) (BT, p. 29)

Not the least revealing factor here is Brecht's idiosyncratic vocabulary. His terms slide from one designation to another: his reference to 'practice' becomes a reference to 'the new subject-matter' which in the following paragraph is glossed as 'the situation', and seems in his remarks on 'the petroleum complex' quoted above, to refer to scientific or technical developments, or what Marxism would term the 'productive forces'. 'Theory' on the other hand is associated with an anticipation of 'humanity's new mutual relationships'; the new social relations of production, as they might be described, which derive from changes in the economy or productive forces. Brecht states clearly enough in his own terms that these latter developments are secondary and dependent on the first. But there is an implication still that 'theory' and thoughts of new human relationships in a total view of social change, run ahead of themselves, or ahead of the material changes in 'practice', 'subject-matter', or 'situation' which would make them possible.

Brecht himself we might say was fast acquiring a 'theory', namely revolutionary Marxism, which embraced 'the entire sequence (entailing no less than 'the transformation of the whole social order' as he puts it in 'The dialectical drama'). He wished however to 'apply' this theory to drama in such a way that it would be understood as participating in the dialectical process of history, but also be seen as an active *dialecticising* agency which would spur on this process by politicising its audiences. The problem being, as the theory of Marxism pointed out, that changes in drama, or in the institution or social relations of the theatre, were themselves involved in a dialectic in which they were secondary. Both theory and theatre apparently waited on history for their realisation ('The reason: art follows reality') though they went beyond it in anticipating 'the entire sequence' and 'humanity's new social relationships'.

To explain this we have to look further than Brecht's personal development. Brecht's 'dialectical' theory arrived at an impasse almost in the same moment that it was conceived, first because of the generally problematic relation between cultural and historical change, but also because of the particular movement of history and the political situation of the late 1920s and early 1930s.. At first sight it would seem that Brecht, as someone newly impressed with the Marxist explanation of capitalism, would be likely to see the political and economic turmoil of these years as a presage of social revolution. John Willett for one, chooses to see Brecht's stress on 'pedagogics' and the appearance of his 'most sharply Communist works' in these years in these terms. Indeed he goes further to suggest that the notes on *Mahagonny* and *The Threepenny Opera* 'should be read in the light of the political and economic crisis which developed in Germany during the second half of 1929, making revolutionary change seem not only desirable but imminent.' (BT, p. 33)

The relevant events of 1929 were the shooting and killing of workers by police on May Day in Berlin, a series of prohibitive decrees against the movement of people in the city's working-class districts which followed, and then from October the economic repercussions of the Wall Street crash. Brecht had watched the clashes between the workers and police from the window of Fritz Sternberg's apartment, and Sternberg later reported his belief that 'it was this experience that was not least influential in bringing him [Brecht] closer and closer to the Communists'.[2]

This experience may well have reinforced a belief on Brecht's part that revolution was 'desirable', but there is nothing in Sternberg's account, or elsewhere, to suggest that Brecht saw it at the same time as 'imminent'. Nor is Willett's interpretation of the political situation the most obvious one. Frederick Ewen, for example, discussing Brecht's *Mahagonny* as a portrait of the anarchy and near collapse of the Weimar Republic, describes the close of the 1920s as follows:

> The impact of the world economic crisis was just beginning to be felt; but there could be no mistaking the meaning of the increased aggressiveness of the nationalists and National Socialists; nor of the secret militarisation of the rightists; nor

> of the weakness of the Weimar regime in the face of these threats. The population was bewildered, especially the working classes, in the face of the innumerable parliamentary crises, changes of government, and most disturbing, the frequent resort by Hindenburg and Brüning to government by decree. Dissensions on the left — the inability of Communists and Socialists to form a common front in the face of mounting unemployment and patent disaster, undermined faith in leadership. Scandal after scandal in high places, involving even officials of the Weimar regime, and several prominent Social Democrats (the notorious 'Sklarek' affair) made for cynicism. That large industrialists and financiers were openly supporting the National Socialists was taken for granted.[3]

Whatever else, this is not a picture of imminent socialist revolution. No more is Brecht's description of *Mahagonny* as a capitalist hell where 'nothing is forbidden', where 'the penniless man/is the worst kind of criminal', and where the working-class lumberjacks are defenders of exploitation.[4] If we accept, all the same, that Brecht did indeed move 'closer to the Communists', the general and growing influence of the Party, as measured in the elections of September 1930 when their vote increased by 50 per cent, has to be set alongside the massive swing to Hitler's National Socialist German Workers Party which increased its vote by 800 per cent in the same elections.[5]

If Marxism, then, and events in Berlin, provided Brecht with a vision of 'changed human relationships', to which a dialecticising theatre would contribute, he was also witness to much which would prevent and forestall its outcome. Both perspectives consequently appear in his early essays, including 'The dialectical drama' which for all its revolutionary ambition runs up against the wall of the class character of existing theatre and the capitalist economy of present society.,

In the end we can perhaps only surmise why the actual term 'dialectics' appeared in the headnote for a projected set of essays and then in 'The dialectical drama', but not in other contemporary and subsequent essays. The weighty political, ideological and economic obstacles Brecht saw in its path must surely have been one reason. In the event he turned away from the project of expressly applying dialectical materialism to the theatre (away from 'theory' one might say) to consider more intrinsic questions of dramatic form and function (as if substituting 'helium' for 'the picture of the world'), which were capable of change and conducive still to the larger aims he saw as necessary and desirable. This would explain too Brecht's descripton of *Mahagonny* as 'nothing more or less than an opera' (BT, p. 37), though he attacks 'opera' in much the same way he attacks the orthodox theatre. He ends the notes on *Mahagonny*

> Perhaps *Mahagonny* is as culinary as ever — just as culinary as an opera ought to be — but one of its functions is to change society; it brings the culinary principle under discussion, it attacks the society that needs operas of such a sort; it still perches happily on the old bough, perhaps, but at least it has started (out of absent-mindedness or bad conscience) to saw it through . . . (BT, p. 41)

A new society could not appear overnight any more than a new tree, nor could the 'old opera' as Brecht says be 'just "wished away" '. The new must appear from the old, and transitional work and thinking would partake of both. To adapt the maxim reported later by Walter Benjamin, Brecht saw that he must start not ' "from the good old things" ' — nor the good future things — but from ' "the bad new ones." ' (UB, p. 121)

If this is a correct version of Brecht's change of emphasis and reorientation, it also implies a reversal of the priorities he had announced in 1929, when he had said 'it is not the play's effect on the audience but its effect on the theatre that is decisive at the moment'. These two effects are quite clearly related and 'in sequence' in Brecht's thinking, but one can see how the increasingly restricted opportunities for securing control of the 'means of production', or even of a venue for such production in a Berlin experiencing Hitler's rise to power, would have turned Brecht's attention from the second to the first as a more practical possibility. His situation in exile from 1933, in Scandinavia and then in America, would have put questions of economic and large-scale social change further beyond the realm of what was immediately and practically possible, even as such changes seemed more urgent. This would make sense too, along with the change from a 'dialectical drama' to an 'epic theatre', of the disappearance in subsequent essays of the themes of the theatre's economic basis and the socialisation of the means of cultural production. By the mid-1930s these interests had been overtaken by Brecht's development of the theory of *Verfremdung*. And this, for all its centrality, also implied a shortening of focus or change of tactics, since *Verfremdung* was designed to fulfil the drama's pedagogic function, precisely by effecting a transformation *in the audience*. This is not to say that *Verfremdung* ruled out the further changes Brecht looked to, beyond the raising of consciousness it was intended to provoke, but that as a theatrical technique it could not guarantee them. Once again, the success of a dialecticising experience in the theatre had to wait upon the operations of the dialectic in history.

A later statement, unpublished in Brecht's lifetime but said to date from the mid-1930s, confirms just this. Brecht writes,

> Up to now favourable circumstances for an epic and didactic theatre have only been found in a few places and for a short period of time. In Berlin Fascism put a very definite stop to the development of such a theatre.
>
> It demands not only a certain technological level but a powerful movement in society which is interested to see vital questions freely aired with a view to their solution, and can defend this interest against every contrary trend. (BT, p, 76)

For the signs of such 'a powerful movement in society' Brecht had to wait until the period of rconstruction after World War II.

Notes

1. *Gesammelte Werke*, 15 (Suhrkamp, Frankfurt am Main, 1967), pp. 211–25. Page numbers for subsequent quotations from this essay are given in the text.

2. Fritz Sternberg, *Der Dichter und die Ratio. Errinnerungen an Bertolt Brecht* (Sachse und Pohl, 1963), pp. 25–6. The relevant passage is quoted in Frederic Ewen, *Bertolt Brecht. His Life, His Art, and His Times* (Citadel Press, New York, 1969), p. 185.

3. Ewen, *Bertolt Brecht*, p. 192.

4. *The Rise and Fall of the City of Mahagonny*, in *Collected Plays*, Vol. 2iii, John Willett and Ralph Manheim (eds) (Eyre Methuen, London, 1979), pp. 27, 57.

5. See Ronald Taylor's account in *Literature and Society in Germany, 1918–1945* (Harvester Press, Brighton, Sussex, and Barnes and Noble, Totowa, New Jersey, 1980), pp. 28, 31. Taylor judges that by June 1932, 'the only power to offer a viable alternative to the Nazis was that of conservative nationalism, backed by the army', p. 32.

3

A 'By No Means Undialectical' Epic Theatre: Brecht's *Gestus*

In referring to Brecht's early notes on a dialetical drama John Willett concludes that 'The term "dialectical" went into cold storage, to be taken out again in a somewhat different context at the end of Brecht's life'. (BT, p. 46)[1] As any reader of Brecht's prose writings can see, however, his interest in dialectics did not disappear in 1929 or 1930. If anything, it was consolidated in the Marxist and philosophical studies conducted from 1926 through to 1941.[2] Here, amongst other topics Brecht examined dialectics in relation to social class and as a method of revolutionary thinking, presenting a sketch of the political role of intellectuals in 'perforating' bourgeois ideology, dialecticising all areas of thought, and developing revolutionary theory, together with a ten-point statement on the relative autonomy of the superstructure.[3] *The Philosophical Notes 1929–1941* contain related sections titled 'On Dialectics' and 'On interventionist thinking' ('eingreifendes Denken') where, in one group of essays, Brecht considers the agenda for a 'Society of dialecticians' — of the kind perhaps which met in his own apartment in the early 1930s, and in another passage titled 'Dialectics' dismisses the mechanical and undialectical idea of progress towards socialism.[4] The essays on 'interventionist thinking' confirm Brecht's view of dialectics as a mode of critical thinking, purposefully oriented towards practice and social change. In an earlier passage titled 'Critical Marxism' he had referred to this as 'die Kunst des praktischen Negierens, . . . die, der Entwicklungsgesetze eingedenk, im Hinblick auf eine bestimmte mögliche Lösung kritisiert.' ('the art of practical negation . . . which, mindful of the laws of development, criticises with a view to a definite possible solution.').[5] Marxism 'lehrt eingreifendes Denken gegenüber der Wirklichkeit' ('teaches interventionist thinking towards reality'), says Brecht, and

Marx and Lenin, in the interchangeable set of terms he explores in these essays, were themselves examples of interventionist, critical, dialectical, and 'correct thinking'.[6]

Elsewhere, aside from the references to dialectics and dialectical materialism in the allegorical *Me-Ti*, Brecht's published writings include a conversation with Hermann Greid, titled 'On dialectics', from 1939, and a short essay rejecting propagandist verse, also from the 1930s, and titled 'The dialectic'.[7] Few direct references to dialectics and drama appear in these essays it is true, but there are significant exceptions even so: notably the programatic notes on 'Dialectics and *Verfremdung*', the argument of which was then confirmed in the later appendices to *The Messingkauf Dialogues* and in at least one entry in Brecht's *Arbeitsjournal.*[8]

My point, however, is not to number references and titles — though these do count for something. What we can say is that the titular concept of a 'dialectical drama' is replaced by that of an 'epic theatre' and thence by a discussion of *Gestus* and *Verfremdung*, with perhaps the explanation for this change I have given previously. My argument here is that the informing principles of dialectics are, nevertheless, never far from Brecht's dramatic theory. We can see in 'The dialectical drama' indeed, how the terms dialectics, epic, *Verfremdung* and *Gestus* were already associated in Brecht's thinking. In that essay Brecht is discussing an 'epic' element in drama, and he refers both to gest and a form of the 'alienation-effect' that was to become *Verfremdung*. Experiments in epic drama, he says, had led to the discovery of the role of the gest ('das Gestische') and this 'was precisely the dialectical element which put the theatrical in the dramatic'.[9] Later in the essay he writes, 'The broad types that were presented in as strange ('fremd') and objective a way as possible (so that one could not identify with them) ought to have pointed through their treatment to other types'.[10]

Statements such as these suggest how close in certain respects Brecht's early conception of the relation between epic and dialectic was to the much later discussion of 'Dialectics in the theatre'. Brecht's theory did of course change between 1931 and the middle 1950s, but his description in the early essay of 'epic' as a 'formal principle' which is nevertheless necessary to a dialectical drama is echoed in the later remark that ' "epic theatre" is too formal a term for the kind of theatre aimed at', though it is at the same time 'a prerequisite for these contributions'. Along with this there was his retrospective comment in the introductory paragraph to 'Dialectics in the theatre': 'in our view', said Brecht, 'and according to our intentions, the epic theatre's practice — and the whole idea — were by no means undialectical'.[11] The implications of this remark for the theory of the 1930s and 1940s are, I think, worth pursuing.

John Willett says of the change in Brecht's theoretical nomenclature around 1930 that 'non-Aristotelian' rather than 'dialectical' 'was a better description of his theatre at this stage, referring as it does above all to the elimination of empathy and imitation (or mimesis)'. (BT, p. 47) Without some account of the grounds for Brecht's opposition to empathy and imitation, however, we are left with a seemingly fussy and aesthetic distinction between dramatic modes. By the term 'non-Aristotelian' Brecht indicated his rejection of the dramatic form — Aristotle talks of tragedy particularly in these terms — whose object was to purge the emotions of pity and fear through the experience of catharsis. Brecht's more immediate target, however, aside from the parlous state of existing German theatre, was the long-standing assumption that whereas 'epic' recorded the world through narrative as completed action in the past, 'drama' portrayed the world through an illusion of reality, as if it were being witnessed in the present. This distinction had been presented by Goethe and Schiller jointly in 1797 in the essay 'On epic and dramatic poetry'. The means and the ends of drama as given in this tradition represented everything to which Brecht was opposed. It was assumed that drama required rounded, believable individuals, an effect of verisimilitude, an emotional identification with leading players themselves lost in their role, and in general a suspension of disbelief whose effect could only be a narcotic dulling of the mind and imagination. Drama of this kind effectively reconciled its audiences to the *status quo* in the form of an accepted and unalterable Fate. Theatrical illusions Brecht realised, 'have an important social function' which they go on fulfilling so long as the situation they meet remains unaltered; 'the drug is irreplaceable; it cannot be done without'. (BT, p. 41) But the vulgarising of Fate to a level 'of reconciling oneself to circumstances' conceals the class function such a concept and resolution now played: 'fate', wrote Brecht in 1929, 'is no longer a single coherent power; rather there are fields of force which can be seen as radiating in opposite directions; the power groups themselves comprise movements not only against one another but within themselves, etc. etc.' (BT, p. 30) Fate has become a matter of 'class-warfare — where one class fixes the fate of the other'. (BT, p. 49)

Just as, in one way, Brecht sees the theatre as a cultural institution which absorbs and neutralises innovative work so as to produce the merchandise of an evening's entertainment as befits a capitalist society, so at another level the drama of illusion is seen to reinforce the ideology necessary to this society. Thus, in its conception of character and in its style of acting, it upholds the notion of the whole and autonomous individual; its plots provide the security of a unitary, linear chain of events moving towards a predictable end, and its structure assumes the value of a harmoniously fused and sacrosanct work of art — removed 'from every process and influence of our time'. (BT, p. 49)

Brecht's opposition to the combined individualism, evolutionism and idealism perpetuated by this drama was evident from the early 1930s. In 1931, he spoke of the individual as being 'now in a state of complete dissolution', of having 'collapsed long ago', and of a contrary view of human beings as experiencing inner 'friction' — ' "the sum of all social circumstances" '. (BT, pp. 45, 46) The epic theatre's methods meant, said Brecht, a 'separation of the elements' rather than their fusion: 'so long as the expression "Gesamtkunstwerk" (or "integrated work of art") means that the integration is a muddle, so long as the arts are supposed to be "fused" together, the various elements will all be degraded'. The 'process of fusion' he added, 'extends to the spectator, who gets thrown into the melting pot too and becomes a passive (suffering) part of the total work of art.' (BT, pp. 37–8) As he put it in his notes to *The Threepenny Opera*, 'the epic drama, with its materialistic standpoint and its lack of interest in any investment of its spectators' emotions' is opposed to 'The dynamic, idealistically-orientated kind of drama, with its interest in the individual'; it follows not 'a single inevitable chain of events' with the emotional security this allows, but 'a different kind of chain, whose course need not be a straight one but may quite well be in curves or even in leaps.' (BT, p. 45)

Some of these ideas come together in Brecht's remarks on *Man equals Man*, and then in the slightly later notes on *The Mother*. Answering objections to Peter Lorre's way of speaking the part of Galy Gay, Brecht writes,

> The speeches' content was made up of contradictions and the actor had not to make the spectator identify himself with individual sentences and so get caught up in contradictions, but to keep him out of them. Taken as a whole it had to be the most objective possible exposition of a contradictory internal process. (BT, p. 54)

He goes on then to distinguish the epic actor's performance from the capacity needed by the older actor 'for coherent and unhurried development'. The epic actor, says Brecht, 'has to be able to show his character's coherence despite, or rather by means of, interruptions and jumps.' (BT, p. 55) It then follows that in the character's development 'the various phases must be able to be clearly seen, and therefore separated'. (ibid.) Finally, the epic actor's 'way of knotting all the separate elements together . . . do not altogether add up to a single unchangeable character, but to one which changes all the time and becomes more and more clearly defined in course of "this way of changing" '. (BT, p. 56)

If the actor must change in what Brecht calls his 'anti-metaphysical, materialist, non-aristotelian drama', so too must the spectator. In the notes to *The Mother* which opens with this description of his contemporary didactic pieces, Brecht writes of how such a theatre, 'Anxious to teach the spectator a quite definite practical attitude, directed towards changing the world . . . must begin by making him adopt in the theatre a quite different attitude from what he is used to.' (BT, p. 57) In Brecht's description, epic theatre's 'indirect impact' is achieved by non-illusionistic staging, which takes an attitude towards the incidents shown, by groupings in 'natural order', and by acting such as Helene Weigel's creation of the part of Vlasova, the Mother, when she 'spoke the sentences as if they were in the third person'. In this way Weigel herself refrained from identifying with the character and also prevented the spectator from transporting himself/herself to a particular scene as if he/she were an 'invisible eye-witness and eavesdropper'. (BT, p. 58) In the terms of Goethe and Schiller's 'On epic and dramatic poetry', Brecht thus elects for the narrative manner of the epic poet, who 'surrounded by a circle of quiet listeners', relates 'what has happened in calm contemplation.'[12] This is akin to the relaxed, yet informed, practical and questioning attitude Brecht wished to inculcate in his audience. In a sense he seems to require no more than 'the taking of an attitude' — just as he had spoken of the separated elements of epic theatre 'adopting attitudes' to its content.

> Once the content becomes, technically speaking, an independent component, to which text, music and setting 'adopt attitudes'; once illusion is sacrificed to free discussion, and once the spectator, instead of being enabled to have an experience, is forced as it were to cast his vote, then a change has been launched which goes far beyond formal matters and

> begins for the first to affect the theatre's social function. (BT, p. 39)

Being forced, as it were, to cast a vote, is not the same as being compelled to vote one way. For all the talk of Brecht's dogmatic communism in the phase of his 'didactic plays', he writes, in his discussion of *The Mother* once more, of the play's 'indirect impact', distinguishing between the epic theatre, Aristotelian drama, and a drama of 'direct impact':

> In calling for a direct impact, the aesthetics of the day call for an impact that flattens out all social and other distinctions between individuals. Plays of the aristotelian type still manage to flatten out class conflicts in this way although the individuals themselves are becoming increasingly aware of class differences. The same result is achieved even when class conflicts are the subject of such plays, and even in cases where they take sides for a particular class. A collective entity is created in the auditorium for the *duration of the entertainment*, on the basis of the 'common humanity' shared by all spectators alike. Non-aristotelian drama of *Die Mutter's* sort is not interested in the establishment of such an entity. It divides its audience. (BT, p. 60)

Just as Brecht saw the individual as the product of contradictory forces and the work of art as 'a bundle of separate elements', so his theatre was consciously directed at dividing its audience — inevitably along class lines.

Statements such as this suggest at the same time how misleading the translation 'didactic play' for Brecht's *Lehrstück* can be. His own suggested English equivalent was 'learning play' and this is generally preferable and more accurate. Epic theatre, as Brecht said in one of many such statements, was designed to teach a 'quite practical attitude, we have to make it possible for him [the spectator] to take a critical attitude while he is in the theatre.' (BT, p. 78) The vital distinction becomes then the one Brecht made in an interview in 1934: 'This isn't', said Brecht, explaining epic drama, 'the same thing as committed art. At most pedagogics.' (BT, p. 67) This is at the heart of his opposition to Aristotelian and neo-Aristotelian categories. He was opposed to empathy and imitation because they were the chief characteristics of an illusionist theatre, and because this theatre induced a passivity which could only serve the ends of social and political conformism or reaction. In short he was opposed to their ideological effect or 'social function'. Hence his argument for a theatre with an educative and politicising function which would help install an informed but questioning general public.

Though the term 'dialectic' does not appear in Brecht's account of epic theatre summarised above, many of its leading features could be glossed from the texts of dialectical materialism as being in accordance with the classic 'laws' of the unity of opposites, the transformation of quantity into quality, and the negation of the negation. Brecht, we can say, was opposed from the 'materialistic standpoint' of epic theatre to the metaphysical idealism of conventional realist drama. As characterised by Engels, metaphysics 'accepted things as finished objects', it 'preferred to investigate *things* as given, as fixed and stable'.[13] In this way in realistic drama (and generally in bourgeois aesthetics) the integrated work of art, the operation of Fate or circumstance, and human nature — as exemplified by the 'coherent ego' of individual characters and an undifferentiated collective audience — are viewed as fixed, stable and unalterable 'things'. Brecht's comments above, on Fate, on the character of Galy Gay, on the 'separation of the elements', on his intention to divide and transform the audience, show how he viewed such supposedly unified and eternal entities as properly a complex of contradictory (class) forces, set in a process of change. His rejection of the abstraction 'Man' with all that this implied finds a precedent in Marx's 6th Thesis on Feuerbach:

> But the essence of man is no abstraction inherent in each single individual. In its reality it is the ensemble of the social relations.[14]

More generally, in perceiving and wishing to present the contradictory, changing sides of actions and events, Brecht was applying what, according to Lenin was 'one of the principal, if not the principal, characteristics [sic] . . . of dialectics'; to wit, 'The splitting of a single whole and the cognition of its contradictory parts'.[15] Even more strikingly, Brecht's conception of the development of character (understood 'as "the sum of all social circumstances" ') and of narrative, echoes to the point of its very phrasing, the view within the texts of dialectical materialism of a progressive, but discontinuous, pattern of change. 'History moves often in leaps and bounds and in a zigzag line' wrote Engels.[16] And Brecht, in 1929: 'Today's catastrophes do not progress in a straight line but in cyclical crises'. (BT, p. 30) Statements by Lenin reinforce and elaborate this view of development. He speaks, writing of Marx and Engels, of their common view of any other principle of development than dialectics as distorting 'the actual course of development (which often proceeds by leaps, and *via* catastrophes and revolutions)', of human knowledge as following 'not . . . a straight line, but a curve, which endlessly approximates a series of circles, a spiral.'[17] Brecht's view of epic theatre as following 'a kind of chain, whose course need not be a straight line, but may well be in curves or even in leaps', and of the epic actor as needing 'to show his character's coherence despite, or rather by means of, interruptions and jumps' are obviously in keeping with this, and belong in the full context of dialectical principles set out by Lenin.

> In our times the idea of development, of evolution, has almost completely penetrated social consciousness, only in other ways, and not through Hegelian philosophy. Still, this idea, as formulated by Marx and Engels on the basis of Hegel's philosophy, is far more comprehensive and far richer in content than the current idea of evolution is. A development that repeats, as it were, stages that have already been passed, but repeats them in a different way, on a higher basis ('the negation of negation'), a development, so to speak, that proceeds in spirals, not in a straight line; a development by leaps, catastrophes, and revolutions; 'breaks in continuity'; the transformation of quantity into quality; inner impulses towards development, imparted by the contradiction and conflict of the various forces and tendencies acting on a given body, or within a given phenomenon, or within a given society; the interdependence and the closest and indissoluble connection between *all* aspects of any phenomenon (history constantly revealing ever new aspects), a connection that provides a uniform, and universal process of motion, one that follows definite laws — these are some of the features of dialectics as a doctrine of development that is richer than the conventional one.[18]

Further direct evidence of the informing influence of Marxism upon Brecht's early dramatic theory appears in the notes to *Mahagonny*. The four characteristics of epic theatre tabled as 'in curves', 'jumps' (as opposed to the 'linear development' and 'evolutionary determinism' of dramatic theatre), 'man as a process' and 'social being determines thought' could all once again be cross-referenced with the statements of dialectical materialism given above. In Brecht's essay they are linked with the ingredients of 'narrative', 'argument', 'montage', 'reason', with epic theatre's view of the human being as 'the object of the enquiry', as 'alterable and able to alter', and with its pedagogic function, which 'turns the spectator into an observer, but / arouses his capacity for action / forces him to take decisions'. (BT, p. 37) Brecht's debt to Marxism here is of a kind to suggest that he is not simply 'quoting' its principles, but has absorbed them and is, moreover, 'applying' them — as he had intended in the project for a dialectical drama. It is this extension of the essential philosophy of Marxism into the realm of art and its 'social duties', to use Brecht's term, which is impressive. And this too, once again, which distinguishes Brecht's means and ends from those of a 'committed art', when this is understood, as most commonly it has been, as an art which treats a topical political subject, or propagandises for a particular political programme or party.

By the date of the *Mahagonny* notes Brecht had introduced the terms *Gestus* and *gestisch* into his theoretical vocabulary. In a rudimentary sense these terms mean what John Willett in *Brecht on Theatre* says they do; they refer to 'both gist and gesture; an attitude or a single aspect of an attitude, expressible in words or actions'. (BT, p. 42) More than this, however, we have seen from 'The dialectical drama' that Brecht associates, indeed identifies *gestisch* with the dialectic. Later in the 1930s this connection was elaborated by his friend and co-exile, Walter Benjamin, in the essay 'What is epic theatre?' Benjamin's essay appears to be largely based on Brecht's notes to *Mahagonny* and *Man equals Man*, plus a performance of that play which he describes as 'a model of epic theatre'. (UB, p. 3) In his own notes on *Man equals Man* Brecht writes of how the actor Peter Lorre's 'manner of speaking had been split up according to gests', of how 'over and above the meaning of the individual sentences a quite specific basic gest was being brought out'. A short film made of the peformance, says Brecht, 'showed how Lorre manages "to mime" the basic meaning underlying every (silent) sentence'. (BT, pp. 54, 55)

These remarks show how close Brecht's idea of 'gestic acting', of presenting a basic underlying attitude or meaning, was to the acting style of the silent cinema, and to the deliberately etched gestures and tableaux of popular melodrama. In fact, though many have found Brecht's term and his description obfuscating, he made a point of referring gest to the authority of common experience. This is evident in his prose and verse accounts of 'the street scene', which remain the best introductions to the technique and purpose Brecht had in mind. (BT, pp. 121–9; P, pp. 176–9) In these texts he presents a 'natural model' from 'everyday theatre' for the instruction of actors in epic theatre. In his main example Brecht describes how in the event of a motor accident a witness will re-enact the scene, imitating exactly but selectively the actions of both driver and victim, while retaining the role of commentator. The purpose of this 'acting' says Brecht, is by no means to identify with the participants or to provoke empathy, but to demonstrate and explain the event, supplying sufficient evidence for the onlookers and listeners to arrive at a judgement, apportioning blame as necessary. In the process the street actor will point out not only what basically happened, but will show too, said Brecht, how it need not have occurred. Imitating the driver and casualty, the eye-witness gives

> Only so much as to make the accident intelligible, and yet
> Enough to make you see them. But he shows neither
> As if the accident had been unavoidable. The accident
> Becomes in this way intelligible, yet not intelligible, for both
> of them
> Could have moved quite otherwise; now he is showing what
> They might have done so that no accident
> Would have occurred. (P, p. 177)

What is entailed in *Gestus* then is the analysis of an underlying (and internally contradictory) social content, the third-person 'quotation' or miming of this content and the undisguised 'knotting together' of a series of social gests in an episodic but progressive and educative narrative. As the name for a repertoire of (self) distancing effects in speech and action, movement and grouping on stage, choral report and the commentary of song, music, costumes, titles and sets, *Gestus* was designed to simplify this narrative of social attitudes and relationships, to make what Brecht called the all important 'story' element of epic theatre, immediately accessible and intelligible. (BT, pp. 200, 202) As the principal vehicle for the necessary 'historicisation' of character and incident, gestic playing eschewed the conventions of psychological portrayal (though Brecht said that the psychological operation of getting into the skin of a character could be used in rehearsal, BT, p. 137) in favour of a more 'finished', external presentation. The resulting separation of character and actor made intellectual and emotional space for the critical observation of familiar social types and stories, and thus for the inference of alternative deeds and destinies. If characters and actions were alterable rather than fixed in nature, and if a dramatic narrative could be interrupted and held up for comment, then it was possible to alter social attitudes and relationships and intervene in the narrative of history.

For many, the ideas of gestic acting, music and staging have proved particularly frustrating. Not only do the forms, and dramaturgical and political effects of *Gestus* appear to be unknowable outside their realisation in the theatre, their only guaranteed example, in practice as in theory, appears to be Brecht himself. Gestic style comes therefore to seem arcane and unrepeatable, a private method frozen in abstracted theory and past time. A common result is that modern theatres aspire to no more than archival productions. Unable to stage authentically 'Brechtian' productions, they 'put on Brecht'. But yet Brecht spoke of the purpose of the model books as being to provoke innovation and development rather than to fix an original. If it is the case that only Brecht could be 'Brechtian', his intentions have obviously come to nothing.

I want to make just two points in this connection, which, though they fall far short of the kind of analysis of theatre history and practice these problems require, nevertheless illustrate that *Gestus* was neither entirely dependent on Brecht's direction, nor exclusive to his own theory and practice. The first concerns the vastly different productions of Brecht's *The Mother* in the early 1930s. Brecht's notes on the first 1932 production in Berlin present this and Helene Weigel's performance as exemplary.[19] The later production by the Theatre Union in New York in 1935, however, was, from his point of view, little short of disastrous.[20] There are several reasons for this. As the last of Brecht's plays to be performed in Berlin before his emigration, *The Mother* came as the culmination, the end of the beginning, of a process of development in Brecht's own work on Lehrstück technique, as well as of developments in German radical and agit-prop theatre. For all the ominous intimations in the early 1930s, Brecht was working in a enriching artistic and political culture. In New York, on the other hand, his ideas and personality (and Hanns Eisler's also, apparently) clashed violently with conventional hierachies in the Theatre Union company and with its Stanilslavskian technique and social realist ambitions.[21] The New York production seemed in short to fail because it was not the

Berlin production. In fact, however, it proved something else. At one level the Theatre Union production failed, quite simply, because of textual distortions, Brecht insisting as much as anything, during rehearsals and in writing, on a return to his text. The point being that, quite aside from questions of acting technique and directorial control. Brecht's text, *as written*, itself ensured certain gestic effects.

The first scene of the play, for example, comprising a speech by the Mother and a chorus, was rewritten, in spite of Brecht's protests, as a dialogue between Vlasova and her son.[22] Of Weigel's performance in the 1932 production, Brecht had written:

> In the first scene the actress stood in a particularly characteristic attitude in the centre of the stage, and spoke the sentences as if they were in the third person; and so she not only refrained from pretending in fact to be or to claim to be Vlassova (the Mother), and in fact to be speaking those sentences, but actually prevented the spectator from transferring himself to a particular room, as habit and indifference might demand, and imagining himself to be the invisible eye witness and eavesdropper of a unique intimate occasion. Instead what she did was openly to introduce the spectator to the person whom he would be watching acting and being acted upon for some hours. (BT, pp. 58–9)

No doubt a great deal of this depended on Helene Weigel's personal skill as an actress and interpreter of Brecht's ideas. Over and above the gestic features of a live performance, however, or rather prior to them, the speaker's third person presentation of herself as a social type ('a worker's widow and a worker's mother') is evident in, and 'directed' by, Brecht's text. So too is the generalising function of the chorus which not only *represents* the Mother's situation, so as to reinforce the picture of her typical devotion and helplessness (she is the 'Vlasovas Of All Countries'), but also, in the change of pronoun in the scene from 'I' to 'you'. simultaneously *addresses* both character and audience. Thus the play's subject, or premise, the customary role and consciousness of the mother figure which the drama will demonstrate as alterable, has already been shown. In the process of political education which then ensues, the 'worker's mother' both shows and experiences the dialectical interaction of common sense with theory in her changing relationship with her son to become no longer the 'eternal' but the revolutionary mother. On returning home after escaping from prison, the son has to find and cut himself some bread in the kitchen while the mother continues with the printing of leaflets. The significance of this reversal and the overall process of change depends on the initial gest of domestic estrangement between mother and son in the opening scene. Here in Brecht's text, the son says nothing. He is absorbed in reading, and, after rejecting the mother's soup, goes out. The conversion of this scene into dialogue, therefore, while it was meant to add realism, in fact subtracted from the social reality of the initial scenic gest and obscured the 'joining up' of scenes in the play's all important 'story', thus putting the play's political theme at risk. In this, and in other cases where Brecht objected to the New York production, gestic content and the demonstration of social attitudes was textually ensured in language as a very material guide to performance. There was, then, such a thing as writing for gest, as well as writing about, or practising it.

The second reason why it is wrong to think of gest as Brecht's personal theory and prerogative, is that others either employed the term or spoke of an equivalent practice. Kurt Weill, for example, had written of the gestic character of music in an essay of 1927 (BT, p. 42), while the arguments for a gestic style of acting had been gaining currency in different left theatre groups in the 1920s in ways which suggested a series of independent but commonly inspired developments. Thus Frederick Wolf, author of the play *Tai Yang Awakens*, which was to influence Brecht's *Good Person of Szechwan*, could write of these developments:

> We must stress again and again that all the left wing plays of the professional theatre — be they 'analytical' like Wangenheim's *Mouse Trap*, or one of Brecht's 'epic' plays, or my own — that all these plays of the 'big form' are unthinkable without the pioneering work of the agitprop troups and Piscator. The essential formal components of our plays — the short scene, the scene montage, the distancing narration and report, the simultaneous scenes . . . the bursting of the boundaries of the proscenium arch and the incorporation of the audience as co-actors and co-workers into the play — they were all fought for by the agitprop troupes and Piscator in hard ideological and practical labour.[23]

Writing to Wolf in 1930, Piscator had called for 'a form of stylised theatre . . . uncompromising and like the Japanese theatre . . .

with basic gestures', and before him, an earlier pioneer, Vsevolod Meyerhold, had spoken in 1910 of the technique of 'stylisation' ('To "stylise" a given period or phenomenon means to employ every possible means of expression in order to reveal the inner synthesis of that period or phenomenon').[24] Meyerhold had drawn on the popular traditions of spectacle, commedia dell'arte, circus and music hall, and these had provided models also for the large number of amateur cabaret and agit-prop groups in Weimar Germany. Of these the most prominent and self-critical were the Berlin Red Megaphone. One of its members, Elli Schliesser, summing up the developments of the twenties in an essay titled 'Looking back and looking forward', criticised both the anarchic ridicule of satiric cabaret and the solemn rigidity of the collective lecture (a form developed by Red Megaphone itself):

> A kind of 'dualism' came about: the belief that one worked either with vivid scenic means . . . but politically superficial — or in a politically serious way, but then in a deadly, dry and boring way . . . recruitment without education and education without appeal, this was the direction in which the cliché would have led.[25]

There must, she writes, be a way, beyond political caricature and simple propaganda:

> We have shown: the Capitalist (mostly with a big belly and a money bag), the (party) Official, the Law — abstractions, concepts which, even in our heads, were not the starting point of a thought process but the final result. We did not represent our thought process on stage — thus developing the concept in the spectator in the same way . . . We must look for forms which enable us to make the relations of class forces visible . . . Away from the cliché, but not back to the 'Old Theatre', the 'Naturalistic Drama', forward to the dialectical play![26]

This is obviously very close to Brecht's own aims in developing gestic acting and gives a new depth to his remark that *The Mother* was both indebted to and went beyond agit-prop in teaching 'the tactics of the class war' in 'a process of development'. (BT, p. 62) Schliesser's words and the work of Red Megaphone and other amateur troupes, along with the innovations associated with Piscator and Wolf in the professional theatre, indicate the kind of shared political culture from which Brecht's own ideas emerged. Others, quite simply, were thinking and working along related lines. And not only was this true of gestic acting, but also, evidently, of the concept of a dialectical drama.

For Walter Benjamin, himself an important figure in that political culture, and an enthusiastic and astute spectator of the first Berlin performance of *The Mother, Gestus* and dialectics were intimately related, and this, indeed, forms the guiding theme of his essays on epic theatre. Some of the forms and effects Benjamin identifies are clear already from Brecht's own writings. For example, Brecht's comment on the way the epic theatre 'divides its audience'. As he put it later, the epic performer is engaged in a discussion about social conditions with his audience, prompting 'the spectator to justify or abolish these conditions according to what class he belongs to.' (BT, p. 139) Benjamin attributes this to *Gestus*; its role being to astonish and therefore interest, but also, as a consequence, to differentiate 'the false and deceptive totality called "audience" ' so that separate, interested parties 'corresponding to conditions as they really are' emerge from within it. (UB, pp. 4, 10) This conforms perfectly, once more, with the dialectical procedure of 'the splitting of a single whole', and as Lenin goes on to describe it, 'the recognition (discovery) of the contradictory, *mutually exclusive*, opposite tendencies in *all* phenomena'.[27]

Secondly, Benjamin writes of how the epic actor's flexible and pluralistic style (changing, as Brecht said, in accordance with a change in the function an actor is fulfilling), is controlled by the dialectic contained in Brecht's repeated directive that ' "The actor must show an event, and he must show himself . . . Although these two tasks coincide, they must not coincide to such a point that the contrast (difference) between them disappear." ' (UB, p. 11) In this 'first commandment of epic theatre . . . that "the one who shows" — that is, the actor — "shall be shown" ', Benjamin finds a similarity with what he calls the 'general educational approach of Marxism', itself 'determined by the dialectic at work between the attitude of teaching and that of learning'. (ibid.)

Thirdly, and this is the main thrust of Benjamin's essay, he suggests that the central dialectic of epic theatre lies in the relation between the encapsulated gest and the continuum which it briefly interrupts. The gest he writes,

> has a definable beginning and a definable end. Indeed, this strict, frame-like, enclosed nature of each moment of an

> attitude which, after all, is as a whole in a state of living flux, is one of the basic dialectical characteristics of the gesture. (UB, p. 3)

Gestus in this sense is like a form of unexpected punctuation which interrupts and retards the 'flow' of events. And this is vital to the functioning of epic theatre, since it is in this way that conditions can be not simply represented on stage but, in a moment of interruption, revealed. What follows is the division of the audience along class lines. This understanding of gest leads Benjamin to conclude:

> the dialectic which epic theatre sets out to present is not dependent on a sequence of scenes in time; rather, it declares itself in those gestural elements that form the basis of each sequence in time . . . The thing that is revealed as though by lightning in the 'condition' represented on the stage — as a copy of human gestures, actions and words — is an immanently dialectical attitude. The conditions which epic theatre reveals is the dialectic at a standstill. (UB, p. 12)

This is an important insight, with implications I shall return to in discussing Benjamin's comments on Brecht's poetry. A qualification which needs to be made at this point, however, is that Benjamin ignores the 'immanently dialectical' combination or 'montage' of a *series* of gests in epic theatre's narrative sequence — what Brecht calls 'this way of joining up'. For if the single gest brings the dialectic to a standstill (revealing contradictory conditions, the separation of actor and character, and gives rise to an informed partisanship on the part of the audience), it also resumes its own momentum beyond the exclamation mark of the enclosed gest. It does this also in a progressive development which clarifies character and event, moving in a 'chain' which is true to the narrative of history as dialectical materialism understands it. To quote Brecht once more on this point, the epic actor 'has to be able to show his character's coherence *despite*, or *rather by means of*, interruptions and jumps'. This does not 'add up to a single unchangeable character but to one which changes all the time and becomes more and more clearly defined in course of "this way of changing" '. (my italics)

There is a further and related dialectical aspect to gest which neither Benjamin's essay nor Brecht's early writings really draw out. This derives from the item Brecht tables under epic theatre in the *Mahagonny* notes as 'he [the human being] is alterable and able to alter'. (BT, p. 37) From an aphoristic maxim this becomes an integrated part of Brecht's description of epic style (the street actor will demonstrate how things might have happened otherwise) until by the end of the 1930s it is translated into practical advice to actors, along with a set of other established technical routines. Thus in the essay 'Short description of a new technique of acting which produces an alienation effect' (1940), Brecht wrote:

> When he appears on the stage, besides what he actually is doing he will at all essential points discover, specify, imply what he is not doing; that is to say he will act in such a way that the alternative emerges as clearly as possible, that his acting allows the other possibilities to be inferred and only represents one out of the possible variants. He will say for instance 'You'll pay for that', and not say 'I forgive you'. He detests his children; it is not the case that he loves them. He moves down stage left and not up stage right. Whatever he doesn't do must be contained and conserved in what he does. In this way every sentence and every gesture signifies a decision; the character remains under observation and is tested. The technical term for this procedure is 'fixing the "not . . . but" '. (BT, p. 137)

To act in such a way as to show 'the alternatives' and 'other possibilities' is to show that actions are the result of decisions, and that, just as in the past tense of epic theatre, so in the present tense of a divided audience, forced 'to take decisions' when their 'capacity for action' is aroused, alternative courses of action are also possible. In this respect gestic acting shows more than the other, contradictory (and suppressed) side of a phenomena as dialectics requires, and argues for more too than a belief that 'the human being . . . is alterable and able to alter.' To put this question in Marx's words, it is not enough to conceive of men as 'products of circumstances' or of 'changed men' as 'products of other circumstances', since this ignores the fact 'that it is men who change circumstances'.[28] Brecht had dramatised the first conception of an alterable humanity in *Man equals Man* but already in expressing his belief in 1927 that a 'new human type' would 'not let himself be changed by machines but will himself change the machine',[29] he was anticipating a less behaviouristic and more dialectical view of social change. It is with this in mind, it would seem, that actors for the epic theatre are recommended in the poem 'Speech to Danish working-class actors on the art of observation' for example, to adopt the view of the 'discontented' section of their audience. Speaking from their 'lower benches' the discontented reject the representation of an external Fate governing men's affairs: 'the word has spread' they cry out

> That mankind's fate is man alone. Therefore
> We now ask you, the actors
> Of our time — a time of overthrow and of boundless mastery
> Of all nature, even men's own — at last
> To change yourselves and show us mankind's world
> As it really is: made by men and open to alteration. (P, p. 234)

To demonstrate through the display of alternatives that the world was alterable 'by men', indeed to assist man 'to master the world and himself' (BT, p. 135) — this then was the full force of the technical procedure of ' "fixing the 'not . . . but ' " '.

Later remarks by Brecht in the 1950s suggest that he had become more openly committed to this broad political aim. Thus he writes on a planned performance of Strittmatter's *Katzgraben*, 'we must infect a working-class audience with the urge to alter the world (and supply it with some of the relevant knowledge)', (BT, p. 247) and in a definition written in 1954 of socialist realism that it 'lays bare the dialectical laws of movement of the social mechanism, whose revelation makes the mastery of man's fate easier'. (BT, p. 269) By this late date Brecht had shifted his ground and terminology somewhat. We can see nevertheless how his announced aim of confirming and engendering a consciousness of, and pleasure in, 'the productivity and alterability of society' was by no means inconsistent with his earlier statements. While his theory had perhaps outgrown the formal descriptions 'epic' and 'gestisch' it had at the same time built upon them. Indeed it is impossible to see how his post-epic, dialectical drama could begin to fulfil its social objectives without these already 'dialectical' means as its artistic prerequisites.

Notes

1. *Brecht on Theatre*, p. 46. Cf. Willett's later discussion in *Brecht in Context* (Methuen, London and New York, 1984), pp. 207–8. Willett's argument here is that dialectics as a conceptual method came to the forefront in 1931 and then not again until the last two years of Brecht's life. He

writes also that the 'outward uses of the term were much less important than the encouragement given to Brecht's natural way of seeing things', p. 207.

2. *Gesammelte Werke* (Suhrkamp, Frankfurt am Main, 1967), 20, pp. 45–178. See T.W.H. Metscher's useful discussion, 'Brecht and Marxist dialectics', *Oxford German Studies*, 6 (1971–2), pp. 132–44. Metscher comments that the publication of Brecht's theoretical writings on theatre, art and politics gave proof of his 'wide interests in philosophical and sociological problems, and of his status as a Marxist thinker', p. 135.

3. *Gesammelte Werke*, 20, pp. 51–4, 64, 76–8.

4. Ibid., p. 151–2, 146-50.

5. Ibid., p. 71.

6. Ibid., 16, p. 531; 12, p. 563; 20, p. 166.

7. Über Dialektik', in *Brecht im Gespräch, Diskussion, Dialoge, Interviews*. Werner Hecht (ed.) (Suhrkamp, Frankfurt am Main, 1975), pp. 53–6; 'Die Dialektik', in *Gesammelte Werke*, 19, pp. 394–5; also in *Über Lyrik*, Elizabeth Hauptmann and Rosemarie Hill (eds) (Suhrkamp, Frankfurt am Main, 1948), pp. 25–6.

8. *Gesammelte Werke*, 15, pp. 341–73; *The Messingkauf Dialogues*, John Willett (trans.) (Methuen, London, 1965), esp. pp. 102–3; *Arbeitsjournal*, vol. 1, 1938–43, Werner Hecht (ed.) (Suhrkamp, Frankfurt am Main, 1973), pp. 138, 216. Cf also the entries, also for 1940, in the *Arbeitsjournal* on pp. 86, 364.

9. *Gesammelte Werke*, 15, p. 217.

10. Ibid., p. 220.

11. Ibid., 16, pp. 869, 923.

12. Goethe and Schiller, 'Über Epische und Dramatische Dichtung', in *Goethes Werke. Band XII* (C.H. Beck, Munich, 1981), pp. 249, 251. I am following the discussion in Esslin *Brecht*, pp. 113–4, here.

13. Engels, *Ludwig Feuerbach and the End of Classical German Philosophy,* in *On Dialectical Materialism* (Progress Publishers, Moscow, and Lawrence and Wishart, London, 1977),p. 176.

14. Marx, 'Theses on Feuerbach', ibid., p. 31.

15. Lenin, 'On the question of dialectics', ibid., p. 381. The first German translation of Lenin's essay appeared in the magazine *Unter dem Banner des Marxismus*, Willie Schultz (ed.), vol. 1, no. 2 (1925), a copy of which was in Brecht's possession. The same issue contained essays by A. Deborin titled, 'Lenin über Dialektik' and 'Lenin als Revolutionärer Dialektiker'. Brecht marked both the second article and a paragraph in the essay by Lenin on Marx's analysis of the exchange of commodities. In his copy of volume three of Lenin's *Samtliche Werke* (1927), Brecht marked this same paragraph, Lenin's remarks on the 'identity of opposites', and the sentences, 'Every individual enters incompletely into the universal, etc., etc.' and at the end of the essay, 'Rectilinearity and one-sidedness, woodenness and petrification, subjectivism and subjective blindness — voilà the epistemological roots of idealism.' It is impossible to say precisely when Brecht read Lenin's essay, but reasonable to assume on this evidence that he read it twice in the late 1920s.

16. Engels, 'From a Review of "Karl Marx, *A Contribution to the Critique of Political Economy*." ' in *On Dialectical Materialism*, p. 50.

17. Lenin, 'From *Karl Marx*', and 'On the question of dialectics', ibid., pp. 373, 385.

18. Lenin, 'From *Karl Marx*', ibid., pp. 374–5.

19. *Gesammelte Werke*, 17, pp. 1036–81. Extracts from these notes are included in *Brecht on Theatre*, pp, 57–62.

20. *Gesammelte Werke*, 17, pp. 1048–62, and in *Brecht on Theatre*, pp. 81–4.

21. See the account in Lee Baxandall, 'Brecht in America, 1935'. in *Brecht*, Erika Munk (ed.) (Bantam Books, New York, 1972), pp. 33–60.

22. The rewritten scene is included in *Gesammelte Werke*, 17, pp. 1042–5. Brecht's text appears in English in *The Mother*, Steve Gooch (trans.) (Eyre Methuen, London, 1978).

23. Quoted in Richard Stourac and Kathleen McCreery, *Theatre As A Weapon. Workers' Theatre in the Soviet Union, Germany and Britain 1917–1934* (Routledge and Kegan Paul, London and New York, 1986), p. 169.,

24. Ibid., pp. 94–9.

25. Ibid., p. 155.

26. Ibid., pp. 155–6.

27. Lenin, 'On the question of dialectics', in *On Dialectical Materialism*, p. 381.

28. Marx, 'Theses on Feuerbach', ibid., p. 30.

29. Brecht, *Man equals Man*, John Willett and Ralph Manheim (eds), Gerhard Nellhaus (trans.) (Eyre Methuen, London, 1979), pp. 99–100.

4

'Only "Actually" is it Familiar': Brecht's *Verfremdungseffekt*

Verfremdung has been described as 'the key concept' of Brecht's theory of theatre.[1] As such it is integral to the more general concept of 'epic', and intimately related to *Gestus*, since gestic acting in its nature and effects was one of the principal vehicles of *Verfremdung*. Brecht's term itself has been variously translated as 'alienation', 'estrangement', 'éloignement', 'distanciation' and 'defamiliarisation'. As he described it, it employed elements of stage design, music and lighting as well as a gestic acting style in a conscious — and in some ways self-conscious — attempt to historicise characters and events. In this way the theatre-goer's practically instinctual tendency to empathise with supposedly 'eternally human' characters and 'universal' situations would be frustrated, and the 'single chain' of a 'timeless' narrative necessary to a conventional illusion of reality would be interrupted. Instead of a unified and pacifying, or even simply 'entertaining' work of art, with all its aesthetic and ideological concomitants, Brecht wished for an epic theatre in which acting, music and design, conceived as 'a bundle of separate elements', would operate autonomously, but at the same time in a relation of commentary and contradiction with each other. The immediate effect of this separation (principally of actor and audience from theatrical character and incident) would be one of surprise, dismay and perhaps discomfort, as the audience's unexamined assumptions about art and society took a jolt. Brecht's audience would then be 'verfremdet', and would react, so Brecht says, in the following way:

> I should never have thought so — That is not the way to do it. — This is most surprising, hardly credible. — This will have to stop. This human being's suffering moves me, because

> there would have been a way out for him. This is great art: nothing here seems inevitable — I am laughing about those who weep on the stage, weeping about those who laugh.[2]

It becomes quite clear, from the many statements made by Brecht, that the function of the *Verfremdungseffekt* is to puncture the complacent acceptance of either character, motive, narrative, incident or resolution, as 'fixed' and 'unchanging', or 'obvious' and 'inevitable'. Thus in his 'Notes to *The Roundheads and Pointed Heads*' he talks of how 'certain incidents in the play should be . . . raised — by means of inscriptions, musical or sound effects and the actors' way of playing — above the level of the everyday, the obvious, the expected (ie alienated)'. (BT, p. 101) In the later essay 'On experimental theatre' he writes that, 'Alienating an event or character means first of all simply stripping the event of its self-evident, familiar obvious quality and creating a sense of astonishment and curiosity about them'.[3] In the *Short Organum* (1948) he talks of the function of the new *Verfremdungseffekte* as being 'to free socially conditioned phenomena from that stamp of familiarity which protects them against our grasp today.' (BT, p. 192)[4] The desired consequence was, as ever with Brecht, to install, beyond surprise and astonishment, 'an attitude of inquiry and criticism' (BT, p. 136) and an appreciation of change — the realisation, as he put it, that 'people's activity must simultaneously be so and be capable of being different'. (BT, p. 71) The *Verfremdungs* process was 'necessary to all understanding'; it was a device by which art 'by its *own* means' could 'further the great social task of mastering life'. (BT, p. 96)

According to John Willett *Verfremdung* entered Brecht's theoretical vocabulary in 1936 with the first publication, in English, of the essay '*Verfremdungseffekte* in Chinese acting'. This followed Brecht's witnessing a performance in May 1935 by Mei Lan-fang and his company in Moscow. It is in this essay that Brecht suggests that the *Verfremdungseffekt* developed in the German epic theatre (uninfluenced, he says, by Asiatic acting) was designed to 'historicise' actors and incidents, and so counteract their 'alleged "eternally human" ' and 'timeless' aspects. The task for actors he says is 'to demonstrate a custom which leads to conclusions about the entire structure of a society at a particular (transient) time', and this will be done, for example, by handing over a character's statements 'for criticism' rather than internalising or possessing them. Only the *Verfremdungseffekt* adopted as a technique of acting makes it possible, says Brecht, 'to underline the historical aspect of a specific social situation'; a changing period demands a 'social point of view' and the *V-Effekt* will assist the new theatre in 'its social criticism and historical reporting of completed transformations'. (BT, pp. 96, 98–9)

In his note on this essay Willett suggests that *Verfremdungseffekt* 'is a translation of the Russian critic Viktor Shklovskij's phrase "Priem Ostrannenija", or "device for making strange" '. (BT, p. 99) Although this idea has been sometimes disputed, it has become an inescapable part of any discussion of *Verfremdung*, with or without reference to Willett's original suggestion.[5] I want here first to respond to Willett's interpretation, and then to consider the broader context in which the term *Verfremdung* appeared, before finally identifying its dialectical aspects.

Returning to the discussion of *Verfremdung* in 1984, Willett was even more confident than in *Brecht on Theatre*: 'the *Verfremdungseffekt*', he says in *Brecht in Context*, 'appears to be a precise translation of Viktor Shklovsky's term *Priëm Ostranenniya*'. He then adds

> there seems to me to be every reason to accept the view of Bernhard Reich who said in his memoirs that he first heard the term *Verfremdung* used that year [1935] by Tretiakov [then representative of the Society of Cultural Relations in Moscow], with Brecht present, and concluded that this inspired Brecht to adopt Shklovsky's formulation as a description first of the Chinese methods and then of his own.[6]

Willett goes on to argue that *Verfremdung* was for Brecht a means of 'gaining new insights into the world around us by glimpsing it in a different and previously unfamiliar light'. He finds precedents for this in Shelley, Wordsworth and Schopenhauer, and concludes, 'In other words it comes close to what is meant by the common clichés "to shed a new light on", "to look with fresh eyes at", or "to open one's eyes to" '.[7]

There are a number of problems with this account. First of all as the essay '*Verfremdungseffekte* in Chinese acting' and other later comments in the *Short Organum* make clear, Brecht distinguishes between Chinese 'alienation effects' and those he aimed at in epic theatre. The first, he said, could only profitably be studied by 'those who need such a technique for quite definite social purposes', (BT, p. 96) and later speaking of the use of *V-Effekte* in classical, medieval and Asiatic theatre, that 'The social aims of these old devices were entirely different from our own' — this difference amounting to the fact that the old *V-Effekte* 'remove the object represented' so that it 'cannot be altered', whereas the purpose of the epic *V-Effekte* was precisely to expose phenomena to change. (BT, p. 192)

Secondly it will not do to paraphrase *Verfremdung* as offering 'new insights into' or 'shedding a new light on'. This is not because *Verfremdung* belongs to the higher reaches of theory where no ordinary language shall reach, but because phrases such as these flatten its meaning into the clichés of perception it was intended not simply to revitalise, but to transform. It is true that Brecht comes close in his discussion 'The *V-Effekt* as a procedure in everyday life' to suggesting that what is involved in *Verfremdung* is the revival of a perception that has sunk into a daily habit, as when, for example, we are recalled to our early astonishment at the mechanism of a watch whose operation we have come to take for granted. But this example, like the similar one Brecht gives of driving an old model T Ford and being newly impressed by cars as 'a triumph of engineering', supposes that we did once possess, but have now lost, an attitude of naïve but genuine enquiry. Also there is a considerable difference between saying 'I forgot I was wearing a watch' and 'so that's how a watch works'. The second is closer to Brecht's theatre practice. Even so, what he was concerned to do in and through the theatre was to generate an attitude of critical enquiry, an alertness to contradiction and a desire for change where these had *not* existed, but had been systematically suppressed, as theatre played its part in producing what Brecht calls 'a cowed credulous, hypnotised mass'. (BT, p. 188) In the *Short Organum*, moreover, where this phrase occurs, Brecht talks repeatedly of being able to 'grasp' or 'interfere' or 'intervene' in social processes so as to 'influence' or 'transform' men and events through an understanding of the laws which govern their activity and movement. The *Organum* in this way directly associates *Verfremdung* with the insights of dialectical materialism. Brecht's argument here begins in Section 44 where he presents the example of Galileo observing a chandelier:

> He was amazed by this pendulum motion, as if he had not expected it and could not understand its occurring, and this enabled him to come on to the rules by which it was governed. (BT, p. 192)

This says Brecht is the 'disconcerting but fruitful' outlook the theatre must provoke; 'fruitful' because it passes from amazement through incomprehension to inquiry and so to a general scientific explanation. Phrases such as 'to shed a new light on' or 'to look with fresh eyes at' simply fail to describe this process fully. In the *Organum* Brecht goes on:

> This technique allows the theatre to make use in its representations of the new social scientific method known as dialectical materialism. In order to unearth society's laws of motion this method treats social situations as processes, and traces out all their inconsistencies. It regards nothing as existing except in so far as it changes, in other words is in disharmony with itself. This also goes for those human feelings, opinions and attitudes through which at any time the form of men's life together finds its expression.
>
> Our own period, which is transforming nature in so many and different ways, takes pleasure in understanding things so that we can interfere. There is a great deal to man, we say; so a great deal can be made out of him. He does not have to stay the way he is now, nor does he have to be seen only as he is now, but also as he might become. We must not start with him; we must start on him. This means, however, that I must not simply set myself in his place, but must set myself facing him, to represent us all. That is why the theatre must alienate what it shows. (BT, p. 193)

Quite clearly Brecht is concerned here once again with change, most directly as far as the theatre goes we might think, with changes in 'human feelings opinions and attitudes'. The difference then between his overall strategy and 'taking a fresh look at things' or 'gaining fresh insight' is, to put these phrases at their highest, the difference set out by Marx between '*interpreting* the world in various ways' (i.e., seeing it differently and shedding new light on it) and *changing* the world. It would be a mistake to suppose that the kind of attitude Brecht describes in this context as 'taking pleasure in understanding things so we can interfere [or intervene]' is itself a familiar, that is to say, common one. If it were, and if (since it amounts to the same thing), Marxism and socialism and a socialist art as Brecht conceived of them, were common currency, then Willett would be justified in wondering why Brecht 'devoted so much effort to explaining and establishing' *Verfremdung*. [8] 'Communism' as Brecht wrote almost in answer, 'is the simple thing so hard to achieve'.[9]

As for *Verfremdung* itself, Brecht wrote enigmatically at the close of 'The *V-Effekt* as a procedure in everyday life', that 'only "actually" is it familiar'. (BT, p. 145) He implies that to become a truly common and effective everyday procedure it needs to be illuminated, explained, and itself 'estranged', as in his own discussion:

> In a sense the alienation effect itself has been alienated by the above explanation; we have taken a common, recurrent, universally-practised operation and tried to draw attention to it by illuminating its peculiarity. But we have achieved the effect only with those people who have truly ('in fact') grasped that it does 'not' result from every representation 'but' from certain ones: only 'actually' is it familiar. (BT, ibid.)

Brecht writes earlier that sentences using 'not . . . but' constructions are the simplest forms of *Verfremdung*, and that the expressions 'in fact' ('tatsächlich') and 'actually' ('eigentlich'), as in 'he wasn't in fact at home' or 'I don't actually agree' are similarly conducive to *V-Effekte*. These double-edged expressions are then applied in his last paragraph to *Verfremdung* itself.

We remember that Brecht recommended that actors practising gestic acting 'quoted' their speeches, putting them into the third person past so as to separate actor and character, and 'historicise' the speech's gestic content. Quotation marks themselves, such as Brecht's own therefore, can be 'alienating'. In this way, in everyday circumstances, words and statements can be at the same time ratified and queried, endorsed and held off (in the 'quotation' of platitudes, truisms and clichés for example), in a gesture which says they are true (on occasion, or for others who say *and* think such things), but not consistently or really true. To put the word 'actually' in quotation marks is therefore to ironise it, to say that *Verfremdung* is familiar in real life (in 'actuality'), but that it is not commonly recognised for what it is (the very mark of its familiarity). It is and is not 'really' common. If *Verfremdung* were indeed, without qualification or quotation marks, truly common, and thus consciously deployed in dramatic and everyday contexts, Brecht would have no use of it or of dialectical materialism. As it is, dialectics is necessary to grasp the simultaneous 'not . . . but' of Brecht's paradoxical 'only "actually" is it familiar'; for it is dialectics, as Engels said, which 'knows no hard and fast lines, no unconditional, universally valid "either-or" . . . and besides "either-or" recognises also in the right place "both this — and that" '.[10]

Willett's attempt to 'over-familiarise' *Verfremdung* is of a piece with his reference to Shelley, Wordsworth and Schopenhauer as precedents for Brecht's use of this device, and for the 'making strange' of Russian Formalism. They shared, he suggests, a view of art 'as a means of productive reorientation'. Shelley's description of poetry as making 'familiar objects to be as if they were not familiar' and Wordsworth's aim to make 'the strange familiar and the familiar strange' alike provide, Willett says, for the complete alienation from the world spoken of by Schopenhauer, 'so that the commonest objects and incidents appear quite new and unknown'.[11] But if there is no distinction between these earlier writers, or between them and Brecht, then presumably there is none either between Brecht's *Verfremdung* and Ezra Pound's adopted dictum 'make it new', or between these writers and any other who 'helps us to see things afresh'. This is truly the clichéd world of humanist aesthetics where all the arts aspire, with 'fresh' variations, to represent the condition of an 'eternal human nature'.

This general position, together with its implications, would seem to follow, as do the other difficulties, from Willett's central conviction that *Verfremdung* is a ('precise') translation of *ostranenie*. The merit of this suggestion is that it opens a vista onto cross-currents and affinities within the arts and across nations in the inter-war period — much of which Willett has himself impressively documented.[12] Indeed it is only in the context of Brecht's artistic and intellectual contacts in the 1930s that one can hope to discover a source of *Verfremdung*, or more correctly, distinguish it from its apparent sources. What has to be considered here, however, is not only Brecht's personal contact with Tretiakov, but the more general question of the relation between Brecht's work and ideas and those of the Russian Futurists, including his related response to the emerging doctrine of socialist realism, as advanced particularly in association with the theories of Georg Lukács. In addition, or in contrast as Willett would see it, there is the obvious possibility which presents itself that Brecht's *Verfremdung*, especially when understood as 'alienation', derives from Marxism. I want to consider these questions in what follows.

To begin with Reich's memoir which Willett refers to. There Reich recalls:

> I was referring to a production detail when Tretyakov corrected me, remarking 'Yes, that is an estrangement [Verfremdung]' and looked conspiratorially at Brecht. Brecht

> nodded. That was the first time I had met the expression Verfremdung. I must assume therefore that Tretyakov provided Brecht with the term. I think that Tretyakov had reshaped the term originally formulated by Shklovsky, *otchuzdenie*, 'distancing', 'alienation'.[13]

Willett sees no reason to deny the suggestion he finds here that Brecht borrowed Shklovsky's formulation. There are three answers to this. The first is that Reich's memory provides only circumstantial evidence, shaped by his own assumptions and reading of the event. Secondly, the passage is not only the product of memory but refers to this event in an ambiguous way; that is to say it could be 'read' differently (i.e. *Verfremdung* was known to both Brecht and Tretiakov prior to this occasion; hence the nod. This implication, together with the use of the German word, suggest that it might even have been Brecht who supplied Tretiakov with the term rather than the reverse.) Thirdly, as Fradkin and Ewen have argued, Brecht's theory was as Ewen puts it 'fully developed', in spirit if not in the letter, before 1935.[14] The meeting with Tretiakov and the exchange of the word *Verfremdung* becomes in this light incidental rather than decisive.

Marjorie Hoover's study of the relationship and correspondence between the two men tends to bear this out. Commenting on Brecht's second trip to Russia in 1935, and on the passage from Reich, she writes, 'So Brecht found on this occasion the name for the thing, "Verfremdung" which he had already long practiced.'[15] She concludes that much as their agreement on the 'dialectic theory of "Verfremdung" . . . appears obvious' Brecht and Tretiakov differed, sometimes radically, on the 'literary means of achieving' their shared political objective.[16] As to the authorship of the term *Verfremdung*, the correspondence, consisting of thirteen letters by Tretiakov, and one by Brecht between his first visit to Moscow in 1932 and 1937, only compounds the mystery. Tretiakov's 'fairly correct German' in Hoover's description, and for whose 'inadequacy' he himself apologised in one letter, make it seem unlikely that he discovered the term, unless perhaps by happy accident. A letter from Brecht, moreover, in the important period between July and September 1934, has not been preserved, nor are its contents known.

Even if we put these considerations to one side, it is a striking, and from Willett's point of view, awkward fact, that Reich goes on in his *Memoir* not to equate but to *distinguish between* Brecht's and Shklovsky's use of the supposedly common term:

> Brecht's *Verfremdung* aims at 'making-aware'. Shklovsky and his followers were recommending this 'making-aware' mainly for the cinema, seeing it as a way of arousing a strong impression in the spectators by means of an extremely formal juxtaposition. Despite the semantic similarity Brecht's conception differs from this quite fundamentally both with regard to its point of departure ('making-aware' in Brecht is a logical necessity since habit and familiarity hinder the recognition of phenomena) and its result (Brecht's estrangement helps one to see better the content of things).[17]

A similar distinction to that drawn here, but one which, like Reich's own, runs quite counter to Willett's interpretation, has been offered by Stanley Mitchell:

> In both theories the (proper) role of art is seen as one of de-routinisation, de-automatisation: art is the enemy of habit; it renews, refreshes our perceptions; by 'making-strange', it defamiliarises. But while Shklovsky's *ostranenie* was a purely aesthetic concept, concerned with renewal of perception, Brecht's *Verfremdung* had a social aim: if the world could be shown differently, ie as having different possibilities, could it not be differently made? Brecht wished to strike not merely at the perceptions, but at the consciousness of his spectators.[18]

Shklovsky had written in 'Art as device' (1917) that the artistic technique of 'making things strange' meant

> To make forms difficult, to increase the difficulty and length of perception because the process of perception is an aesthetic end in itself and must be prolonged.[19]

Mitchell describes this as belonging to a 'perceptual aesthetics', and Tony Bennett, commenting on the same statement in his study of Russian Formalism and Marxism, writes that in Shklovsky's view 'defamiliarisation . . . was not thought to be motivated by any consideration beyond that of promoting a renewed and sharpened attention to reality. The category of defamiliarisation was thus invested with a purely aesthetic, and not with any ideological significance'.[20]

Few would disagree with Bennett's description, but once again it draws attention to the superficial resemblance, and profound difference, between *ostranenie* and Brecht's *Verfremdung*. Brecht's social purpose was unmistakable: 'To think, or write', he had said in 1931, 'or produce a play also means: to transform society, to transform the state, to subject ideologies to close scrutiny'.[21] Russian Formalism, on the other hand, dominated within the 'Society for the Study of Poetic Language' *(Opoyaz)* by Shklovsky, was concerned with the purely aesthetic task of isolating the defining features, or 'literariness' *(literaturnost)* of poetic language. Formalism argued that rather than simply reflecting reality, literature 'estranged' habitual forms of perception by means of the linguistic and formal mechanisms unique to it. By definition, this would embrace Shelley and Wordsworth, and each and every other writer who counted as 'literature'. Brecht, however, would have been amongst the last to agree to such a universaling description; to apply it to *Verfremdung*, moreover, is to fly in the face of his attempt, precisely *via* this category, to historicise customs, attitudes and events. To insist then, as Willett does, on a direct equivalence between *ostranenie* and *Verfremdung*, aestheticises Brecht's concept, effectively neutralising his conscious politicisation of art and the pedagogic function he attributed to it.

In his essay Stanley Mitchell puts the difference between Brecht and Formalism itself in ideological terms. The Formalist assumption of the (illusory) autonomy of art was, he suggests, only the mirror image of the (illusory) freedoms of the market economy; it therefore reinforced alienation and the 'fetishism of commodities' which converts perceptions from processes into things. Brecht on the other hand developed his theory of *Verfremdung* 'as a means to shock people out of a passive-fatalistic acceptance of authoritarian and manipulative politics'. Mitchell concludes that 'Of all the "modernist" theories, Brecht's *Verfremdung* constituted the most appropriate response to capitalist alienation'[22] His answer to the apparent synonymity of Shklovsky's and Brecht's terms is that they shared 'similarities of implication'. The important connection therefore lies not between Brecht and Russian Formalism, but between Brecht and the generation of Futurist writers and artists associated with *Lef*, and *Novy Lef* in the 1920s, who helped realise those implications. Figures such as Mayakovsky, Tretiakov himself, Arvatov and Eisenstein are seen therefore as developing the components of a revolutionary aesthetic (using montage, documentary and agit-prop) which can be said to have politicised the concepts of Russian Formalism. *Verfremdung*, similarly, appears as a politicised form of *ostranenie*.[23]

Summarising this development in Russia, Osip Brik wrote:

> Art was still 'a device'; what had changed from the original Formalist interpretation was the application of the device. The emphasis was shifted from the aesthetic function of the device to its use in the service of a 'social demand'. All the manifestations of the device . . . were now considered in the light of their potential utility.[24]

This certainly comes close to Brecht's own emphasis. It is true too that the set of ideas developed within Futurism — of writers responding to a 'social demand' of being 'proletarianised' in a newly conceived relation to the artistic means of production, of exploiting new forms and technologies in the service of working-class revolution — find echoes, point for point, in Brecht's theory. But this is not to say, if we are going to be precise about Brecht's development that he was *consciously* engaged, as Russian artists were, in politicising the concepts of Formalism. 'Nothing comes out of nothing' as Brecht acknowledged, but the sources of his own theory and practice were extremely heterogeneous. Amongst Russian artists this included Meyerhold, and perhaps Mayakovsky and Eisenstein (but nowhere explicitly Shklovsky), and in terms of the development of the theory of *Verfremdung*, the English writers Christopher Marlowe and G.B. Shaw. If we were to follow these sources, or others, such as (from a list by Ernst Schumacher) the acting of Herr Steinrück, Piscator's political theatre, American behaviourism, scientific socialism, Charlie Chaplin, Eastern Asian Theatre, agitprop, Bavarian and Scandinavian folk theatre, Helene Weigel, and detective stories,[25] we would see that Brecht's ideas, development and purpose as a *German* poet and playwright would have to be distinguished from the circumstances and career of, for example, either Mayakovsky or Eisenstein, with whom, in general terms, he might be thought to share a revolutionary aesthetic.[26]

Nor, to press this further, is this simply a matter of the independent development of individual artists. Russian Futurism, first of all, did not represent an homogenous and unchanging body of aesthetic or political opinion. As Richard Sherwood has described it:

> The 'Left Front of the Arts' was therefore a rather heterogeneous grouping of artists in many fields who felt that the new art spread over and blurred the old dividing lines of art. The term 'left artist' could only be defined roughly as

> an artist influenced by Futurist, Formalist or Constructivist theories on art, ie a general hostility to imitation of life, in favour of 'creation' or 'construction' of life; hostility to realism in art, or a tendency to utilarianism; rejection of 'belles-lettres' in literature, or 'pure' or 'easel-art' in painting, and of 'applied art' (in the sense of art 'applied' to a ready-made object). The term 'left' artist does not, of course, imply any specific political allegiance on the artists' part. The range of theories too numerous to discuss in detail, went from the 'trans-sense' poetic experimentation of some of the Futurists, supported by a part of Formalist theory, all of which was impatiently dismissed by the most rapidly evolving section of Constructivists as 'laboratory work', to the 'production art' theory of these same Constructivists, that was already not only an anti-aesthetic tendency, but one leading rapidly to an anti-art programme.[27]

Added to this there were the differences between *Lef* and *Novy Lef*. *Lef*, under Mayakovsky's editorship, ceased publication in 1925. He then began *Novy Lef* in 1927 but resigned the editorship in July 1928 to Tretiakov under whose direction the magazine proclaimed 'factography' — i.e. the newspaper report, newsreal, photograph, travel sketch and documentary film, as the most valid revolutionary art forms. Sherwood comments, 'Futurism had therefore passed through a whole revolution in outlook, from the original "art for art" view of the earliest experimental verse, through "art in production", utilitarian or "production" art and constructivism, and on to mere reportage of "literature of fact" '.[28] Also, as Ben Brewster points out, the politicisation of art within Futurism occurred within a broader set of trends, calling in turn for a traditional socially-conscious realism and an agitational and specifically proletarian art and culture.[29] The second of these was associated with the *On-Guard* group of the 'All-Union Association of Proletarian Writers' (VAPP — later RAPP, the 'Russian Association of Proletarian Writers'). In Germany the equivalent of RAPP was the Communist organised 'League of Proletarian Writers' whose magazine was *Die Linkskurve*. This embraced those who advocated traditional realism; a proletarian group (influenced, says Brewster, by German 'Neue Sachlichkeit' and with agitational and documentarist aspects) of which Ernst Ottwalt was an example; and, thirdly, revolutionary dadaists such as John Heartfield, Wieland Herzefelde, George Grosz and Erwin Piscator.[30]

One could 'associate' Brecht with these latter tendencies and personalities, but one would have to distinguish him from them as well, and by the same token, distinguish him from Russian developments, with which Ottwalt and Piscator were more closely connected. Brecht's work was neither so directly agitational nor documentary as theirs. Of 'Neue Sachlichkeit' ('new objectivity' or 'matter of factness'), for example, which shared certain aesthetic and political assumptions with Tretiakov's 'factography', Brecht said revealingly in the late 1920s, that as regards the theatre it was a 'quite necessary and inevitable step forward' but was at the same time 'reactionary'. (BT, p. 17) Of his own play *The Mother*, he said it 'owed much to the agit-prop theatre', but 'none the less remained distinct from it', being less concerned with stimulating immediate action than with teaching 'the tactics of the class war'. (BT, pp. 61–2) Nor was Brecht ever unequivocally involved with the League of Proletarian Writers, or with the Communist Party. The League he saw, according to Völker, as a 'sorry left-wing species of organisation', while *Die Linkskurve* was in its turn critical of Brecht's two most 'committed' early plays, *The Measures Taken* and *The Mother*.[31]

If there are these complications in situating Brecht in a left cultural and political context in Germany, they are accentuated and multiplied when related to developments in Russia. In the end Brecht cannot be simply enlisted into the ranks of Russian Futurists as he is in Brewster's statement that 'Brecht and Mayakovsky . . . transformed the aesthetic concepts they derived from their avant-garde origins'.[32] Nor can *Verfremdung* be seen with any real historical accuracy, as summing up, in Mitchell's view 'an entire history of the (socialist) politicisation of Shklovsky's original notion of *ostranenie*.'[33] What we can say is that there were certain parallels: that theoretically, as a left modernist, Brecht shared a set of problems and emphases with artists in a certain phase of Russian Futurism, and that these similarities emerged within an international, and at some points, undoubtedly interlocking cultural and political network. One of the most fruitful comparisons along these lines would probably be between Brecht and Eisenstein, whose theory of 'montage' and of a dialectical cinema emerged in the same years as Brecht's early thoughts on a dialectical drama and epic theatre.[34] Nevertheless, once again we have to say that Moscow was not Berlin, that revolutionary and post-revolutionary Russia, and Weimar and Nazi Germany, were not, and were not seen by Brecht to be the same; and that, as a matter of detail, his artistic principles, methods and purposes were developed independently.

This mixture of sameness and difference is confirmed by Walter Benjamin's contemporary theorisation of progressive developments within the European and Russian *avant-gardes* in his essay 'The author as producer'. This refers to both Tretiakov and Brecht, and was read by Brecht in 1934, when he saw it as applying (exclusively) to artists of his own type 'of the upper bourgeoisie'.[35]

Benjamin distinguishes in his essay between the kind of political commitment expressed in propagandist or tendency literature, and that which a writer can express by adapting changing techniques or means of production. Commitment in itself, he adds, is necessary but insufficient; a writer must also 'have a teacher's attitude'. (UB, p. 98) These thoughts echo and may in part derive from the development of a 'production aesthetic' and of 'factography' in Russian art, but they also look back directly to Brecht's own ideas in essays written in the late 1920s and early 1930s. In their main thrust, they enlarge too on the distinction between 'committed art' and 'pedagogics', which Brecht had made as recently as March 1934, a month prior to Benjamin's delivery of his paper in Paris. The precedents, that is to say, for the productive aesthetics Benjamin was concerned to clarify in the early 1930s existed, in Brecht's case, in his own earlier writing and practice. Indeed, Brecht's epic theatre, as *already* established, is Benjamin's primary example of this aesthetic. If Brecht in this way was an exemplar, summing up 'the (socialist) politicisation' of artistic forms and techniques, there is no sense in Benjamin's account that this had, for Brecht, involved a transformation of specific Formalist categories.

Behind Benjamin's essay there is the narrative of his own relationship with Brecht, and Brecht's with Tretiakov, both involving demonstrable personal contact and the exchange of ideas. In this respect, the implication of Benjamin's essay, written as it was in 1934, is that the formative moment in this second relationship, when an artistic and political kinship was recognised, and was recognisable, had occurred when Tretiakov first visited Berlin with *Scream China* in Meyerhold's production in 1930, and then in the following year, when his *Field Captains* was published and he was involved in discussions with German intellectuals and artists, including Brecht and Benjamin.[36]

In the absence of any record of these conversations, we have Benjamin's 'The author as producer', and Tretiakov's introductory essay on Brecht, both of 1934. Neither, once again, makes any reference to Shklovsky. What they do do is confirm that the important dates for the development of Brecht's theory are *earlier* than Willett suggests, that Russian Formalism as such had very little to do with it and that the relationship between Russian Futurism, in the representative person of Tretiakov, and Brecht, amounted to two independent movements which in these years met, first in Berlin and later in Moscow, to fructify and confirm but not to merge one with the other.

The relationship between Brecht and Russian aesthetics took a further twist as the 1930s advanced, since it was also in 1934 that A.A. Zhdanov announced the doctrine of 'socialist realism' at the First Soviet Writers Congress. This called for a commitment to the political orthodoxies of the Party and for a realist aesthetic, which, as it was put forward by Georg Lukács in a series of essays between 1935–9, presented the nineteenth-century bourgeois novel as its apogee. Writers such as Tretiakov, Ernst Bloch, James Joyce, Hanns Eisler, and Brecht also, were attacked in these articles as 'decadent' and 'formalistic'. Brecht replied in at least two (at the time unpublished) articles in 1938 for the Russian-based magazine *Das Wort* of which he was nominally an editor.[37] Here he reversed the terms of Lukács's attack, arguing that it was 'formalist' to 'abstract the one and only realism from certain given works'. Instead, he wrote 'we . . . shall make a lively use of all means, old and new, tried and untried, deriving from art and deriving from other sources, in order to put living reality in the hands of living people in such a way that it can be mastered.' (BT, p. 109) Unpublished though it was, Brecht's reply was a defence of a 'broad and political' concept of realism which had been developing, along a generally common front, within left modernism. By the late 1930s such views, and those who held them in Russia, were being systematically purged — a fact which may well account for Brecht's caution. Already, by the mid-1930s Tretiakov was out of favour, and Meyerhold obstructed in his work. Tretiakov's arrest, and the arrests of Ernst Ottwalt and Carola Neher, soon followed.[38]

The debate between a socialist-modernist, and a narrowly defined, socialist-realist aesthetic took place therefore within an increasingly hostile political environment. Brecht's participation in this debate as himself an outsider, in exile, confirms his distance from formalism, in whatever guise; and aligns him expressly with Russian left Futurists against an official and punitive aesthetic dogma. This occurs also, we might note, not in the period of the formation of a shared 'productive aesthetic' but in the period of its distortion and suppression. Even then, however, Brecht's position was complicated by his reluctance to engage publicly in acrimonious debate, or in outright criticism of the Stalinist regime.[39] 'Probably all that can be said initially', he remarked on early developments, 'is that the Bolsheviks do not understand how to develop a literature. One should not even conclude that their methods have failed in this field; perhaps it is enough to say that the methods they applied in this field have failed'. Later he could plainly see the crippling and divisive effects of an authoritarian and legalistic literary policy, commenting, 'It is clearly not an atmosphere in which a vital, militant, exuberant literature could survive'.[40] The fact is, nevertheless, that though Brecht joined in the defence of left Futurists and other left modernists, and generally shared an aesthetic and political commitment with a figure such as Tretiakov, he publicly kept his counsel, and kept his distance, as far as Russian art and affairs were concerned.

To return to Brecht's concept of *Verfremdung*. In the essay 'The popular and the realistic' which was one of his replies to Lukács, Brecht defines 'realist' as, firstly, 'laying bare society's causal network'. (BT, p. 109) This is in telling contrast with the 'laying bare of the device' described by Shklovsky as the process by which literature draws attention, self-reflexively, to its own manufacture as an end in itself. Brecht's phrase is also very close to the description he gives to *Verfremdung* in the passage from the *Short Organum* quoted above. He says there that

> This technique allows the theatre to make use in its representations of the new social scientific method known as dialectical materialism. In order to unearth society's laws of motion this method treats social situations as processes and traces out all their inconsistencies. (BT, p. 193)

In these terms, Brecht's conception of realism shared no less than the aims and methods of Marx's *Capital*; seeking to apply these to the realm of 'human feelings, opinions and attitudes'. (ibid.) The artistic 'device' of *Verfremdung*, therefore (if we understand the word 'device' not as a formal or technical device but as the 'social measure' Brecht termed it[41]), adopts the mode of analysis that characterises dialectical materialism to produce what Brecht called 'the representation of truth, of the real mechanism of society'. (BT, p. 110) More is involved in this process than 'making the familiar strange' even if this is imbued with a political purpose. *Verfremdung* amounts to a 'seeing *through*' the customs and habits of mind which constitute ideology; a 'perforation' or 'intervention' in Brecht's words, so that reality can be 'grasped' and so 'mastered'.

In Benjamin's essay 'The author as producer' epic theatre is described in similar terms; as setting out 'not so much to fill the audience with feelings — albeit possibly feelings of revolt — as to alienate the audience in a lasting manner, through thought, from the conditions in which it lives.' (UB, pp. 100–1) These conditions, Benjamin says,

> are not brought close to the spectator; they are distanced from him. He recognises them as real — not, as in the theatre of naturalism, with complacency, but with astonishment. Epic theatre does not reproduce conditions; rather, it discloses, it uncovers them. (UB, p. 100)[42]

These disclosures Benjamin adds are effected by 'interruptions' which, as we have seen earlier, he identifies particularly with gestic acting and thence with the capture of the dialectic, as at a standstill. From statements such as these, from Benjamin and from Brecht, we can say that *Verfremdung* served as an analytic and politically motivated technique which employed the methods of dialectical materialism so as to expose the 'real' dialectic, the real contradiction in attitudes, processes and events, where these lay beneath a world of familiar, settled and seemingly eternal appearances presented by ideology.

We ought also to note once more the date of Benjamin's essay. Here, in 1934, there is a description of the 'alienation effect' — as it was evident to Benjamin from Brecht's epic theatre — before the latter's visit to Russia in the following year. Benjamin's essay confirms that *Verfremdung*, in effect, if not in name (since Benjamin's word is '*entfremden*'), was already a recognisable part of Brecht's practice, regardless of events and conversations in 1935. It suggests too that this 'alienation effect', if understood aright, was not simply in embryo in the early 1930s, but was already compatible with Brecht's 'mature' theory.

The connection which emerges between *Verfremdung* and dialectics from this discussion helps answer the second common speculation that Brecht's term is derived from the concept of alienation (*Entäusserung* and *Entfremdung*) as used by Hegel and developed by Marx. Brecht did on occasion use the term *Entfremdung* with to all intents and purposes the same meaning as *Verfremdung*.[43] In referring to one of these examples in Brecht's essay 'Theatre for pleasure or theatre for instruction', Ronald Gray, following Jan Knopf, says that 'it seems very likely that Brecht did have Hegel in mind at that moment'.[44] In the same way, it is presumably with Marx's use of the term in mind that Stanley Mitchell talks of *Verfremdung* as 'the most appropriate response to capitalist alienation'.[45]

Marx had explored the theme of alienation in his early texts, particularly the *Economic and Philosophic Manuscripts of 1844* (first published in Berlin in 1932). Here he analysed the alienation of the labourer from the product of labour, from himself, from Nature and from others. It is quite likely that Brecht knew the *Economic and Philosophical Manuscripts* or the *German Ideology* which also discusses alienation. There is some evidence too of his specific reference to 'alienation' as a general condition under capitalism. He talks thus of the poems in *Hauspostille* as a record of the 'dehumanisation' which Marx had identified with the proletariat,[46] and in the essay '*Verfremdungseffekte* in Chinese acting' (where the word first occurs according to Willett), he describes the environment as 'something remarkably inhuman; it exists in fact apart from man, confronting him as a coherent whole'. (BT, p. 97) On one occasion also he used the term 'alienation' in a recognisably Hegelian-Marxist sense, referring to Kafka as being terrified by 'the thought of men being alienated from themselves by the forms of their life in society'.[47]

These statements do not take us very far, however, in suggesting a link between the socio-economic category 'alienation' and Brecht's *Verfremdung*. Given, moreover, that the effect of Brecht's theatrical device is to *uncover* and combat 'alienation' rather than enforce it, we can only translate his term as '*de*-alienation' if we wish to retain a trace of the Hegelian and Marxist concept. There is little authority for suggesting an actual debt, or intended supersession of this kind, however. To this extent, John Willett is justified, when he says that Brecht's word was 'not of Marxist-Hegelian descent', if it is then going too far to say that it 'had nothing to do with the political-philosophical-psychological aspects of *Entfremdung* or "Alienation" as used by other writers'.[48]

A more promising suggestion would seem to be that Brecht's term derived if not directly from Marx or Hegel, then from Brecht's association with Karl Korsch, his acknowledged 'Marxist teacher'.[49] This cannot in the end be proved either way. Nevertheless, the relationship between Korsch and Brecht is an interesting and important one; with, I would suggest, a definite bearing on the meaning, if not the strict etymology, of the term *Verfremdung*.

Brecht had known Korsch in Berlin and the two men were

neighbours in 1935–6 in Skovsbostrand, Denmark. The contact between them then continued until Brecht's death, and was peppered with an exchange of ideas, mutual advice, theoretical agreements and political differences. In Skovsbostrand, Korsch was engaged on his volume *Karl Marx*. Aside from this work, Brecht undoubtedly knew Korsch's *Marxism and Philosophy* (1923, reissued in 1930), the essay 'Why I am a Marxist', and possibly additional essays.[50] In *Marxism and Philosophy*, Korsch had argued that the philosophical sources of Marx's ideas in Hegel had been ignored in favour of the economistic orthodoxy adopted by the Second International, and particularly by Karl Kautsky. As a consequence the status of Marxism as a guide to revolutionary action had also been lost sight of. Korsch directed attention in this way to certain early Marxist texts, but this did not mean that he wished to retain an early concept such as 'alienation' as a 'philosophical' category, which had prefigured and then been superseded by Marx's more general economic category of 'commodity fetishism'.[51] What Korsch chiefly wished to emphasise was the source of Marx's dialectical materialism in Hegel's idealist dialectic, and the error of ignoring the question of ideological preconditions for proletarian revolution. Marxism, he insisted, united theory and practice, and conceived of the relation between the ideological superstructure and the economic base in dialectical terms. It was historically specific, critical, and revolutionary.[52]

The political disagreements between Brecht and Korsch concerned their estimates of Lenin (who Korsch persisted in seeing as a mechanical materialist in spite of evidence of his debt to Hegelian dialectics), the role of the Party and of the centralised state in Russia.[53] For his part Brecht was prepared to accept Russian Statism and what he termed 'dictatorship *over* the proletariat' as long as that state could be seen as 'a *workers'* state' and the dictatorship over the proletariat seen as 'useful' to the proletariat.[54] In spite of their differences, however, Brecht shared Korsch's objections to Party orthodoxy, and in his own terms, learnt from and developed Korsch's interpretation of Marxism as an active, transformative critique of bourgeois society.

This had little to do with the concept of 'alienation' and everything to do with the importance of ideological struggle and dialectics. The general evidence of this exists in the essays by Brecht that I have discussed. In addition a specific relation between dialectics and *Verfremdung* appears on at least three occasions: in the note 'Dialektik und Verfremdung', in an appendix to the *Messingkauf*

Dialogues, and in an entry dated 20.12.40 in the *Arbeitsjournal*. The first and last of these are worth presenting in full. In 'Dialectic and *Verfremdung*', Brecht lists nine points, in abbreviated fashion, as follows:

1. Verfremdung als ein Verstehen (verstehen — nicht verstehen — verstehen), Negation der Negation.
2. Häufung der Unverständlichkeiten, bis Verständnis eintritt (Umschlag von Quantität und Qualität).
3. Das Besondere im Allgemeinen (der Vorgang in seiner Einzigartigkeit, Einmaligkeit, dabei typisch).
4. Moment der Entwicklung (das Ubergehen der Gefühle in andere Gefühle entgegengesetzter Art, Kritik und Einfühlung in einem).
5. Widersprüchlichkeit (dieser Mensch in diesen Verhältnissen, diese Folgen dieser Handlung!).
6. Das eine verstanden durch das andere (die Szene, im Sinn zunächst selbständig, wird durch ihren Zusammenhang mit andern Szenen noch als eines andern Sinns teilhaftig entdeckt).
7. Der Sprung (saltus naturae, epische Entwicklung mit Sprüngen).
8. Einheit der Gegensätze (im Einheitlichen wird der Gegensatz gesucht, Mutter und Sohn — in 'Mutter' — nach außen hin einheitlich, kämpfen gegeneinander des Lohnes wegen).
9. Praktizierbarkeit des Wissens (Einheit von Theorie und Praxis).

(1. *Verfremdung* as understanding (understanding — not understanding — understanding), negation of the negation.
2. The accumulation of incomprehensible things until understanding occurs (the transformation of quantity into quality).
3. The particular in the general (the process in its singularity, uniqueness, thereby its typicality).
4. The moment of development (changing feelings into feelings of an opposite sort, criticism and empathy in one).
5. Contradictoriness (this man in these relations, these consequences of this action!).
6. Understanding one thing through another (the scene, with at first an independent meaning, is discovered through its connection with other scenes to share in another meaning).
7. The jump (saltus naturae, epic development with jumps).
8. The unity of opposites (in unity the opposite is sought, Mother and son — in *Mutter*, — outwardly unified, struggle against each

other because of the reward).

9. Applicability of knowledge (unity of theory and practice).)[55]

The entry in Brecht's *Arbeitsjournal* (as printed in that text) runs as follows:

> klar, daß das theater der verfremdung ein theater der dialektik ist. jedoch sah ich bisher keine möglichkeit, durch anwendung des begriffsmaterials der dialektik dieses theater zu erklären: es wäre für die theaterleute leichter, die dialektik vom verfremdungstheater her als das verfremdungstheater von der dialektik her zu verstehen. anderseits wird es wohl nahezu unmöglich sein, die forderung,die realität so darzustellen, daß sie meisterbar wird, zu erheben, ohne auf den widerspruchsvollen. prozessualen charakter der zustände, vorgänge, figuren hinzuweisen, denn ohne erkennen ihrer dialektischen natur ist die realität ja eben nicht meisterbar. der v-effekt macht diese dialektische natur darstellbar, das ist seine aufgabe; durch sie erklärt er sich. schon beim aufstellen der *titel*, welche das szenische arrangement ermöglichen sollen, genügt es zb nicht, bloß eine soziale qualität zu verlangen; die titel müssen auch eine kritische qualität enthalten, einen widerpruch anmelden, sie müssen voll arrangierbar sein, also muß die dialektik (widersprüchlichkeit, prozessualität) konkret werden können.
>
> die welträsel werden nicht gelöst, sondern gezeigt. was die wirkung betrifft: die emotionen werden widerspruchsvoll sein, ineinander übergehen usw. in jeder beziehung wird der zuschauer zum dialektiker. da ist ständig der sprung vom besonderen zum allgemeinen, vom individuellen zum typischen. vom jetzt zum gestern und morgen, die einheit des inkongruenten, die diskontinuität des weitergehenden. hier wirken die v-effekte.

> (It is clear that a theatre of *Verfremdung* is a dialectical theatre. Yet I previously saw no possibility of explaining this theatre through the application of dialectical concepts: it would be easier for theatre people to understand dialectics from a *Verfremdung* theatre than a *Verfremdungs* theatre from dialectics. On the other hand it will be practically impossible to require that reality is shown in such a way that it is capable of being mastered without indicating the contradictory and changing nature of conditions, processes, figures, since

> without recognising its dialectical nature reality is simply not open to control. The *V-Effekt* makes this dialectical nature apparent, that is its task; in this way it becomes explicable. Already by putting up the titles which facilitate the scenic arrangement, it is not enough for example to desire merely a social quality; the titles must also contain a critical quality, announce a contradiction. They must be completely arrangeable, therefore the dialectic (contradictoriness, changeability) must be able to become concrete. The puzzles of the world are not solved but shown.
>
> What this effect involves: the emotions become contradictory passing into one another, etc. In each connection the spectator becomes a dialectician. There is the continual leap from the particular to the general, from the individual to the typical, from now to yesterday and tomorrow, the unity of what is incompatible, the discontinuity of what is ongoing. This is how the *V-Effekt* works.)[56]

These statements confirm much that has been said, as well as reinforcing the view that *Verfremdung* was the cental device of epic theatre. The first note also, cryptic though it is, adds something in its reference to the 'negation of negation' which is quite crucial to the dialectical aspect of *Verfremdung*, and crucial too to its difference from other forms of estrangement. As Brecht describes it elsewhere, in less explicit but still thoroughly dialectical terms: 'What is obvious is in a certain sense made incomprehensible, but this is only in order that it may then be made all the easier to comprehend.' (BT, p. 143) The process therefore that *Verfremdung* sets in motion is the inherently dialectical one by which whatever is obvious, self-evident, or 'natural', is 'negated', i.e. made to appear first strange, unfamiliar and incomprehensible, but then, in the 'negation of the negation', returned; transformed as the newly intelligible. What, theoretically, Brecht also associates with this process is the dialectical progression to a higher state, the change from quantity to quality, as the spectator is re-positioned in relation to ideology and history. As a newly class-conscious and politicised individual, the spectator is thus brought to the point, potentially at least, of collective political action.

This raises large questions in itself of course about the relation between art and social change. Whatever else, however, it is puerile to accuse Brecht, as Martin Esslin has done, of failure on the grounds that his theatre audiences have not been converted to socialism. We may as well say Marx 'failed' in writing *The Communist Manifesto* or *Capital*. Brecht certainly desired the advent of socialism. But he also realised that it would depend on more than the efforts of the theatre, just as the theatre itself was dependent on forces and events external to it: the arts, he said, could 'help' and 'contribute to' social change and in so doing 'regain their old powers', for 'Nothing but the advance of the workers, and furthering the advance of the workers can lead to their own advance.' (BT, p. 240) The ideological struggle in which Brecht participated could only be fully realised 'outside the limits of the performance',[57] and was thus dependent on further ideological, social and economic factors over which epic theatre and *Verfremdung* could themselves have no control. We cannot therefore describe *Verfremdung* as the 'negation of the negation', and intend by this that it negated alienation under capitalism. (Mitchell comes close to suggesting this but adds, correctly, that its negation of the negation occurred 'in terms of the spectator's consciousness.[58]) It could not of itself negate this condition, but only 'uncover' its socio-economic mechanism: *Verfremdung* could not as Brecht says 'solve' the riddle of the world, only 'show' it.

This is to return once again to the difference between Brecht's pedagogic and dialecticising art, and a committed or agitational art. In more than one sense Brecht's work was a 'primer' of social change, not that social change itself; nor yet a blueprint or direct stimulation of it. As such it could only be ideally completed by an actively participating audience, newly equipped or reinvigorated by Brecht's pedagogy for the task of practically changing the world. To put this another way, and specifically in relation to *Verfremdung*, Brecht saw that there must be a 'return from alienation'; that is to say, a full enactment of the progressive sequence entailed in the 'negation of the negation', so that in the words of the early catalogue of aims, epic theatre 'turns the spectator into an observer, *but* / arouses his capacity for action'. (BT, p. 37 my italics) Brecht suggests that *Verfremdung* of the kind employed in Dada and surrealism did not guarantee this return from alienation,[59] but his reservation could be levelled equally at *ostranenie* which as a formalist strategy estranges the familiar into the non-referential, the non-active world of aesthetic sensation.

A valuable distinction along these lines is drawn by Fredric Jameson between *ostranenie* and the Marxist dialectic, and this is the way finally we should respond to the idea that the Russian 'making strange' and *Verfremdung* are equivalent. Dialectical thinking Jameson characterises as ' a moment in which thought rectifies itself, in which the mind, suddenly drawing back and including itself in its new and widened apprehension doubly restores and *regrounds* its earlier notions in a new glimpse of reality.'[60] To achieve this, dialectical thinking passes from the self-consciousness of the Hegelian dialectic to its materialist and Marxist form. At this stage there is 'a consciousness of ourselves as at once the product and the producer of history, and of the profoundly historical character of our socio-economic situation as it informs both solutions and the problems which gave rise to them equally'. Jameson concludes:

> . . . it seems to me that even such aesthetic concepts as the *ostranenie* or 'making-strange' of Russian Formalism (as well as its American version, 'make it new'), indeed the profound drive everywhere in modern art toward a renewal of our perception of the world, are but manifestations in aesthetic form and on the aesthetic level, of the movement of dialectical consciousness as an assault on our conventionalised life-patterns, a whole battery of shocks administered to our routine vision of things, an implicit critique and reconstruction of our habitual consciousness. What distinguishes such concepts *philosophically* from genuine dialectical thinking is of course their failure to account for the initial numbness of our perception in the first place, their inability to furnish a sufficiently historical explanation for that ontological deficiency which they can only understand in ethical and aesthetic terms. Yet such intellectual distortion, such structural repression of an essential element in the situation, is amply accounted for by the Marxist theory of ideology, which posits a kind of resistance of *mauvaise foi* that grows ever stronger as we draw closer and closer to that truth of the socio-economic which, were it realised in all its transparency, would immediately obligate us to praxis.[61]

Brecht identified this 'initial numbness' as the 'general passive acceptance' of ruling ideology which he wished to transform into a 'state of suspicious inquiry'. (BT, p. 192) In inculcating an attitude of 'productive criticism', a dialectical attitude through *Verfremdung*, he wished to bring us 'closer to that truth of the socio-economic', and so, precisely, 'obligate us to praxis'.

This aim was entirely consistent with Korsch's view of the

philosophical and political character of Marxism. The last word on this, however, somewhat ironically, should go to Sergei Tretiakov — quoting Brecht. As early as 1934, Tretiakov credited Brecht, as wanting, under Lenin's influence, to change reality by changing the spectator. He chose to introduce Brecht to a Russian readership using Brecht's own words:

> 'the spectator should be changed, or rather the seeds of change should have been planted in him, seeds which must come to flower outside the limits of the performance. It should not be a circular performance in which everything is completed, in which the heroes and villians are balanced; it should rather be a spiral performance, a tilted circle rising to another horizon, and a spectator who is thrown out of balance.'[62]

Notes

1. Reinhold Grimm, *Bertolt Brecht: Die Struktur Seines Werkes* (Hans Carl, Nuremberg, 1959), p. 14, and Keith A. Dickson, *Towards Utopia. A Study of Brecht* (Clarendon Press, Oxford, 1978), p. 250. Dickson offers a particularly astute discussion of *Verfremdung*, pp. 240-8. I have retained the German forms *Verfremdung* and *Verfremdungseffekt(e)* rather than pre-empt the discussion by adopting a particular translation.

2. I have adopted Martin Esslin's translation of this passage, *Brecht. A Choice of Evils* (Methuen, London, 1959, revised 1980), pp. 119–20. Cf. *Brecht on Theatre* p. 71.

3. *Gesammelte Werke,* 15 (Suhrkamp, Frankfurt am Main, 1967), p. 301. The translation is Dickson's, *Towards Utopia*, p. 241.

4. A better translation than Willett's 'our grasp' for Brecht's 'dem Eingriff' (*Gesammelte Werke*, 16, p. 681) would be 'intervention'.

5. See Reinhold Grimm, 'Verfremdung. Beiträge zu Wesen und Ursprung eines Begriffs', *Revue de littérature comparée*, 35 (1961), pp. 207–36; Ernst Bloch, '*Entfremdung, Verfremdung*: Alienation, Estrangement', in Erika Munk (ed.), *Brecht* (Bantam Books, New York, 1972), pp. 3–11; and Majorie L. Hoover, 'Brecht's Soviet connection, Tretiakov', *Brecht Heute / Brecht Today*, 3 (1973), pp. 39–56. In an otherwise very careful discussion, Hoover lets slip a description of 'ostranenie' as 'the Russian equivalent of "Verfremdung"', p. 44. For a recent, but brief, and on this point again over-casual presentation see Eugene Lunn, *Marxism and Modernism* (University of California Press, 1982; Verso, London, 1985), pp. 122–3.

6. John Willett, *Brecht in Context* (Methuen, London and New York, 1984), p. 219.

7. Ibid., pp. 220, 221.

8. Ibid., p. 221.

9. *Gesammelte Werke*, p. 463.

10. Engels, 'From *Dialectics of Nature*', in *On Dialectical Materialism* (Progress Publishers, Moscow; Lawrence and Wishart, London, 1977), p. 137.

11. Willett, *Brecht in Context*, p. 220.

12. Willett, *The New Sobriety. Art and Politics in the Weimar Period, 1917–33* (Thames and Hudson, London, 1978).

13. Bernhard Reich, *Im Wettlauf mit der Zeit* (Henschel, East Berlin, 1970), p. 371, quoted and translated in Stanley Mitchell, 'From Shklovsky to Brecht: some preliminary remarks towards a history of the politicisation of Russian Formalism', *Screen*, 15:2 (Summer, 1974), p. 81.

14. I.M. Fradkin, *Bertolt Brecht: Put i Metod* (Moscow, 1965), p. 135; quoted in Dickson, *Towards Utopia*, p. 244; Frederic Ewen *Bertolt Brecht. His Life, His Art, and His Times* (Citadel Press, New York, 1969), pp. 224, 225.

15. Hoover, 'Brecht's Soviet connection Tretiakov', p. 44.

16. Ibid., p. 55.

17. Bernhard Reich, quoted Mitchell, 'From Shklovsky to Brecht', p. 81.

18. Mitchell, ibid., p. 74.

19. Shklovsky, 'Art as technique', in L.T. Lemon and M.J. Reis (eds), *Russian Formalist Criticism: Four Essays* (University of Nebraska Press, Lincoln, 1965), p. 12.

20. Tony Bennett, *Formalism and Marxism* (Methuen, London, 1979), p. 31.

21. Quoted Ewen, *Bertolt Brecht*, p. 199.

22. Mitchell, 'From Shklovsky to Brecht', pp. 76, 78.

23. This connection is developed by Ben Brewster, 'From Shklovsky to Brecht: a reply', *Screen*, 15:2 (Summer, 1974), p. 82–102. Further useful discussion of the relation between Brecht and Soviet production aesthetics is contained in David Bathrick, 'Affirmative and negative culture: the avant-garde under ''actually existing socialism — the case of the GDR', *Social Research*, 47:1 (Spring, 1980), esp. pp. 174–82.

24. 'Osip Brik: selected writings', *Screen*, 15:3 (1974), p. 51.

25. Ernst Schumacher in Hubert Witt (ed.) and John Peet (trans.), *Brecht As They Knew Him* (Seven Seas Books, Berlin; International Publishers, New York, 1974, 1977; Lawrence and Wishart, London, 1974, 1980), p. 226.

26. See Käthe Rülicke-Weiler's comments on Brecht's relationship with these artists, 'Since then the world has hope', in ibid., pp. 198–9; also Roland Barthes, 'Diderot, Brecht and Eisenstein', in *Image-Music-Text.* Essays selected and translated by Stephen Heath (Fontana, London, 1977), pp. 69–78; and Rainer Friedrich, 'On Brecht and Eisenstein', *Telos*, 31 (Spring, 1977), pp. 155–64.

24. 'Documents from *Lef*', translated, edited and introduced by Richard Sherwood, in *Screen*, 12:4 (Winter, 1971/2), p. 31.

28. Ibid., p.32.

29. 'Documents from *Novy Lef*', edited and introduced by Ben Brewster, *Screen*, ibid., pp. 60–61.

30. Ibid., p. 63.

31. Klaus Völker, *Brecht: A Biography* (Marion Boyars, London and Boston, 1979), p. 160; and cf. Ewen, *Bertolt Brecht*, pp. 254, 275.

32. Brewster, 'From Shklovsky to Brecht: a reply', p. 82.

33. Ibid., p. 79.

34. See in this context and in addition to the articles cited above, Eisenstein's 'A dialectical approach to film form' and 'Methods of montage', both written in 1929, in Sergei Eisenstein, *Film Form*, Jay Leyda (ed. and trans.) (Denis Dobson, London, 1963), pp. 45-63, 72-83.

35. Benjamin, 'The author as producer', in *Understanding Brecht*, p. 85-103. Brecht's comment is reported on p. 105.

36. See Völker, *Brecht*, p. 161.

37. The text quoted here appears as 'The popular and the realistic' in *Brecht on Theatre*, pp. 107-115. This and three other related essays are translated in Perry Anderson *et al.* (eds), *Aesthetics and Politics* (New Left Books, 1977), pp. 68-85. These and other of Brecht's essays on realism from 1938 and 1939 are contained in *Gesammelte Werke*, 19; cf. esp. pp. 287-382. For two astute and informative discussions of the many which have appeared on this theme, see David Roberts, 'Brecht: epic form and realism. A reconsideration', *Thesis Eleven* (Philip Institute of Technology, Victoria, Australia), nos. 5/6 (1982), pp. 32-58; and Eugene Lunn, *Marxism and Modernism*, 'Part Two', pp. 75-145.

38. Völker, *Brecht* pp. 204, 205.

39. See Völker, ibid., p. 239, and Benjamin, 'Conversations with Brecht', in *Understanding Brecht*, pp. 116-17.

40. Völker, *Brecht*, pp. 247, 246.

41. Brecht, *The Messingkauf Dialogues*, John Willett (trans.) (Eyre Methuen, London, 1965), p. 104, and see Benjamin, *Understanding Brecht*, pp. 87-8.

42. In the 'second version' of the essay 'What is epic theatre?', first published in 1939, Benjamin writes again that the 'task of epic theatre' is to '*uncover*' and not 'reproduce' conditions, adding '(One could just as well say: to *make them strange* [verfremden].) This uncovering (making strange, or alienating) of conditions is brought about by processes being interrupted.' (p. 18) My point has not been to deny the relevance of the description 'making strange', but to clarify Brecht's concept, and distinguish it where necessary from apparent equivalents in Soviet aesthetics. As other essays by both Brecht and Benjamin prove the Formalist concept of 'making strange' was not *necessary* to *Verfremdung*.

43. In 'Theatre for pleasure or theatre for instruction', dated as 'about 1936', with the suggestion that there were earlier drafts, *Brecht on Theatre*, pp. 69-76; and in the note 'Episches Theater, Entfremdung', *Gesammelte Werke*, 15, p. 372.

44. Ronald Gray, *Brecht. The Dramatist* (Cambridge University Press, 1976), p. 75. Joseph Franklin Dial has discovered that Brecht wrote 'V-Effekt!' by the side of a passage in the Preface to Hegel's *Logik*. The passage in translation runs:

> Instinctive action is distinguished from intelligent and free action broadly by this, that the latter is accompanied by clear consciousness; when the content of that which stirs the mind is drawn out of its immediate unity with the Subject, and made an Object for it, then

there begins Freedom for the mind. (Hegel's *Science of Logic*, vol. I, translated by W.H. Johnston and L.G. Struthers, Allen and Unwin, London; Humanities Press, New York, 1929, 1966, pp. 45-6.)

Dial says that Brecht annotated Hegel's *Logik* in March 1937, and writes that 'one can recognise in this passage from Hegel the philosophical premises on which Brecht's theory of the *V-effekt* is based.' Elsewhere he states that 'a close investigation of Brecht's theory reveals . . . that the concept of *Verfremdungseffekt* is absent until 1937'. *The Contribution of Marxism to Bertolt Brecht's Theater Theory* (Doctoral thesis, Harvard, 1975), pp. 104, 105, 63n. As I and others have suggested, the concept and the term were present before 1937. It seems much more likely that Brecht was bringing the concept to this passage in Hegel rather than discovering it there.

45. Mitchell, 'From Shklovsky to Brecht', p. 78.

46. Brecht, 'Über die Hauspostille', in *Über Lyrik*, selected and edited by Elizabeth Hauptmann and Rosemarie Hill (Suhrkamp, Frankfurt am Main, 1964), p. 74.

47. Benjamin, *Understanding Brecht*, p. 108. Cf. the discussion and further citations in Brewster, 'From Shklovsky to Brecht: a reply', p. 92-3.

48. Willett, *Brecht in Context*, p. 220.

49. On the relationship between Brecht and Korsch, see Wolfdietrich Rasch, 'Bertolt Brechts marxistischer Lehrer', *Merkur*, XVII (1963), pp. 988-1003; Heinz Brüggemann, *Literarische Technik und Soziale Revolution* (Rowohlt, Reinbek bei Hamburg, 1973), esp. Ch.6; Roland Jost, *Er War Unser Lehrer* (Pahl-Rugenstein, Köln, 1981), esp. pp. 137-58; and Arnold Schnölzel, 'Korsch, Brecht und die Negation der Philosophie', in *Brecht 1983. Brecht und Marxismus. Dokumentation* (Henschelverlag, East Berlin, 1983), pp. 32-44. The fullest statement by Brecht was his 'Uber meinen Lehrer'. Here Korsch is described as 'ein enttäuschter Mann' ('a disappointed man') and criticised for his political caution: 'Er ist sehr für den Kampf, aber er selber kämpft eigentlich nicht. Er sagt, es sei nicht die Zeit dazu.' ('He is much in favour of the struggle, but he doesn't himself actually engage in struggle. He says it isn't the time for it.') *Gesammelte Werke* 20, p. 65-6. On this and other references to Korsch in *Me-Ti*, T.W.H. Metscher comments, rightly I believe, that Brecht was 'critical, albeit affectionate', 'Brecht and Marxist dialectics', *Oxford German Studies, 6* (1971-2), p. 135n.

50. Cf. Schnölzel, 'Korsch, Brecht und die Negation der Philosophie', pp. 35-6; and Brecht *Gesammelte Werke*, 20, pp. 70-1.

51. Karl Korsch, *Karl Marx* (Russell and Russell, New York, 1938, 1963), 'Part Two', Ch. VII. Korsch worked on the draft of this chapter while staying with Brecht in Denmark. See Patrick Goode, *Karl Korsch. A Study in Western Marxism* (Macmillan, London, 1979), p. 141.

52. See 'Why I am a Marxist', included in Karl Korsch, *Three Essays on Marxism*, (Pluto, London, 1971). Brecht's emphasis on the importance of ideology and of the ideological struggle is everywhere apparent, but see the essays, 'Theses for a theory of the superstructure', 'Pedagogy' and 'The proletarian dialectic', the last of which appeared in 1965 in a version altered by Korsch, *Gesammelte Werke*, 20, pp. 76-80, 150-1, 370.

53. Patrick Goode, *Karl Korsch*, pp. 125-35.

54. Wolfdietrich Rasch, 'Bertolt Brechts marxistischer Lehrer', p. 999; Benjamin *Understanding Brecht*, p. 121.
55. *Gesammelte Werke*, 15, p. 360–1.
56. Brecht, *Arbeitsjournal*. vol. I, 1938–1942, Werner Hecht (ed.) (Suhrkamp, Frankfurt am Main, 1973), p. 216.
57. Brecht, quoted by Tretiakov 'Bert Brecht', in Witt and Peet, *Brecht As They Knew Him*, p. 78.
58. Mitchell, 'From Shklovsky to Brecht', p. 78.
59. *Gesammelte Werke*, 15, p. 364.
60. Fredric Jameson, *Marxism and Form* (Princeton University Press, New Jersey, 1971), p. 372.
61. Ibid., pp. 373–4.
62. Brecht, quoted by Tretiakov, in Witt and Peet, *Brecht As They Knew Him*, p. 78.

Part Two
In and Above the Stream

5

'Bad Time for Poetry'

John Willett's book *Brecht in Context* draws attention away from the conventional view of Brecht's work as an individual artistic achievement to his use of sources, his collaboration and differences with other artists, the relation between his theatre and other media, and the historical context of his political views. His aim he says at one point is to see how Brecht could bring an everyday subject briefly and simply to a political point. Accordingly he turns to the poem 'The fishing tackle' to suggest how its rhythm and economy serve as a basis for Brecht's comment on the Californian Japanese interned in World War II. The poem 'is political. It is poetic. Neither aspect interferes with the other; it is perfectly fused right down to its elements.'[1]

In reviewing Willett's book Stephen Spender acknowledged the evidence for Brecht's intellectual independence and critical view of Stalin. He concludes, however, that 'Obviously the case of Brecht is not closed,' and that 'the writings themselves, because they include great poems and plays, submit themselves to judgement by some ultimate criterion different from that by which we judge the man.'[2] Spender does not tell us what this criterion is, but we can guess. It would probably have something to do with timeless aesthetic value, with the poet's unique expression of universal sentiments, and the unity of formal beauty with humanising content.

These are the kind of 'ultimate' criteria Esslin invokes to separate Brecht the 'poet' (his general description of the artist) from the man (and Marxist). The art which is thus 'rescued' from history and politics is the art of liberal humanism, its aesthetic a loose derivation of Aristotelian categories of mimesis and universality and romantic subjectivism. Artistic value is thought to be inherent in the transcendent and fetishised art object, which stands above and apart from the life it nevertheless imitates.[3]

Willett cannot be accused of wanting to separate Brecht the poet from Brecht the man, or either from the artistic and political contexts in which Brecht's work was produced. On the contrary, he sees the poetic and the political as 'perfectly fused'. In that very judgement, however, he simplifies their relationship and merely extends the traditional criterion of organic unity until it more securely embraces rather than prohibits politics.

But to say this is a simplification in Brecht's case is itself misleading. Romantic individualism has proved a tenacious general ideology, as have the aesthetic conventions of mimesis, transcendence, and organic unity associated with it. Brecht was opposed to their implications and effects, but there are signs of the lingering influence of this aesthetic on his thinking all the same. Some of his early comments particularly, suggest also that he took a much more traditioal attitude to poetry than to the theatre. An early interview from 1926, for example, reports Brecht as saying that his poetry was a 'more private' area of work and expression than his drama. Since his theatre was 'sober and matter-of-fact' and appealed to reason, the implication is that his poetry is a realm of mood and feeling, and 'Feelings are more private and limited.' (BT, pp. 14, 15) His instructions to readers of his first volume of poems, the *Hauspostille* in 1927, where he writes, facetious though the general tone is, of the 'first Lesson' as being 'directly aimed at the reader's emotions', would seem to bear this out. A decade later in the 'Logic of poetry', he begins his commentary on Fritz Brügel's 'Whispering song', in a concession to the prime tenets of conventional aesthetics, by saying, 'that the poet's emotional involvement was not sufficiently deep and consistent for some thorough, compelling logic to bring his poem into equilibrium.' (P, p. 477) He then embarks on an unflinching pursuit of faulty and mixed metaphors in Brügel's poem of which any English or American New Critic would be proud. The poem 'Bad time for poetry' might similarly be thought to endorse the view (though I do not think it does) of poetry as a separated and unchanging artistic form. The poem can be construed as saying therefore that an effect of the 'dark times' of the 1930s has been to drive the use of rhyme and conventional 'poetic' sentiments ('Delight at the apple tree in blossom') temporarily, but only temporarily, into abeyance. In the context of Brecht's work as a whole the very large number of poems unpublished in his life time would seem itself to argue that he regarded poetry as a more private, and more occasional, secondary, activity.[4]

Some of this evidence is ambiguous. Many other comments also, and by far the majority, suggest how Brecht resisted conventional assumptions and definitions of poetry. In a further early comment he refuted the suggestion that his poetry was the best argument against his political drama and that he should have been a poet not a dramatist. His poetry, he said, already made the case against existing drama.[5] In the essay 'Theatre for pleasure or theatre for instruction', also, he neatly side-stepped the widespread conception of the poet as romantic genius and seer:

> People are used to seeing poets as unique and slightly unnatural beings who reveal with a truly godlike assurance things that other people can only recognise after much sweat and toil. It is naturally distasteful to have to admit that one does not belong to this select band. (BT, p. 73)

Brecht's own view of art, and of poetry in particular, he summed up, in response to an example of Romantic poetry, in a note of August 1940. He begins with the reservation that to describe Wordsworth's 'She was a phantom of delight' as a ' "petty-bourgeois" idyll' is 'hazardous', for the petty bourgeoisie is composed of conflicting tendencies. Moreover, lines from Wordsworth's poem can help conjure up contrary states 'less unworthy of the human race' than those which presently prevail. 'Art *is* an autonomous sphere,' Brecht writes, 'though by no means an autarchic one.' There then follow three 'criteria' or conditions for art. Art's function, it is said, is to enrich the individual's capacity for experience and for expression or communication. But this individual is to be understood as one 'who goes ahead and is then overtaken by the masses', while on the matter of expression, 'the question is to what extent the How is linked to the What, and the What bound up with specific classes.' His third point is that

> Poetry is never mere expression. The absorption of a poem is an operation of the same order as seeing and hearing, i.e. something a great deal less passive. Writing poetry has to be viewed as a human activity, a social function of a wholly contradictory and alterable kind, conditioned by history and in turn conditioning it. It is the difference between 'mirroring' and 'holding up a mirror'. (P, p. 483)

Brecht therefore sees the individual writer or reader in 'specific classes', and poetry in its 'social function', as comprising a series of active, contradictory and unevenly developing relationships. Other essays confirm that this dialectical view extends to the artistic and political 'contexts' Willett intends by his title. Brecht does not look for a 'fusion' of poetry with other arts, or with society and politics, however, but, as in 'epic theatre', for a 'separation of the elements.' Thus he talks of how a poem will be 'tested' by its musical setting, and of how individual poems will disagree with and complement others when brought together in a collection. (P, pp. 461, 484–5) The coherence he ascribes to his poems is not that of formal organic unity, however far this is extended, nor is it attributable to the author, since 'poetry is never mere expression.' As he wrote to Wieland Herzfelde, the editor of *A Hundred Poems*.

> As every poem is the enemy of every other poem it demands to be published on its own. At the same time they need one another, derive strength from each other, and can consequently be grouped. That 'same hat' under which they are normally brought is the author's hat, in my case a cap. But there is a risk here too: maybe the poems in question describe me, but that was not what they were written for. It's not a matter of 'getting acquainted with the poet' but of getting acquainted with the world, and with the people in whose company he is trying to enjoy and alter it. (P, pp. 462–3)

Brecht's conception here of the poet, and of how his work should be presented, is consistent with his advice to working-class actors, that 'you should/On no account show yourselves only but/The world.' (P, p. 234) That world, certainly from the late 1920s, Brecht thought of as contradictory and alterable. It became poetry's task, therefore, as it was the theatre's, to demonstrate and assist this process in the interests of a liberated humanity. In the major essay on his verse technique, 'On rhymeless verse with irregular rhythms', published in 1939, Brecht says of his earlier work,

> My political knowledge in those days was disgracefully slight, but I was aware of huge inconsistencies in people's social life, and I didn't think it my task formally to iron out all the discordances and interferences of which I was strongly conscious. I caught them up in the incidents of my plays and in the verses of my poems; and did so long before I had recognised their

> real character and causes. As can be seen from the texts it was a matter not just of a formal 'kicking against the pricks' — of a protest against the smoothness and harmony of conventional poetry — but already of an attempt to show human dealings as contradictory, fiercely fought over, full of violence. (P, p. 465)

Brecht's protest against a conventional aesthetic and against conventional poetry was, as this suggests, a purposeful, but also intuitive and progressively conscious one. Often the result has been seen as an anti-individualistic and uncompromisingly functional verse. Thus to H.R. Hays in his Introduction to the *Selected Poems* of 1947, Brecht 'became the enemy of emotional self-indulgence to a fanatical degree. To counteract softness, impressionism and decorative lyricism, he attempted to create artistic forms out of didacticism itself. He discovered aesthetic values in functionalism.'[6] This is to impute an extremism to Brecht he did not possess, however; since, as we can already see, his antagonism to romantic individualism amounted neither to an outright denial of the individual writer or reader, nor of the integrity and value of the single poem, even the Romantic nature poem. What is clear is that Brecht historicised the production and function of poetry. He did not join art and politics therefore, so much as politicise art; in the process coming to reassess and radicalise its conventional categories. Poetry could therefore express emotion, but was more, and less, than a vehicle for mere self expression or for unlocated 'universal' emotion; it would express and 'show . . . conflicting feelings', directly and with sobriety, in poems which adopted 'the emotional form proper to them.' (P, pp. 465, 470)

Brecht similarly re-defined rather than rejected aesthetic beauty. Poetry would exhibit and demonstrate more the 'functional beauty' Hays speaks of, than the beauty supposedly inherent in an art object and apprehended through disinterested contemplation. Hays likens this to aesthetic concepts in the fields of architecture and design, but Brecht's comments on architecture show that he had more than contemporary functionalism in mind as a model for poetry. The new buildings were like 'prisons' to the workers who had to live in them, and neglected to provide for more than their practical needs. We need the concept of beauty, Brecht says, but are embarrassed by its vagueness and ambiguity and its apparent dependence on the notoriously individual concept of 'taste'.[7] Brecht's alternative, socialising aesthetic lay in the discovery of beauty in objects (including poems), according to the shapes and value they had acquired through use. Thus he writes in 'Of all the works of man.'

> Of all the works of man I like best
> Those which have been used
> The copper pots with their dents and flattened edges
> The knives and forks whose wooden handles
> Have been worn away by many hands: such forms
> Seemed to me the noblest . . .
> Absorbed into the service of the many
> Frequently altered, they improve their shape, grow precious
> Because so often appreciated. (P, p. 192)

Works of labour are valued aesthetically, and works of art as forms of productive labour. Amongst other things, this criterion informs Brecht's rejection of the perfected and finished work of art of conventional expectations. The enduring poem, for Brecht, was not the timeless and ostentatiously 'useless' object, but the incomplete, open, and still serviceable work. Works endure 'As long/As they are not completed' and are granted duration by 'Those who'll be alive then' he writes in 'About the way to construct enduring works.' (P, p. 193, 195) It was on this kind of premise that Brecht explained to Herzfelde that he ought to present his poems as '(as it were) famous' or 'as if they were famous (or were going to be)'. The reader, thus introduced to the poems and provided with a way of reading them, could join with the poet in 'trying to enjoy and alter' the world, (P, p. 463) The poems would then become in a new sense 'famous', acquiring enduring value according to their continued use.

Several other poems substantiate the integrated aesthetic and social implications of Brecht's materialist criterion of value, including the American poem 'The fishing tackle' which Willett examines and the 'Song about the good people' referred to earlier. In the first poem the 'traces of use and of work/Lend great dignity to the stick', a bamboo cane, bound with cord and with an iron hook which Brecht's son had acquired, second-hand, and given him as a birthday present. Brecht reads the gift as a sign, a metonym, bearing a history of labour and associated political persecution. Its value lies in this associated history, but also in the function it continues to have in prompting 'so many/Unsolved but not insoluble/

Questions of humanity.' (P, p. 386) Brecht does not indulge himself in an extrapolated history, but neither is this history written on the stick, since history and politics do not adhere spontaneously to the poetic or everyday object but have to be actively and imaginatively constructed from them.

The political and aesthetic meanings Brecht discovers as a double mark of the stick's enduring value are separated but corrected and the poem remains open on both counts not 'fused'. In 'About the way to construct enduring works', Brecht's criterion of use-value is extended to human activities and to people: those who are valued are 'Those who ask questions . . . He who has not spoken' and those who appear insignificant, but 'Are/The powerful ones of tomorrow' (p. 195). Similarly, elsewhere, it is the 'active discontented' and the 'doubters' who are appealed to and win Brecht's praise. Just as enduring works 'inviting further work' last 'as long as/They invite and reward', so also in the 'Song about the good people', the good people are those who 'Invite one to improve them', who 'are of use to us.' Their work, aimed at changing the world, is incomplete, and like the fishing tackle, brings with it both solutions and continuing problems. (P, p. 337)

The concept of 'aesthetic beauty' was therefore socialised and materialised in Brecht's thinking; redefined in terms of art's 'use-value' as a purveyor of enjoyment and knowledge, sensuous pleasure and rational logic, as both crafted form and dialectical argument, (the titles of three essays on these themes in the volume *Über Lyrik* run 'Underrating the formal aspect', 'The lyric poet need not fear reason', and 'There is no separation between instruction and amusement'). As such, Brecht's general aesthetic (though this itself was incomplete, and certainly more occasional than systematic before the *Short Organum*) was opposed on every major count to the theoretical tenets and common sense derivatives of philosophical aesthetics. In practice, and politically, it was opposed too to the implications of an aestheticist perfection of the kind Brecht spotted, for example, in the opening stanzas of Ezra Pound's *Hugh Selwyn Mauberley*. Borrowing the title of the first section of Pound's poem, Brecht both parodies and warns of Pound's pretentions to a monumental stone-mason's art:

E.P., Election de son sepulcre

The production of petrifactions
Is an arduous business and
Expensive. Whole towns must be reduced to rubble
And at times in vain
If the fly or the fern
Was badly placed. Furthermore
The stone of our towns is not lasting
And even petrifactions
Can't be relied on to last. (P, p. 384)

To abbreviate Walter Benjamin (and given that Pound is presenting a persona in *Hugh Selwyn Mauberley*), aestheticism, when it encounters the political sphere, is conducive to fascism.[8] Brecht's open, provisional, and expendable verse was, on the other hand, the politicised art of change and future communism (whose actual forms, since 'men make history' were properly beyond its control).

Brecht saw the German poetic tradition and his own verse and thinking on poetry as 'conditioned by history and in turn conditioning it'. In truth, however, and especially in the traumatic changes occurring in European society and the world economy in Brecht's years, history conditioned poetry more than the reverse. The dialectic, as it were, while acknowledged and in operation, was unequal in its application. Brecht is led in a distant response to this to exclaim, in a note in his *Arbeitsjournal* in August 1940, on the decline of German verse after Goethe. He sees it as dividing along respectively secular and pontifical lines in Heine and Karl Kraus, and Hölderlin and Stefan George. Both tendencies are 'anti-bourgeois', but both are 'one-sided'. (P. pp. 460–1). In two notes, on his own *Svendborg Poems* in 1938, and the *Hauspostille*, again from August 1940, he sees his early poems as the verse of decline and decadence, dehumanisation and excess. (P, pp. 458, 458–9) 'From the bourgeois point of view', the *Svendborg Poems* are more 'one-sided, less ''organic'', cooler, more self-conscious (in a bad sense)'. The conditions and concepts have however changed, or are in need of revision. Where ('from the bourgeois point of view'), there was 'richness' in the *Hauspostille* poems, there is now, says Brecht, 'a rich choice of battlefields'; where there was 'originality', there is now an 'originality of problems'. The *Svendborg Poems* were less decadent because 'Capitalism has forced us to take up arms', but a militant poetry exacted its own costs: 'I no longer go off to "commune with Nature in the woods" ' and 'literature is not blooming' (P, pp. 458, 459). But then says Brecht, in a further reversal, 'the notion of "bloom" is too one-sided,' power and greatness have nothing to do with 'an idyllic conception of organic flowering'. There is, after all, as far as conditions allow, a dialectic of loss and gain, withdrawal and advance for individuals and their works.

Brecht evidently felt the difficulty of revising the conventional notions of verse and of working with the consequences, particularly in the early war years. In another journal entry of August 1940, he reflects on his slow production:

> At present all I can write is these little epigrams, first eight-liners and now only four-liners. I am leaving *Caesar* on one side, since the *Good Person* isn't finished. When I open the *Messingkauf* for a bit of a change it's like having a cloud of dust blow into one's face. Can you imagine that sort of thing ever coming to mean anything again? That's not a rhetorical question. I *should* be able to imagine it. And it isn't a matter of Hitler's current victories but purely and simply of my own isolation so far as production is concerned. When I listen to the news on the radio in the morning, at the same time reading Boswell's *Life of Johnson* and glancing out at the landscape of birch trees in the mist by the river, then the unnatural day begins not on a discordant note but on no note at all. (P, p. 460)

It was indeed a 'bad time for poetry' (as for other work), because as these notes and essays tell us, Brecht's poetry was 'one-sided' in form and argument. As he writes in the poem 'To those born later':

> And yet we know:
> Hatred, even of meanness
> Contorts the features.
> Anger, even of injustice
> Makes the voice hoarse. Oh, we
> Who wanted to prepare the ground for friendliness
> Could not ourselves be friendly. (P, p. 320)

Similarly, in 'Bad time for poetry' itself,

In my poetry a rhyme
Would seem to me almost insolent.

Inside me contend
Delight at the apple tree in blossom
And horror at the house-painter's speeches.
But only the second
Drives me to my desk. (P, p. 331)

There is in the background of these poems a shadowy residue of an essentialist conception of poetry, but this did not mean that Brecht looked for a return to the smooth and seamless harmonies and 'splendid unity' of Goethe. For this too was 'full of contradictions'. (P, p. 460) Nothing suggests either (how could it?) that Brecht anticipated a verse combining the secular, liberal idealism of a Karl Kraus with the pontifical, subjective, and counter-revolutionary tendency exemplified by Stefan George. Neither was progress served, a 1930s essay suggests, by committed, conventionally propagandist verse: 'Flach, leer, platt werden Gedichte', Brecht writes, 'wenn die Dinge, von denen sie handeln, nicht in ihrer lebendigen, d.h. allseitigen, nicht zu Ende gekommenen und nicht zu Ende zu formulierenden Form auftreten' ('Poetry becomes dull, empty, flat . . . if it does not treat the things that it deals with in their living, that is to say all-sided, incomplete and indefinable form'). The result otherwise is '*bad* tendency poetry' ('*schlechte* Tendenzdichtung').[9]

The poetry Brecht proposed and anticipated could not consistently be other than a unity of opposites; and this was indeed how he discussed its internal relations, the relations between poems, and the development of a changing poetic tradition, regulated by history. Present conditions required, even necessitated an expendable poetry, contorted and coarsened by anger and hatred, but which from the perspective of a better future might be regarded with 'forbearance' by those born later. Best of all, of course, 'when the time comes at last/And man is a helper to man' (P, p. 320), and in a scandalous affront to traditional aesthetic assumptions, it could simply be forgotten, having served and outlived its usefulness.

Notes

1. John Willett, *Brecht in Context* (Methuen, London and New York, 1984), p. 210.

2. Stephen Spender, 'Brecht's historic compromise', *Guardian*, 2 Feb. 1984, p. 8.

.3 Cf. Rainer Friedrich, 'On Brecht and Eisenstein', *Telos*, 31 (Spring 1977), pp. 156–7; Tony Bennett, 'Really useless knowledge: a political critique of aesthetics', *Thesis Eleven*, 12 (1985), pp. 28–52.

4. Philip Brady in a review of the two volumes of *Gedichte aus dem Nachlass* (Suhrkamp, Frankfurt am Main, 1982), concludes that 'Poetry . . . was obviously still, for Brecht, a place for more private gestures, for the unplanned, the throwaway.' *TLS*, 27 May 1983, p. 550.

5. Bertolt Brecht, *Über Lyrik*, E. Hauptmann and Rosemarie Hill (eds) (Suhrkamp, Frankfurt am Main, 1964), p. 58.

6. H.R. Hays, 'Brecht, anti-individualist', *Selected Poems* (Grove Press, New York, 1947), p. 6.

7. Brecht, *Über Lyrik*, p. 51.

8. Benjamin writes, 'The logical result of Fascism is the introduction of aesthetics into political life . . . Communism responds by politicising art', 'The work of art in the age of mechanical reproduction', in *Illuminations*, Hannah Arendt (ed.) (Fontana, London, 1973), pp. 243–4.

9. Brecht, *Über Lyrik*, p. 25.

6

Alienating Verse

The main devices of *Gestus* and *Verfremdung* developed for the theatre were consistent, as we have seen, with the proposals for a dialectical drama and with the tenets of dialectical materialism. I want to suggest here that the forms and metrical innovations Brecht developed for poetry can be similarly understood, as the functional devices of a verse composed in and for specific social and political conditions, and as themselves examples or extensions of 'gest' and *Verfremdung*.

Superficially the signs are against this. Brecht's writings on poetry were fewer, and his poetry was arguably more occasional than his essays on the theatre, or his plays. There is some sense too in which his poetry lagged behind the theory and practice of 'epic' theatre, or was, apparently, a lower priority. Brecht's first volume, the *Hauspostille*, published in 1927, was, for example, closer in its cynical hedonism to *Baal* (1918), from which several of its songs were indeed drawn, than it was to Brecht's politicised consciousness in the later 1920s. Thereafter also, Brecht published only two collections of poetry and three post-war selections in his lifetime.

It would be a mistake, however, on account of this 'uneven development', to regard Brecht's poetry as a separate artistic realm, and thoroughly wrong to think that its less public character gave it an ideological purity over his other writings. If anything, the reverse is true, since the tenets of organicism, universality and subjective expression cling more persistently to poetry than to the theatre. As a poet Brecht had consequently to pull away from a more deeply naturalised and adhesive literary ideology. There are many ways besides, in which his poetry and theatre were related, and did in fact synchronise, or syncopate, one with the other. The 'Theatre Poems' designated for *The Messingkauf Dialogues*, for example, defy classification as poetry or theory. They play an integral part in the development of Brecht's general arguments on the theatre, and though written, somewhat confusingly before and after, as well as during the main years of composition of *The Messingkauf Dialogues* in 1939–1940, do also have in the context of that incomplete work, a projected dramatic setting.

The 'test' of poetry, moreover, as Brecht said, was its setting; just as performance was the test of a play. (P, p. 485) Many of his poems over his whole career were accordingly set to music. They were written for plays of course, or for film in the case of *Kuhle Wampe*, as songs, with guitar or banjo accompaniment in Brecht's early years, or later, as marching songs for propaganda purposes. In a general sense therefore we might say that Brecht's poetry was already 'gestic'; employed as a functional device in counterpoint or contradiction with an action or incident, so as to interrupt and estrange the dramatic or historical narrative in which it was set. This function was differently inflected in different types of poetry and setting, however; both as a factor of altered conditions and as a matter of conscious strategy. I want to examine some of these changes in the following chapter, but first of all to outline here some of the more formal means by which poetry, as a particular range of artistic conventions and possibilities, was brought to join in common cause with Brecht's dialectical and dialecticising drama. This does not mean that at some point, 'in the last analysis', Brecht's poetry did indeed comprise a separated and autonomous artistic realm, nor that it was on the other hand a 'prop' simply for his drama; a kind of private sketch pad of ideas and techniques worked up into the final products of his plays. Brecht's drama and poetry were engaged in different dialogues with literary tradition and convention, and therefore differently angled in what was nevertheless a common exposure of the deceptions of general and aesthetic ideology.

One of Brecht's chief targets in this respect was the figure of 'the poet' and the idea of 'the poem', as these have been both theorised in philosophical aesthetics (by philosophers who did not want to change the world), and popularly understood. The ironic descriptions quoted earlier announce just this purpose. Brecht's comments unsettle the view of poets 'as unique and slightly unnatural beings' who ' "commune with Nature" ', the enemies of reason, logic and analysis, whose poems express the transcendent self, in 'self-contained' consolingly regular rhythms and rhymes. These traditional, commonsense ideas are 'alienated', but so too is the bourgeois individualism which had given this hotch-potch of ideas and expectations an ideological home.

From early on in his career, and with this same end in view, Brecht adapted and parodied standard verse forms such as the hymn, the chorale, the sonnet, the ballad and epigram, or in the *Hauspostille*, the unitary form of the Prayer Book, to produce what one German critic saw as a 'devil's' version.[1] The plebeian, or elitist, or devotional associations of these forms were therefore reinforced or subverted. An early example was the poem 'Great hymn of thanksgiving', modelled on a seventeenth-century hymn by Joachim Neander, which H.R. Hays says Brecht insisted on his including in the *Selected Poems* of 1947, 'because it was uncompromisingly atheist and provided the basis for the Marxist work which followed.' (P, p. 519) Brecht's atheism surfaces through the sententious platitudes of its opening stanzas, 'Lo! Grass and beasts / Like you partake of life's feasts / Like you they must also perish', to expose Heaven's true indifference and man's true worthlessness:

> Worship the cold and the dark and calamity
> dire!
> Scan the whole earth:
> You're a thing of no worth
> And you may calmly expire. (P, p. 74)

Brecht confounds piety in its own idiom, using Neander's hymn against itself and for his own purposes, just as over a period of years he was to 'use' Goethe, Villon, Rimbaud, Kipling, Ezra Pound, Po Chü-yu, Horace and Lucretius. The results traverse a range of tones across what were in Brecht's work the overlapping genres of poem, song, drama and essay. As a series of *formal* innovations and experiments this was perfectly in keeping with his argument against Lukácsian *formalism*. As he wrote in that context,

> Reality alters; to represent it the means of representation must alter too . . . Anybody who is not bound by formal prejudices knows that there are many ways of suppressing truth and many ways of stating it: that indignation at inhuman conditions can be stimulated in many ways, by direct description of a matter-of-fact kind, by narrating stories and parables, by jokes, by over-and understatement. (BT, p. 110)

On this same question, Brecht talks in the essay 'Where I

learned' of the usefulness of folk art, the national classics, the works of the progressive bourgeoisie and of the USSR. Brecht was consistently wary of the concept of the 'folk' and of claims for the authenticity of so-called 'popular' art and the 'popular' heritage. In this essay he recalls how in childhood he heard people sing 'cheap hits and interminable ditties about noble robbers' which, debased though the songs might be, bore traces of an older tradition:

> the singers would still add words of their own. The women workers in the nearby paper factory would sometimes fail to remember all the verses of a song and make improvised transitions from which much could be learned. Their attitude towards the songs was also instructive. They never let themselves be naively carried away. They would sing individual verses or entire songs with a certain irony, putting quotation marks, as it were, round a lot that was cheap, exaggerated, unreal. They were not all that far removed from those highly educated compilers of the Homeric epics who were inspired by naivety without being themselves naive. (P, p. 473)

These habits of the people served Brecht in further undermining 'popular' ideas of the poet and poetry, for here he had discovered a plebeian model for his own appropriation of existing and traditional forms. The women workers employ, moreover, the estrangement, irony, and putting in quotation marks, the showing and being shown of the epic style of acting. This 'way of playing' presents itself therefore for adoption by the poet, just as elsewhere, in the theatre poem 'Everyday theatre' and the essay 'The street scene', the use of 'mask, verse and quotation' (themselves 'common, but uncommon') are recommended to the actor. (P, p. 179)

There was a congruence therefore between gestic acting and Brecht's performative verse, both of which took instruction and authority from the complex simplicity of everyday song and non-aristotelian 'imitations' of 'street' theatre where people have 'a point to put across'. (BT, p. 176) Brecht developed this most fully, in relation to poetry, in the essay 'On rhymeless verse with irregular rhythms'. 'I was always thinking of actual delivery', he stresses again here: 'And for this delivery (whether of prose or of verse) I had worked out a quite definite technique. I called it "gestic" '. (P, p. 465) 'Gest', as discussed above, is the critical demonstration of an attitude, the social 'gist' of which is revealed in its gestural display. In employing this device Brecht could frustrate as he contextualised the traditional subjectivism of lyric poetry. The 'I' of the lyric poem becomes the voice of a narrator, character, or teacher, or it moves across these, while the poem's content becomes a social gest, a quoted instance of typical significance. Brecht's developed answer to lyric verse therefore was neither anonymity nor didacticism, but illustrative verse, deploying socialised voices and narratives in counterpoint and contrast.

This technical innovation and intervention at the level of poetic voice and subject is supported by the use of irregular rhythms or rhymeless verse, such as had appeared from the time of Brecht's first volume, and then by their combined use from the time of the poem 'Born later' to the writing of the *German Satires* and *Svendborg Poems*. Poetry without rhyme, as Brecht remarks at the beginning of the essay 'On rhymeless verse', does not look or sound like 'poetry'. But in conjunction with standard verse forms or regular rhythms, or in its shape on the printed page, Brecht's rhymeless poetry retains the rhythmical or physical shadow of 'poetry', and thus satisfies while it estranges expectations. Brecht comments in the 'Appendix' to his essay that he did not feel that in using irregular rhythms he 'was moving away from poetry.' What he was doing, I suggest, was moving poetry away from 'poetry'; away from what he describes in the same passage as the 'disagreeably lulling, soporific effect' of very regular rhythms, and away too from 'the prevalent aesthetic [which] wanted to restrict poetry merely to the expression of feeling.' (P. p. 470)

Rhymeless verse and irregular rhythms therefore assisted the 'gestic way of putting things'; following the tension and tussle of feelings and attitudes along the rough contours of human speech and action so as to stimulate, in Brecht's words, 'actual thoughts' and 'the emotional form proper to' poetry. In the course of the essay Brecht looks again to examples from street culture: to advertising slogans, the cries of street sellers, and shouted political slogans. The ear and acoustic environment have changed he says. Jazz and the noises of a machine room are in an 'astonishingly close relationship', and jazz is associated too with the liberation of the American Negro. Of his own verse he cites the *German Satires* for whose performance over the radio, rhyme and regular rhythms seemed too smooth and restrictive. Rhymeless verse and irregular rhythms, on the other hand, gave 'the tone of direct and spontaneous speech.' (P, pp. 469, 470).

This was to give 'gestic verse' a truly occasional 'social function'.

Its more enduring political effect, useful still beyond the commands of a topical social content, lay in the way it could show 'human dealings as contradictory, fiercely fought over, full of violence'; in the way it could record and produce conflicts of emotion and consciousness. (P, pp. 464–5) In introducing contrast and contradiction across the different levels of a poem, gestic verse therefore became potentially, and crucially, a dialogic, politicising verse, rather than the monologic lyric verse of bourgeois individualism. A number of effects contributed to this: the presence or absence of rhyme and rhythm, the play of irony against naivety, the relations of co-ordination and contrast between an individual text and its musical setting or performance, or between itself and neighbouring poems or a past work. Gestic verse, in short, discovered and unpicked the seam of the 'seamless artistic whole'; opening up the contradictory space between what had been, what was, and what might be, in form, feeling and ideology. At its most radical, the social gest of the poem could draw on these jointed effects of presence and absence or affirmation and denial in structure, tone, and setting, and thus enter a dialectic with social history.

We can see what in one way this came to mean in Brecht's practice (where the gestic principle was sometimes fully active, sometimes not), if we look at changing representations of the self, as these occur in the 'self-expressive' first person voice of conventional lyric verse, and in the Bertolt Brecht persona. The *Hauspostille* volume, first of all, is a self-conscious display of bohemian camaraderie and nihilism, indebted to the image of the *poete maudit*, and in particular to Villon and Rimbaud. The result is a gutter poetry, marginal and alien, full of sharks and carrion, excrement, piss, bad behaviour, bad health, and above all of wind, streams, rivers, lakes and oceans. Everywhere there is liquid and liquor. The personalities and the first person speaker of the poems are outcasts, whores and libertines; drifting, oblivious and empty in poem after poem. Thus the ruined Evelyn Roe 'gave herself to the dark waves' (P, p. 7), while in 'The Ship', a poem indebted to Rimbaud's 'Bateau Ivre, 'I tossed and shed direction, cast off gravity . . . abandoned in my watery prison' (P, p. 25), and the friends in 'Ballad of friendship', 'like two pumpkins floating seaward/Decayed . . . just drifted' (P. p. 52). In similar vein, 'The ballad of Hannah Cash' tells how 'with the wind she came and with the wind she went . . . She washed into the city like a half-drowned cat' (P. p. 69) and the 'Ballad of the love-death' speaks of two lovers who 'Drift, soaked in love, like some rain-sodden hulk' (P. p. 73).

This is the ego in the process of dissolution Brecht spoke of in 1926. But the individual, the poet, and poem, are more symptom, in their vacancy and decadence, than analysis. They have no more solidity than solidarity, as in retrospect Brecht understood. It is only in his much later self-criticism, however, that the poems are historicised, and, having thus entered a dialogue with history, become themselves a social gest. In a diary note of 1940 Brecht described the *Hauspostille* volume as follows

> This is where literature attains that stage of dehumanisation which Marx observed in the proletariat, along with the desperation which inspires the proletariat's hopes. The bulk of the poems deal with decline, and the poems follow our crumbling society all the way down. Beauty founded on wrecks, rags becoming a delicacy . . . The poet no longer has any sense of solidarity, not even with himself. Risus mortis. But it doesn't lack power. (P. p. 458)

The symptom and theme of the loss of self persisted through Brecht's poems of the 1920s and early 1930s, the poet acting either as muse for a Godless condition of personal emptiness and transparency, or, under newer political imperatives, as the medium and inspiration for collective anonymity. In a cancelled stanza of the transitional poem 'Of poor B.B.', written in 1922, for example, the Brecht persona is typically isolated, perhaps lost 'to paper and women' and 'the asphalt city'. The only consolation he finds is in 'my own pale sky . . . And a black stillness in me and a roar of pines'. (P. p. 538) The stanza in which these lines occur is very close to the published poem 'Song on Black Saturday at the eleventh hour of Easter Eve', where 'part animal already/I went down into the black cities/Papered inside with chilly words to say. (P. p. 97) The figure who speaks the poem fills himself with animals, screams and water, but remains cold, 'light and empty as before.' He is both victim and vessel: 'Nothing inside but masses of space and silence . . . I must be a paper man . . . Into me it rained . . . Wild pigs have coupled in me. Ravens/of the milky sky pissed often into me.' The poem concludes,

> Weaker than clouds are! Lighter than the winds!
> Invisible! Solemn, brutish, light
> Like one of my own poems I flew through the sky
> Along with a stork of somewhat faster flight! (P. p. 98)

We might expect the later, published form of 'Of poor B.B.' which Brecht revised between 1924 and the end of 1925, to confirm these signs of self-objectification, active motion, and new birth. But it does not. The poet in 'of poor B.B.' has found less a new identity, than a new pose. He takes his (more moderate) pleasures, is comfortable and agreeable, ready to accept that both he and others 'are animals with a quite peculiar smell.' (P. p. 107) Beneath this sociability, however, there lies an unfocused anxiety ('I . . . worriedly go to sleep'), a premonition of catastrophe (expressed in the naturalising image of 'earthquakes to come'), and unending 'coldness . . . inside me'. The wind which has swept through the asphalt cities is all that will remain of them. 'And after us there will come: nothing worth talking about.' (P. p. 108)

There is no protest here, only politeness, conformism, wry acceptance and the lowest of ambitions: 'embittered or no', he hopes only that his cigar will stay alight. The 'friendliness' with which poor B.B. now greets the world (I'm polite and friendly to people') is in the end an insignificant advance on the 'windy world of chill distress' of the earlier 'Of the friendliness of the world'. (P. p. 28) 'Coldness' in this world is the temperature of suspicion and indifference. Thus people are 'cold right through', not 'nice and kind' in the poem 'Falada, falada' (P. p. 33). If B.B. is more agreeable in the later poem, this only means that he does not ruffle his companions' complacency. Thus the 'gentlemen' gathered around him at evening put their feet up 'And say: things will get better for us. And I don't ask when.' (P. p. 108) No questions are asked, and no future is expected much as in the earlier poem 'Born later'. 'I admit it', Brecht writes there, 'I/have no hope . . . facing us/Sits nothingness.' (P. p. 59) Brecht stresses in this poem that he 'sees', while only 'The blind talk of a way out', but there is no vision, neither in 'Born later', nor in the bulk of the *Devotional Poems*, because there is no history. Instead there is a sense of general process, a flow or flux, imaged as an ongoing stream or unrelenting wind, and with it the bland acceptance that 'everything passes'. (P. p. 42) Everything is thus borne along an unchanging stream towards the nothingness of its beginning.

The political songs, which seem to represent such an infusion of vigour and commitment in Brecht's writing and thinking, are in the end politicised versions of this same relation to the world: only here 'everything passes' along the uninterrupted road to revolution and a new beginning. Whereas the personages of the earlier poems, including B.B., are 'filled' with animals, noises, the elements, and the city's debris, the singers of verses such as 'Solidarity song' and the 'United front song' are 'filled' with conviction. They become solid in becoming one with the mass. In the process, the individual is discounted — although it would be truer to say that there is no *process* involved at all, for there is simply no personal voice in the poems to take account of: only 'you' and 'us' and 'we' and 'our'; demonstrative plurals joined in untroubled chorus:

Black or white or brown or yellow
Leave your old disputes behind.
Once start talking with your fellow
Men, you'll soon be of one mind.
   Forward, without forgetting
   Where our strength can be seen now to be!
   When starving or when eating
   Forward, not forgetting
   Our solidarity! (P, p. 185)

These are not the sentiments of a dialogic, gestic verse, which demonstrates rather than simply expresses an attitude. Brecht's political songs are *evidence* of political attitudes, of course, but they don't *show* that they know they are, in the self-consciousness dialectics builds into itself. In other words they are propaganda, and as such belong with the proletcult tendencies of the late 1920s and early 1930s. In this context, the performance of 'Solidarity song' by 'Red Megaphone' and the Communist Party Workers Sports Organisation in the film *Kuhle Wampe* was, and remains, stirring and politically 'useful'.[2] This kind of performance suggested too, one might say, how the bourgeois poet could be disinherited, and his individual product collectivised. But this does not alter the fact that 'mass songs' of this kind (a title given to 'Solidarity song' in typescript) reinforce a collective unity, a 'oneness', which swallows up the observing/participating individual. And '*the art of observation*', Brecht said to a company of Danish working-class actors, is 'The first thing you have to learn.' (P, p. 235) If this was a criterion for gestic acting, it did not apply apparently to political songs. The results are effectively 'monologic verse' writ large: political certainly, but hardly politicising.

The political songs reverse the quietism and lack of hope there is in the early poems, but remain, as far as conceptions of personal and social identity are concerned, within the same problematic:

the individual is an empty vessel, or a cipher, pulled by the tide of nihilism or revolutionary sentiment. In its earlier extreme form this empty life was the life of the opium smoker 'vowed to nothingness in future', who 'when she sees herself she'll wonder who/On earth that was'. (P, pp. 114, 115) In one way, the woman of this poem is a further projection of 'poor B.B.', but she is also more than this, and like other figures ('the harlot Evelyn Roe', Marie A., and Hannah Cash) to some degree an objectified type, a case study in destitution. Figures such as these are presented for note, if not yet for action; for sympathy perhaps, but not for empathy. In the early poems, partly owing to their homogenising similarity of tone and theme, these attitudes are conflated and confused rather than distinguished. Brecht had neverthless discovered a mode of social observation, distinct from the conventions of both lyric and self-evidently propagandist poetry, from which there could evolve a form of politicised narrative or journalism in verse.

This development occurred in a planned set of 'Songs of the proletariat' and then in the three 'Tales of the Revolution'. A poem perhaps meant for the initial group, 'Eight thousand poor people assemble outside the city', published in John Heartfield's newspaper *Der Knüppel* in 1926, is based on a newspaper report of eight thousand unemployed miners encamped outside Budapest and threatened with military violence. It was, as John Willett notes, 'the first of Brecht's poems to deal with an explicit incident in the class struggle' and was, significantly, in Brecht's own plans, to be separated from the *Hauspostille*, and instead reserved for 'another collection dealing with the new man.' (P, p. 541–2) Other poems were similarly based on newspaper and prose accounts: 'Three hundred murdered coolies report to an international' (also published in *Der Knüppel*, in January 1927), and then the later 'Tales of the Revolution', comprising 'The carpet-weavers of Kuyan-Bulak honour Lenin', 'The Internationale' (though this was cut on proof) and 'In Smolny during the summer of 1917'. Brecht referred to the first of these 'Tales' as displaying 'one of the many great gests of the Russian proletariat after it had freed itself through the Revolution'. (P, p. 548) Both the 'proletarian songs' and the 'Tales' are, as Brecht's own and Willett's comments suggest therefore, dramatised footnotes to incidents in working-class history, the first transforming the reports on which they are based into a first person plural narrative, while the two published 'Tales' retain the third person form of journalistic report.

In the essay 'On gestic music', Brecht wrote that 'subject-matter in itself is in a sense somewhat banal, featureless, empty, and self-sufficient. It is only the social gest — criticism, craftiness, irony, propaganda etc — that breathes humanity into it.' (BT, p. 105) Gest gives humanity to the emptiness of subject-matter, and, one might add, to the emptiness of the human subject in Brecht's earlier poetry. The 'proletarian songs' and 'Tales' are in this sense 'gestic' verse — but still of a limited kind. In these poems the poet as reporter invites identification with and endorsement of the social gest he presents; the incidents are historicised and illustrative, indeed exemplary. 'Tales of the Revolution', as one application of Engels' 'typical characters in typical circumstances' would, one suspects, have won the warm approval of the later defenders of socialist realism. In this respect there is little difference between these poems and the later 'The Moscow workers take possession of the great Metro on April 27, 1935', only that this is a tale of the Revolution, apparently, effectively in place. The point is of course that the 'definite attitude' Brecht takes towards his subject in these poems — and by which he means to distinguish his 'realism' from the documentarist assumption that an historical incident will speak for itself — has no room for the word 'apparently'. These poems are therefore once again propagandist gests, but allow no room for the other forms or attitudes associated with the social gest — criticism, craftiness, irony, for example — though Brecht lists these and propaganda together.

In other words, these poems are not pedagogic in the full sense that Brecht brought to this term. The 'Tales' in particular do not present, or produce, a 'critical attitude' towards the example of the Russian Revolution. One might ask, in the case of the carpet-weavers of Kuyan-Bulak for example, whether this incident was a genuine gest of local democracy. Did the people and the authorities and Lenin truly think as one? Brecht's poem answers 'yes', and it might be heartening, instructive and 'useful' to accept this. If we consult the newspaper report on which the poem was based, however, we find a different account. For here it is said that Gamelev, the Red Army officer, and not the people (as Brecht's poem tells us) proposed the idea of a statue to Lenin. Only later did he suggest that the villagers instead burn the dump that was producing fever — once they had produced the money for the statue. (P, p. 548) The newspaper report may not itself be reliable of course, but we can only begin to ask questions, raise doubts, and read history and its narratives critically if information of this kind is included rather than withheld. A fully gestic poetry would awaken its readers to different perspectives, ironies and contradictions, and provoke, precisely, in Brecht's own terms and in the spirit of scepticism he found in the 'Marxist classics', a questioning, productively doubtful attitude. These poems, however, at this time in the late 1920s and early 1930s, with Russian themes as their subject-matter or gests, and hence with conspicuous implications for Brecht's political attitude, do not do this.

Walter Benjamin looks elsewhere for the development of Brecht's politicised verse. The poet of 'Of poor B.B.' he describes as 'a gate', an 'archway', through whom the reader can pass without obstruction: 'he stands in no-one's way' and nothing can come of him, Benjamin suggests, until he decides to stand *in* the way, to intervene. This Brecht does, Benjamin says, 'letting go of himself' to take up the cause of the class struggle in the cycle of poems titled *Aus einem Lesebuch für Städtebewohner*. (UB, p. 58)[3] The poems in this sequence Benjamin describes as studies in 'crypto-emigration' and 'object lessons in underground activity and emigration'. Of the poems he discusses, the first in the series with its refrain 'Cover your tracks' offers, he says, 'A precept for the underground political worker'; the third poem 'We do not want to leave your house' presents Nazi anti-semitism as a sadistic parody of the revolutionary workers' treatment of their true exploiters; and the ninth poem 'Four invitations to a man at different times from different quarters' shows that 'a certain courtesy of the heart' survives alienating social conditions and progressive economic impoverishment. (UB, pp. 58–64)

I believe that Benjamin overestimates the revolutionary consciousness of these poems and simplifies their shifting tones and unidentified voices. The poems often close, for example, in a separated parenthesis, somewhat like the titles of Brecht's drama, or indeed like traditional dramatic asides, and these abruptly twist and confuse perspectives and loyalties. The first poem ends in this way with the line '(That is what they taught me)'. But it is simply not clear who 'they' are, or what the speaker of the poem's attitude to 'them' is. If, as Benjamin's reading suggests, 'they' are a revolutionary cadre, it is still not clear whether their advice to 'cover your tracks' is being followed with unqualified commitment, or mechanically, or resentfully. And who is the poem addressed to, since it cannot be 'they', but must be some third party?; Is 'their' precept being passed on as good advice, or is it being dismissed in the contemptuous tone of 'that's what *they* told me to do'?

The third poem ends '(That is how we speak to our fathers)', and the poem, spoken by this 'we' becomes a gest of the child's betrayal of its parent:

> But when they come for you we shall point
> And shall say: That must be him.
>
> We don't know what's to come, and have nothing better
> But we want no more of you.(UB, p. 61)

If this is a gest of 'why National Socialism needs anti-semitism' in Benjamin's words, (UB, p. 62) then the youths of the Hitler Jugend, as the speakers of the poem appear to be, are, curiously for Benjamin's argument, Jews like their parents. Also if the poem itself, rather than Nazi anti-semitism, is to be taken as a parody and not as a more straightforward piece of self-accusation, then everything depends on being able to understand the way 'we *speak* to our fathers' as being different from the way we act towards, or think of them. If the children say, 'you we shall kill', then they do not mean it; they are speaking the 'lies we are forced to believe' which they act out, but do not in fact believe. The poem then becomes, in a reading provoked entirely by the jolt of its last line, a gest of Nazi bad faith, or, even, an example of how it is possible to follow orders and betray *these* to one's condemned parents (thus giving them the chance to 'vanish').

The particular significance of the final parentheses in this group of poems is that they are examples, in 1926 or 1927, and thus well before the date usually found for its theoretical formulation, of *Verfremdung*. The speakers in the poems show themselves; they perform inside their roles and then step outside them, as self-observers, to offer a situating comment or judgement. In some poems an additional, final voice performs a similar function, such as in the lines '(That's something I heard a woman say)' or '(That's something I've heard people say before now.)' (P, pp. 136, 137). This device, in these two forms, provokes surprise, puzzlement and (self-) removal from the 'I' or 'we' in the body of the poems with whom the reader is by habit and convention induced to identify. In terms of the requirements of 'epic' performance in the theatre poem 'Everyday theatre', the social gest in these poems is 'quoted' in a 'cadenced' irregular and rhymeless verse, by a 'masked' self-dramatising speaker. The summary and quite key political effect of this is simultaneously to fracture the ideology of the unified self and to put some distance between the disoriented, and perhaps now questioning reader, and the accepted or common version of things.

This is obviously to put a different political complexion on these poems than Walter Benjamin does. All the same it offers more of an 'ideal' than true account of what taken together is less an accomplished group of gestic poems than a transitional series. The characters or 'actors' in the poems shift about in an alien urban environment, and have to contend with what are called their 'enemies'. It's on this basis presumably that Benjamin finds signs of 'crypto-emigration' and firm commitment on Brecht's part to the class struggle. The basic psychology of the gests these poems present, however, remains at the relatively unpoliticised level of 'I' versus 'them', rather even than of 'us versus them'. As social types the personages of the poems are more the itinerant unemployed, the broken husband, the deserted woman, or irrepressible whore, than the undercover revolutionary. Oddly, given Benjamin's own literary interests, there is, one might say, more Kafka here than Marx, at least as Brecht understood Kafka in 1934. His remarks on Kafka's *The Trial*, as Benjamin reports them, are in fact a fair description of his own poems 'for those who live in cities'. They point, however, to a quite contrary political tendency than that which Benjamin finds in the poems:

> What it conveys above all else . . . is a dread of the unending and irresistible growth of the great cities. He claims to know the nightmare of this idea from his own intimate experience. Such cities are an expression of the boundless maze of indirect relationships, complex mutual dependencies and compartmentations into which human beings are forced by modern forms of living. And these in turn find expression in the longing for a 'leader'. (UB, p. 111)

Brecht was, one might say, presenting this particular, Kafkaesque gest of urban alienation, and introducing some added distance or 'alienation' in his own sense, on its possible political consequences rather than intervening positively on the side of the class struggle.

This is a measure of the transitional character of these poems. There are other things too which suggest a gradual politicisation of, rather than abrupt break with, the tones and motifs of the early poems and 'Of poor B.B.'. First of all, the desire for invisibility and the lack of hope there are in the earlier poems evidently persist in the asphalt of Berlin. In poem 1, for example, of the 'Ten poems from a Reader for those who live in cities' which Benjamin discusses, invisibility is an advantage:

The man who hasn't signed anything, who has left no picture
Who was not there, who said nothing:
How can they catch him?
Cover your tracks. (P. p. 131)

And in a distinct echo of lines in 'Of poor B.B.', poem 6 of the group Willett collects as 'Belonging to a Reader for those who live in Cities', opens:

If you had read the papers as carefully as I do
You would have buried your hopes
That things may get better. (P, p. 144)

The difference is that these attitudes appear now to arise from a different source: less from a personal and anarchistic desire for oblivion than from the social pressure, in the anonymity induced by the city, to conform; to submit to being nothing. A further sign of Brecht's development is the distinctions these poems make between those who lack a consciousness of their emptiness, or self-alienation (the person who is a 'flathead', for example, by definition does not know that he is one, P, pp. 144–46); those, secondly, who are helpless before this knowledge ('It seems/I have moved out,' says one, 'some one else/Is living here now and/Doing so in/My linen.' P. p. 143); and those who are roused to effect some self-renewal. An example is poem 5 of the 'Reader':

I'm dirt. From myself
I can demand nothing but
Weakness, treachery and degradation
Then one day I notice
It's getting better; the wind
Fills my sail; my time has come, I can
Become better than dirt —
I began at once. (P, p. 135)

The change here comes from an act of personal stock-taking and self-reflection ('I looked/Like a boneless bedspread./Then I saw myself in the glass —/And stopped it at once'). Often in fact the passive, urban, self-alienation which is what this character acts upon so as to reverse, is experienced in the poems as a non-identity, a sense of non-recognition, in which the self is neither reflected upon, nor reflected back by the world. These nobodys indeed leave no tracks; they have no self-image and can make no impression. Poem 10 of the 'Reader' offers the most general statement of this:

When I speak to you
Coldly and impersonally
Using the driest words
Without looking at you
(I seemingly fail to recognise you
In your particular nature and difficulty)

I speak to you merely
Like reality itself
(Sober, not to be bribed by your particular nature
Tired of your difficulty)
Which in my view you seem not to recognise. (P, p. 140)

The alienated city-dweller does not recognise her/his individuality, in reality, but might in the poem which speaks of this very condition in reality's accents (cold, impersonal, dry, sober). The poem 'I hear' which Willett relates to the 'Reader' tells us more about the new tones of this reality and of Brecht's own verse. Significantly, Elizabeth Hauptmann also relates this poem to another, unpublished Ms, titled 'Of inner emptiness' which ends, typically for this sequence, 'Here is/The man it was not.' (P, p. 540) In the poem 'I hear' the speaker responds to rumours in the market place that his time is up with the reflection,

But the worst is this: I myself
Notice that I have grown
Harsher to people. (P, p. 113)

'Harshness' and its related tones was from around the middle twenties contrasted in Brecht's poetry with 'friendliness'. In the most striking example, in the poem 'To those born later', completed in the late 1930s, Brecht writes,

And yet we know:
Hatred, even of meanness
Contorts the features.
Anger, even against injustice
Makes the voice hoarse. Oh, we
Who wanted to prepare the ground for friendliness
Could not ourselves be friendly. (P, p. 320)

Similarly, in 'Bad time for poetry', once again, only the voice of the happy man is good to hear, but of the two contending attitudes of delight and horror, only the second now 'drives me to my desk.' (P, p. 331) Walter Benjamin's discussion of Brecht's poems in the 'Reader' is also connected in the end with this theme. Of the ninth poem of the sequence, 'Four invitations to a man at different times from different quarters', Benjamin writes,

> The friendly indifference which is common to all four invitations is worthy of note. By the fact that the harshness of the offer leaves room for such friendliness, we recognise that social conditions confront man from outside, as something alien to him . . . The inhumanity to which they are condemned has not been able to take from them a certain courtesy of the heart. (UB, p. 64)

Whatever we make of Benjamin's judgement of this poem, it will not serve as a representative comment on this cycle of poems. Nor is it particularly helpful in understanding Brecht's political development. The distinction between 'harshness' and 'friendliness' is, however, a political one, arising from a significant political decision. 'Friendliness' Brecht assigned to workers for the revolution and the new society, and therefore, in certain poems, to the Soviet Union. Thus, the 'main objective' of the Bolsheviks in the poem 'In Smolny during the Summer of 1917', was 'to be treated as friends by these people'. (P, p. 202) Similarly, Hanns Eisler assigned to a performance of 'The carpet-weavers of Kuyan-Bulak' in 1957 an earlier motto from Brecht which stated, 'it is most essential that profound matters should be handled cheerfully, and authorities greeted with friendly benevolence.' (P, p. 548)

We might say that Benjamin's interpretation of the 'Reader' was over sanguine and one-sided; that where he saw revolutionary cadres there was the lumpen-proletariat with a quite different political potential, and where he saw friendliness, there was coldness, impersonality and harshness. But then Brecht too was 'one-sided', though in a different direction. It was a bad time for 'poetry', and Brecht was 'one-sided' — 'from a bourgeois point of view', but also from his own, since 'friendliness' had to be postponed for the society of the future. Soviet society, though with some reservations, continued to represent this future. Accordingly, workers are shown confidently awaiting the Second Five Year Plan, in the poem of that title. (P, p. 204) And in the same vein Brecht hoped in 'I need no gravestone' to be remembered as a poet who made proposals or suggestions for the future which others would put into action. 'Friendliness', that is to say, belonged less to this world than to the next. In the present dark times, of the late 1920s, of Hitler and the war years, poetry had an instructive and analytical function: there would 'be singing/*About* the dark times' (P, p. 320), my italics), and the gestic voice which would speak and show this reality needed to be sober, dry, angry and harsh.

The poem 'Solely because of the increasing disorder' which Willett and Manheim use to open their section 'The first years of exile' explains this further:

Solely because of the increasing disorder
In our cities of class struggle
Some of us have now decided
To speak no more of cities by the sea, snow on roofs, women
The smell of ripe apples in cellars, the sense of the flesh, all
That makes a man round and human
But to speak in future only about the disorder
And so become one-sided, reduced, enmeshed in the business
Of politics and the dry, indecorous vocabulary
Of dialectical economics
So that this awful cramped coexistence
Of snowfalls (they're not merely cold we know)
Exploitation, the lured flesh, class justice, should not engender
Approval of a world so many-sided; delight in
The contradictions of so bloodstained a life
You understand. (P, p. 255)

To become 'one-sided' is to write selectively and critically. The agenda of conventional subjects and sensory pleasures which would console bourgeois man and make him 'whole' ('round and human') are put into abeyance; the poetry which 'some of us' have determined upon is to be neither consoling nor utopian. To become one-sided is also now, some seven or eight years after the 'Reader for those who live in cities', to 'take sides' in the sense that Benjamin understands it in the earlier poems, since the cities here are 'our cities of class struggle'. Nevertheless, the expression 'one-sided' in the poem requires the quotation marks which in the original accompany the word 'unwürdige' ('indecorous') used to describe 'dialectical economics'. This was only 'indecorous', as Brecht was in one sense 'one-sided', from a bourgeois point of view. It was this point of view and its associated poetry which were truly limited and unrealistic. In taking sides and in being in his own sense 'one-sided', it is possible, Brecht's poem says, to see the many sides of existence which bourgeois humanism rounds off, and to see them as, in fact, contradictory. The one-sided man in fact sees more than the rounded man because he sees at least two sides. What is more, in adopting the voice of criticism, craftiness and irony, such a man can see and say two things at once.

The 'social gest' which 'breathes humanity into' emptiness, and featureless self-sufficiency, is therefore, we cay say, in certain modes propagandist, but in others more than this. The difference lies in *Verfremdung* which, like dialectics, shows this against that, 'the not . . . but', and requires the two-sidedness of 'criticism, craftiness, irony' to secure the justice of its committed, political perspective. *Verfremdung* parodies the bourgeois truism that there are two sides to every question, to show up the falseness of its even-handedness, and the truth of conflict and contradiction. It becomes necessary therefore to take sides.

'The splitting of a single whole and the cognition of its contradictory parts' as Lenin, once more, said, 'is the *essence* of dialectics.' The perception of the unity and struggle of opposites furnishes a knowledge of the ' "self-movement" ' of things; 'it alone furnishes the key to the "leaps", to the " break in continuity", to the "transformation into the opposite", to the destruction of the old and the emergence of the new.'[4] In Brecht's poetry, the use of irregular rhythms and rhymeless verse, of narrative and the irony which helped comprise the *critical* form of 'social gest' assist the political process of transformation Lenin describes, by effecting a 'self-movement' in the forms and subject-matter of 'poetry' and the conception of the poet and reader. Its chief political effect lies not in the announcement of solidarity or in the statement of 'correct' political attitudes, but in the way it contests the unifying strategies of bourgeois aesthetics and ideology: in its 'splitting of the single whole' of the bourgeois self and its would-be stabilising perspective on the world in the interests of change and a fuller humanity and friendliness to come. At best, to borrow Brecht's words on his drama, this form of political verse is pedagogics. Its purpose, as the poem 'Solely because of the increasing disorder' tells us, is to engender in its readers not 'Approval of a world so many-sided' but a keeness for its terrible contradictions. Brecht's poem 'Ballad on approving the world', written in 1932, can fittingly serve therefore as a test and example of his, at best, self-educating, self-alienating, gestic verse:

I'm not unjust, but not courageous either:
They pointed out their world to me today
I only saw the bloody pointing finger
And quickly said I liked the world that way.

I stood facing their world, beneath their truncheons
And spent the whole day judging what I saw.
Saw butchers who seemed suited to their functions
When I was asked 'D'you like it?' I said 'Sure'.

. . .

I saw a world which worships God and profits
Heard hunger shout: Give something! Saw a pair
Of pudgy fingers pointing up to heaven.
Said: There you are, there must be something there.

My friend George Grosz's men with heads like bullets —
You know them from his drawings — are, it seems
About to slit the human race's gullets.
I give my full approval to their schemes.

I saw the murderers and the victims also
And, lacking courage but not sympathy
Observed the murderers picking out their victims
And shouted: I approve wholeheartedly!

I see them coming, see the butchers marching
Would like to bawl out 'Stop!, but as meanwhile
I know their agents are beside me watching
I hear my own voice bawling at them 'Heil!

Since poverty and baseness leave me cold
My pen falls silent; times are on the move
Yet all that's dirty in your dirty world
Includes, I know, the fact that I approve. (P, pp. 196, 200–1)

Notes

1. Martin Esslin, *Brecht: A Choice of Evils* (Eyre Methuen, London, 1959, revised 1980), p. 251.

2. Cf. Richard Stourac and Kathleen McCreery, *Theatre as a Weapon* (Routledge and Kegan Paul, London and New York, 1986), p. 166, and John Willett's notes to 'Solidarity song' and the 'United front song' in *Poems*, pp. 550, 556.

3. For Willett's account of the composition of this series and related poems, see *Poems*, pp. 495–6. The title to the sequence is given as *Handbook for City-Dwellers* in *Understanding Brecht*, and as *A Reader for Those who Live in Cities* by Willett.

4. Marx, Engels, Lenin, *On Dialectical Materialism* (Progress Publishers, Moscow, and Lawrence and Wishart, London, 1977), pp. 381, 382.

7

'The Art . . . of not Submitting'

Walter Benjamin sees Brecht's poem 'Legend of the origin of the book Tao-Te-Ching on Lao-Tsû's road into exile' as an instance of 'the special role which the quality of friendliness plays in the author's imagination.' (UB, p. 72) The exiled philosopher Lao-Tsû halts at a customs post and at the customs officer's cheerful request sets down his accumulated wisdom in the form of 38 maxims. His boy relates the sage's discovery

> 'That yielding water in motion
> Gets the better in the end of granite and porphyry.
> You get me: the hard thing gives way.' (UB, p. 71)

Benjamin argues that none of this would have happened but for the friendliness of the participants. These lines confirm Brecht's 'minimum programme of humanity'. he says, and concludes:

> The lesson or advice here is never to forget about the inconstancy and changeability of things, and to align oneself with those things which are inconspicuous and sober and inexhausible, like water. The materialist dialectician will be reminded of the cause of the oppressed. (It is an inconspicuous thing for the rulers, a sober one for the oppressed and, in its consequences, the most inexhaustible of all.) Lastly, apart from the promise and the theory, there is a moral in the poem. Whoever wants to make the hard thing give way should miss no opportunity for friendliness. (UB, p.74)

Stanley Mitchell, in his introduction to *Understanding Brecht*, supports Benjamin's interpretation of this poem and of Brecht's politics.

So, indirectly, do a number of other critics.[1] Mitchell writes, 'Brecht and Benjamin start with the anonymous man and encourage his resilience, so that the "hard thing" may give way . . . Brecht's drama and poetry form a humanist *vademecum* for dark ages. His "heroes" are resourceful, humorous nobodies.' (UB, p, xii)

Mitchell links this, justifiably given Benjamin's discussion of epic theatre, with the figure Galy Gay in *Man equals Man*. Galy Gay's personality is dismantled and reassembled 'like an automobile'; transformed from docker to soldier, he shows just how far man can be manipulated and manoeuvred. In hs own words in the play:

> And I, the one and the other I
> Are used and accordingly usable.
> . . . I shall close an eye to what concerns myself
> And shed what is not likeable about me and thereby be pleasant.[2]

Mitchell writes that 'Galy Gay learns his lesson, masters his situation, and for all his adaptability, indeed because of it, proves the only humane person in the play; able to show "friendliness" to the man whose identity he allowed himself to rob.' (UB, p. xv) For Benjamin, Galy Gay is the 'wise proletarian'; he is

> a man 'who can't say no'. And this too is wise, for he lets the contradictions of existence enter into the only place where they can, in the last analysis, be resolved: the life of a man. Only the 'consenting' man has any chance of changing the world. (UB, pp. 8–9)

Already, in Benjamin's description, Galy Gay sounds more like the 'poor B.B.' who stands in no one's way than the individual who stands out, the better to defend a cause. In fact, of course, Galy Gay is in no way a defender of the proletarian cause. He is cannon-fodder, and though 'strong in the mass' and a 'winner' in Brecht's own ambiguous account of 1927, is seen, even at this time, as an 'ancestor' only of the 'new human type'. This new type, Brecht writes, 'will not let himself be changed by machines, but will himself change the machine'; adding that 'he will above all look human.'[3] Whatever else, this cannot be seen as a description of Galy Gay, who surrenders his ego and 'lets go of himself' to become a passive, pliant soldier. He is 'used and usable' rather than 'useful', and looked in Peter Lorre's performance in Brecht's 1931 production, above all like a dehumanised fighting machine.

Benjamin's interpretation of this poem and play are misleading in a more important respect, however. Mitchell suggests that Benjamin's thinking was dominated in his last years by the concepts of *Jetztzeit* and *Ermattungstaktik*. The first, Mitchell reports, is '(''the presence of the now''), a *nunc stans*, in which time stands still, where past and future converge not harmoniously, but explosively, in the present instant . . . *Jetztzeit* entailed the ability to intervene in events, whether as politician or intellectual, to ''blast open the continuum of history'' '. *Ermattungstaktik*, the ' (''tactics of attrition'')', Mitchell identifies with 'the belief that in the end ''The hard thing gives way''.' (UB, p, xviii)

Benjamin, and following him Mitchell, therefore associate an attitude of passive consent, of patient non-resistance, a belief that since everything does change, it will in the end change for the better, with Brecht's poem, and with Brecht. There are early statements and works certainly, in the *Hauspostille*, and including *Man equals Man*, which suggest a belief that the world is so entirely in flux that human actions and opinions are a matter of indifference, or that change is in itself a good thing.[4] There are also poems of naive optimism, not far removed from the general spirit of *Man equals Man* and *Mahagonny*, which invoke America as the land of growth and opportunity, and which in futurist vein associate the 'new man' with New World technology and labour processes. The poems 'Germany', 'Song of the machines' and 'Song of a man in San Francisco', for example, and poem 12 of *Poems Belonging to a Reader for Those who Live in Cities* present America in this fashion as Germany's present contrary and inevitable future.[5] By the late 1920s, however, and the poem 'Late lamented fame of the giant city of New York', Brecht's Americanophilia had been dramatically checked by the Wall Street crash. New York, the city of granite skyscrapers, 'built on the rock and hence/Indestructible (P, p. 171), the symbol of success and prosperity, had fallen into bankruptcy. The hard thing had indeed given way, but this was a consequence evidently of economic collapse, not of some natural process of change or erosion, analogous to the effect of 'yielding water in motion'.

Benjamin's judgement that Brecht advised consent and patience to 'the contemporary reader' of 1938, the year of the composition of 'Legend . . . on Lao-Tsû's road into exile', is in fact a quite extraordinary and unconvincing one. The attitude he discovers in the poem and in Brecht is best explained by their Italian contemporary

Antonio Gramsci in a passage from *The Modern Prince*:

> When one does not have the initiative in the struggle and the struggle itself is ultimately identified with a series of defeats, mechanical determinism becomes a formidable power of moral resistance, of patient and obstinate perseverance. 'I am defeated for the moment but the nature of things is on my side over a long period', etc. Real will is disguised as an act of faith, a sure rationality of history, a primitive and empirical form of impassioned finalism which appears as a substitute for the predestination, providence, etc. of the confessional religions.[6]

Brecht's poem 'Thoughts on the duration of exile' (written around 1937) comes closest of any poems Benjamin might have known to expressing this mood. There seems to be little point while living in exile, the poem says, in banging in a nail, in caring for or planting a tree, or in struggling with a foreign language, for 'Tomorrow you'll go back home.' The first part ends:

> As whitewash peels from the ceiling
> (Do nothing to stop it!)
> So the block of force will crumble
> That has been set up at the frontier
> To keep out justice. (P, p. 302)

Yet the second part of the poem tells how this advice has not been taken. A nail *has* been knocked in the wall, and a chestnut tree *is* being watered. The poem in fact enacts the tensions of exile, over its two parts, and in its twisting dialogue between the speaking voice of conscience or inner hope and the acting subject. The second continues to write 'Day after day . . . for the liberation', while the first questions the usefulness of this work and probes the other's true feelings.

By this date and the date of 'Legend . . . on Lao-Tsû's road into exile', Brecht had been arguing for some ten years for an interventionist art. When exile made this in any direct sense impossible, there are poems 'about the dark times', such as these same two poems. Yet Brecht's later poem on Benjamin's death, suggests that even in these circumstances, where quite plainly neither man held 'the initiative in the struggle', the 'tactics of attrition' were still felt to be inadequate and ineffective against the 'hard thing' of fascism:

Tactics of attrition are what you enjoyed
Sitting at the chess-table in the pear tree's shade
The enemy who drove you from your books
Will not be worn down by the likes of us.[7]

'The likes of us' Brecht writes. Nevertheless, and for all the 'friendliness' there was between the two men, their tactics were quite different. Brecht spells out his own in the poem 'Driven out with good reason' written within a month or so of 'Legend . . . on Lao-Tsû's road into exile'. He betrays the tricks of his 'own class', he says, to the 'insignificant people', the class 'enemy', with whom he is politically allied.

Yes, I give away their secrets. I stand
Among the people and explain
Their swindles. I say in advance what will happen, for I
Have inside knowledge of their plans.
The latin of their corrupt clergy
I translate word for word into the common speech, and there
It is seen to be humbug. (P, p. 317)

The character Galy Gay saw no difference between 'the one I and the other I', and indeed they were 'equal' in their common exploitation. In this poem, however, as elsewhere in gestic verse and performance, the double persona is the active rather than passive subject of contradiction. Class origin is turned to political advantage against itself, and in the interests of the dispossessed. And this tactic, employing irony and craftiness, is more useful the poem implies than the 'tactics of attrition', for as the people who hide him say, he has 'been driven out *with/Good reason*' (my italics).

The poem 'Legend of the origin of the book Tao-Tê-Ching on Lao-Tsû's road into exile' begins therefore to read like a gest of 'mechanical determinism' in Gramsci's phrase, for which the contemporary sage Walter Benjamin was more the example than Brecht. Benjamin's 'appropriation' of the poem remains curious all the same in the light of his description of the epic techniques of montage and gest in terms of dialectics and the contrary principle of *Jetztzeit*. In *Jetztzeit* time stands still; it intervenes to 'blast open the continuum of history'. Epic gesture Benjamin describes as enclosing 'each moment of an attitude which, after all, is as a whole in a state of living flux . . . in epic theatre the dialectic is not born of the contradiction between successive statements or ways of behaving, but of the gesture itself.' (UB, pp. 3, 12) At the close of the first version of the essay 'What is epic theatre?' in which these statements occur, Benjamin writes:

> The damming of the stream of real life, the moment when its flow comes to a standstill, makes itself felt as a reflux: this reflux is astonishment. The dialectic at a standstill is its real object. It is the rock from which we gaze down into that stream of things which in the city of Jehoo 'that's always full and where nobody stays', they have a song about:
>
> > Rest not on the wave which breaks against your foot,
> > So long as it stands in the water, new waves will break against it.
>
> But if the stream of things breaks against this rock of astonishment, then there is no difference between a human life and a word. In epic theatre both are only the crest of the wave. Epic theatre makes life spurt up high from the bed of time and, for an instant, hover iridescent in empty space. Then it puts it back to bed. (UB. p. 13)

This appears to assign more resistance than resilience to Brecht's theatre. Benjamin's argument is confused, all the same, both by his earlier description of Galy Gay as a type of 'the "consenting" man' who alone 'has any chance of changing the world', and by his persistent association of epic theatre and the dialectics of gest with the incompletely dialectical *Man equals Man*. The immediate problem in the passage, however, lies in the conception of dialectics as the process by which the stream of life is brought to a standstill (although it is also the dialectic which is brought to a standstill), thrown up momentarily into 'empty space' (though this seems also to be the place of the rock of astonishment from which in epic theatre 'we gaze down at that stream of things') before it is set down again in 'the bed of time' (to sleep? or to flow again along its now uninterrupted course).

Benjamin was obviously attracted to the concept and imagery of 'the stream of life'. So, one might say, was the early Brecht. Benjamin quotes in this passage from the 'Song of the flow of things', in *Man equals Man*, and probably owes something in the rest of it to Brecht's words in the essay 'Literalisation of the theatre' which he otherwise draws on very closely in 'What is epic theatre?' Discussing the need for the spectator of epic theatre to be able to do more than pass along a single track, Brecht advises 'Some exercise in complex seeing is needed — though it is perhaps more important to be able to think above the stream than to think in the stream.' (BT, p. 44) Brecht's qualification here is an important one, and the way he develops it in later writings distinguishes his use of this image from Benjamin's own and from the *Ermattungstaktik*. In 'The short description of a new way of acting', for example, Brecht writes of the critical attitude that it 'is active, practical, positive. Criticising the course of a river means *improving* it, *correcting* it. Criticism of society is ultimately revolution'. (BT, p. 146 my italics) In similar vein, of two important uses of this image in the *Short Organum*, Brecht likens the critical attitude to 'regulating' a river in paragraph 22, and in paragraph 41, in an analogy with the way in which the historically defined stage character 'will retain something of the rough sketching which indicates traces of other movements and features', he writes,

> It is the same as when an irrigation expert looks at a river together with its former bed and various hypothetical courses which it might have followed . . . And while he in his mind is looking at a new river, the socialist in him is hearing new kinds of talk from the labourers who work by it. And similarly in the theatre our spectator should find that the incidents set among such labourers are also accompanied by echoes and by traces of sketching. (BT, p. 191)

As we can see, Brecht does not endorse the conceptions of art or life as water and rock, or the reverse, in the forms in which these occur in Benjamin's essays. He thinks of art as interventionist, as instilling a critical attitude which will correct or alter the 'stream', or see it both as it is and might otherwise be. Moreover this 'stream' is not life in general, but the already contradictory attitudes and conduct which comprise character, and shape the narratives of human history. In this view, the dialectic is never 'at a standstill', and if there is any sense of one thing or perspective being 'above' another, it is by way of the spiralling self-consciousness of dialectical thinking which raises 'Everyday things . . . above the level of the obvious and automatic.' (BT, p. 92) Brecht's words here describe the ideological effect of *Verfremdung* and this, needless to say, is hardly intended to send spectators or the river of history unaltered to their beds. The dialectic in which Brecht's verse and drama are 'embedded' is one which moves critically and productively in, and outside, and against the stream of the obvious and expected in class society. It is in other words rooted in the states of consciousness and social conditions it seeks to defamiliarise, regulate and alter. To recall Fredric Jameson's words, Brecht's work is 'obligated to praxis': it is prompted by social conditions (only Hitler 'drives me to my desk') and returns to them (unlike Dada and surrealism). It is this very rootedness in 'social content', indeed, and its consequent 'use-value', which makes Brecht's art a dialectical *and* materialist art.

Benjamin and Mitchell associate Galy Gay's alterability and passivity, and then Lao-Tsû's recommendation of these same things with friendliness and change. The message is really for man rather than the 'hard thing' to give way, for once again, 'only the "consenting" man has any chance of changing the world.' Unfortunately, there are other problems here than those already pointed out. Brecht associated friendliness, as we have seen, with ordinary people and with a socialist future. He detected this even in the 'continuing dark times' and hell of California:

> Hard humanity, uncaring
> Like fishfolk long in ice
> Yet the heart's still quick to answer
> And a smile melts the face. (P, p. 383)

Brecht's image is clearly very close to that of the key stanza in 'Legend . . . on Lao-Tsû's road into exile', but a sign of friendliness, expressing an underlying sympathy of interests is not the same as consenting, for now, to the way things are because time will cure all. The first is a gest of basic solidarity, vital perhaps to a 'minimum programme of humanity'; the second is little short of blind faith. Only in Brecht's attitude towards the Soviet Union could we think of the two together. Thus, we might say that Brecht 'consented' to and and was 'friendly' (i.e. uncritical) towards the 'hard thing' of Stalinism in the belief that this was for the best in the long term. Even so, the evidence for a 'consenting' Brecht in this sense is rather slender and inconclusive, as we shall see. Nor was it this attitude, after all, which Benjamin had in mind in his reading of 'Legend . . . '. The 'hard thing' in this context is not Stalinism, but fascism. And in this context in Benjamin's own record of their conversations in Svendborg, Brecht described himself as 'manic'; at best 'a *moderate* manic', but not 'wise' like Galy Gay or Lao-Tsû. The 'Colossal crimes' of fascism moved him, Benjamin writes, to 'vehemence' (harshness?). Brecht's feeling was that ' "We must neglect nothing in our struggle against that lot . . . They're out to destroy everything . . . That is why we too must think of everything". ' (UB, p. 120).

We have already noted some of the methods ('criticism, craftiness, irony, propaganda etc.') Brecht developed to use against 'that lot'. These devices and tones can, it is true, give his voice and persona an ambiguity and slipperiness (though not of water) which make him appear, as many have said, 'two-faced' and hypocritical. Dialectics cannot stretch to include this latter meaning, if it was ever appropriate to Brecht, but 'two faced', like 'one-sided' did have in his own terms another application, and one which is especially pertinent to the theme of friendliness and Brecht's struggle against fascism. In a typescript version of the third section of 'To those born later', in sentiments close to the published version already quoted, but in words which are a quite precise reply to the political accent Benjamin gives to 'Legend . . . of Lao-Tsû's road into exile', Brecht writes:

> We two-faced people! the one friendly
> We turned towards the oppressed, but to the oppressors
> The other filled with hate. How could there be wisdom
> In our summonses to battle? In our angry words
> Was no mildness. Oh, we
> Who wanted to prepare the ground for wisdom
> Could not ourselves be wise. (P, p. 574)

Unfortunately, the two-faced poet did not think of our convenience and produce harsh poems one day and friendly ones the next. Although, over the sweep of his whole career, from the *Hauspostille* to the 'dark' and 'darkest' then 'difficult times' of the 1950s, the emphasis and force of Brecht's verse changed, he typically spoke in the middle and later periods in two voices at once; apparently, both friendly and cynical, consenting and dissenting, approving and disapproving. This is the case of course with 'Ballad on approving of the world', a poem which exposes rather than countenances petty-bourgeois pusillanimity though it speaks in its accents. Elsewhere too Brecht speaks with the advantage of 'inside knowledge': translating the foreign idiom of (his own) corrupt ruling class into the common tongue where 'it is seen to be humbug'

(P, p. 317). Or there are poems where we are told of this aim and tactic, and where the first person 'I' is presented effectively as a third person 'he'. One voice and attitude is therefore set off against, or shadowed by its contrary; like the alternative course of a river an irrigation expert hypothesises, or the alternative character types and destinies a spectator mentally sketches. Poems of this kind are written in the attitude of critical demonstration, of showing 'what is; but also . . . what could be and is not'. (P, p. 308) But what then, in relation to Benjamin's argument Brecht especially demonstrates, and what gest and *Verfremdung* are especially adept at correcting and regulating, is, precisely the attitude of consent.

This, in the end, is what makes Benjamin's (mis)reading so galling: that Brecht not only did not advise consent, but strove to undermine just this, since popular consent and acceptance had made Hitler possible, and helped establish Nazism as 'what is'; installing it as the prevailing and seemingly unalterable reality. In circumstances such as this, what is more, where, as Brecht writes in 'The world's one hope', 'Oppression, it would seem, is like the moss and unavoidable', when 'The more there are suffering, then, the more natural their sufferings appear', a further ironic consequence was that the 'kindness' and 'compassion' of the oppressed was itself eroded. (P, p. 328) Accordingly, like a pupil of Gautama the Buddha, Brecht rejected 'the art of submission' for 'that of not submitting':

> . . . no longer concerned with the art of submission
> Rather with that of not submitting, and putting forward
> Various proposals of an earthly nature, and beseeching men to shake off
> Their human tormentors, (P, pp. 291–2)

This is why there is, for Brecht, beauty in 'the shaking of heads/Over the indisputable truth' and why 'the most beautiful of all doubts' in the poem 'In praise of doubt',

> Is when the downtrodden and despondent raise their heads and
> Stop believing in the strength
> Of their oppressors. (P, p. 334)

Brecht encouraged questions not quietism, a shaking of heads, not keeping your head down. His verse was designed to estrange the official logic and definitions of Hitler's Europe (and, as I want to show, anticipated and extended this practice before and after Hitler) so as to give history and the possibility of change back to the 'bad times' which had come to seem natural and unalterable; since, 'When evil-doing comes like falling rain, nobody calls out "Stop'!" '.(P. p. 247) His target therefore was the mentality of resignation which had so penetrated people's minds as to comprise society's dominant 'common sense', its prevailing view of reality and of the possible. In its place, much like Antonio Gramsci who theorised the role of 'common sense' in maintaining political and cultural hegemony in the era of fascism, Brecht wished to install a reconstructed 'good sense'. If in the following passage from Gramsci, we substitute 'poetry' and 'poet' (or indeed 'art' and 'artist') for Gramsci's 'philosophy' and 'philosopher' we have a description of Brecht's own political objective, the proximity of their thinking suggesting how Brecht too, like Gramsci, was contributing to a revolutionary Marxist tradition:

> A philosophy of praxis cannot but present itself at the outset in a polemical and critical guise, as superseding the existing mode of thinking and existing concrete thought (the existing cultural world). First of all, therefore, it must be a criticism of 'common sense', basing itself initially, however, on common sense in order to demonstrate that 'everyone' is a philosopher and that it is not a question of introducing from scratch a scientific form of thought into everyone's individual life, but of renovating and making 'critical' an already existing activity.[8]

Walter Benjamin discusses the transforming dialectic between spontaneous common sense and systematic knowledge, between practice and theory, in his discussion of the relationship between Vlassova and her son in Brecht's *The Mother* (UB, pp. 33–6). Another example, where the relationship is between proletarian 'experience' and bourgeois literacy, occurs in the same play when, in scene six, the workers are 'taught' to read such key terms as 'class struggle' and 'exploitation'. Benjamin describes the 'outer' form of this dialectic, involving actors and audience, as 'the supreme dialectic . . . namely, the dialectic between recognition and education'. (UB, p. 25) Borrowing Brecht's term, we could call the mode of dialectic employed in *The Mother*, didactic. A poem such as 'Song of the SA man' is similar in that it too shows something (though only the beginnings in this case) of the educative process by which 'class consciousness' overtakes 'false consciousness', or 'good sense' replaces 'common sense'. This would distinguish both poem and play from the 'propagandist' songs which begin and end in the single voice of the already converted, and distinguish them too from the individual odes in *The Mother* ('Praise of Communism', 'Praise of learning', for example) which tend to confirm a stage already arrived at in the mother's political education.

Brecht employed other modes than the didactic and propagandist, however, and I believe his own political education and intended politicisation of his readers can usefully be followed through them. We see in this way, *pace* Benjamin, how the arts of *not* submitting emerged and developed through a differently articulated and directed, but sustained, attempt to undermine consent to bourgeois and fascist ideology. This I want to illustrate in what follows.

Brecht's earlier poems and plays are neither consciously 'epic' nor dialectical. They are 'anti-social' in their bohemian cynicism and tales of low life, and they are anti-authoritarian. From a quite early date, Brecht's poems begin, for example, to subvert religious ideology, patriotism and national unity, all of them major forces in organising consent to bourgeois society. The *Hauspostille* poems are blasphemous in concept and in detail, and strike at a range of religious forms, moral pieties and habits of faith, which 'exist' even if God does not. As his 1919 poem 'Hymn to God' puts it,

> You let the poor stay poor for year after year
> Feeling that their desires were sweeter than your paradise
> Too bad they died before you had brought them the light
> But they died in bliss all the same — and rotted at once.
>
> Many of us say you are not — and a good thing too.
> But how could *that* thing not be which can play such a trick?
> If so much lives by you and could not die without you —
> Tell me how far does it matter that you don't exist? (P, p. 9)

'The Great hymn of thanksgiving' (P, p. 74) is, as we have seen, another example of Brecht's subversive atheism, as is 'Report on a tick' (P, p. 34) which presents God, or his priestly agent, as an avaricious bloodsucker. Elsewhere, in the poems 'Mary' and 'Christmas legend' (P, pp. 98, 99), the 'miracle' of the Nativity is plebeianised, and the rituals of Christmas put down to Christ's fanciful imagination, or the compassion of the poor though they are 'thrown out by Heaven'.

We might see these poems as belonging to Brecht's 'Feuerbachian' phase. He denies the existence of God, and sees how 'heaven' is a consoling mirror-image of a better world from which the poor are excluded. He 'starts out', as Marx says of Feuerbach, 'from the fact of religious self-estrangement, of the duplication of the world into a religious, imaginary world and the real world. His work consists in resolving the religious world into its secular basis.'[9] Brecht's display of the beast in man and angel, and the hell in heaven was, all the same, more provocative than Feuerbach's 'resolution' of one world into the other. Moreover, in Marx's words, 'the chief thing still remains to be done.' Brecht, accordingly, turned in the direction Marx indicates: beyond Feuerbach, to a recognition of 'the inner strife and intrinsic contradictoriness of this secular basis' and its removal through revolutionary practice.

Brecht's 'anti-war' poems, from 1919 through to the early 1930s, illustrate this process of secularisation and increasing politicisation. In the early, politically unfocused, and soon to be jettisoned 'Song of the soldier of the Red Army', the soldiers are duped as much by religious as by political rhetoric. 'Freedom' does not come; their life is a series of self-renewing hells, and 'if the heavens came now/Those heavens would be much the same.' (P. p. 23) In 'Legend of the dead soldier', composed most probably in the early 1920s, both Kaiser and Church collaborate in resuscitating the dead soldier and in enforcing obedience even beyond the grave.[10] In 'Legend of the unknown soldier' (1926), the burial of the unknown soldier is seen less as an homage than a concealment of the injustice of war for which 'all of us' are responsible (P, p. 122); in 'At Potsdam, "Unter den Eichen" ' (1927), the patriotic motto 'Fit for heroes to live in' is exposed as one of 'the tricks/of the Fatherland' (P, p. 157), and in 'Song of the SA man' (1931), the soldier is seen as both misled and self-deceiving. In this last poem the soldier falls in to the tune of the Third Reich:

I went the way that he ordered
And blindly tagged along. (P, p. 191)

only to discover by the end of the poem that his enemy is his brother, and that they are united in hunger and defeat. Brecht's poem does not blame 'them' or 'us', but sets out the conditions and effects of blind consent, of being used, bringing the soldier (unlike Galy Gay) to a point of dawning self-consciousness.

Brecht comes thus to appreciate and document the nature and

effects, the truly 'inner strife' of ideology. Two contemporary poems, 'Article One of the Weimar Constitution' and 'The ballad of paragraph 218' (P. pp. 182, 186), further expose the 'intrinsic contradictoriness' of the 'secular basis' in the workings of the bourgeois progressive state. State power eliminates 'the People' who question its actions, but in whose name it ostensibly rules, and it coerces women to raise the birth-rate. Brecht therefore calls on the people to withdraw their consent and act in their own interests:

> Are you being fobbed off? Are you being consoled?
> The world is waiting for you to put your demands.
> It needs your discontent, your suggestions. (P, p. 185)

Having by this date absorbed Marxism, but lost 'the initiative in the struggle', Brecht turned, beyond didacticism and propaganda, to the 'harsh' tones of satire in attacking Hitler and Nazism. The alliance between Marxism and satire was one Benjamin had acutely perceived in relation to Brecht's *Threepenny Novel*:

> Marx, who was the first to illuminate with criticism the debased and mystified relations between men in capitalist society, thereby became a teacher of satire; and he was not far from becoming a master of it. It is with Marx that Brecht has gone to school. Satire which has always been a materialist art, has with Brecht become a dialectical one. (UB, p. 84)

The uses to which Brecht was to put his dialectical materialist satire, however, were once again the reverse of 'mechanical determinism' or the 'tactics of attrition'. In the 'Hitler Chorales' of 1933, for example, in poems based on Lutheran hymns which parody the tunes of faith and submission, Brecht employs 'naive' verse to ridicule consent to Hitler and to exploitation as itself utterly naive and self-sacrificing. The 'Hitler Chorale I' begins:

> Now thank we all our God
> For sending Hitler to us;
> From Germany's fair land
> To clear away the rubbish
> We've done with the old ways
> The new paint's spick and span
> So thank we all our God
> Who sent us such a man. (P, p. 208)

And in the first two stanzas of the 'Hitler Chorale III', Brecht writes,

O Calf so often wounded
Direct your steps to where
His knife is being sharpened
Whose dearest charge you are.
He who devised new crosses
On working men to lay
He'll find a way to butcher
You too some sunny day.

In his sight you've found favour
O anxious, panting calf.
It's you above all others
He's claiming for himself.
Just wait in hope, not fretting
Nor try to jump the queue
For now his knife he's whetting
He'll soon be calling you. (P, p. 210, my italics)

Later, in the 'German war primer', using, to borrow Benjamin's word for these poems, the most 'lapidary' common speech (UB, p. 65), Brecht sets the maxims of the established regime or 'those at the top' against their real, underlying meaning; a line or stanza of simple truth and good sense thereby undercutting the official rhetoric which means to squash it:

THOSE AT THE TOP SAY:
This way to glory.
Those down below say:
This way to the grave. (P, p. 288)

GENERAL, YOUR TANK IS A POWERFUL VEHICLE
It smashes down forests and crushes a hundred men.
But it has one defect:
It needs a driver. (P, p. 289)

Gramsci speaks of how the 'criticism of "common sense"' needs to base itself on 'common sense' so as to renovate and make ' "critical" an already existing activity'. An already diffused and spontaneous good sense needs to be reaffirmed and strengthened so as to give it 'coherence and sinew'.[11] Often one of the voices or the implication of Brecht's poems derives from this source in 'good' common sense. The poems in the 'German war primer' offer the simplest examples of this, but there are several others. The pregnant woman in 'The ballad of paragraph 218', for example, speaks the truth of her economic condition ('now we're homeless . .. no job or dwelling . .. There's such unemployment') in an uneven exchange with the 'official' common sense which would brow-beat and silence her ('You're a simply splendid little mummy/Producing cannon fodder from your tummy', P, p. 187). Unlike this woman, the workers in 'Questions from a worker who reads' and 'A worker's speech to a doctor', have the advantage over public officials and official accounts. They speak the truths and doubts of Brecht's 'active discontented' directly and without interruption.

> Every page a victory.
> Who cooked the feast for the victors?
> Every ten years a great man.
> Who paid the bill? (P, p. 253)

asks the first worker, while the second confronts the doctor with,

> Too much work and too little food
> Makes us feeble and thin.
> Your prescription says:
> Put on more weight.
> You might as well tell a bullrush
> Not to get wet. (P, p. 293)

These poems voice 'the open word from a simple man'; the unblanched truth of the dissenting, truly wise proletarian. It was precisely this, says Brecht's poem 'The anxieties of the regime', which the Third Reich, built on fear, anxiety, suspicion and guilty consent, itself feared. (P, pp. 296–8)

Brecht's 'renewed common sense possessing the coherence and sinew of individual philosphies', in Gramsci's words, was itself of course close cousin to Marxism. One result, when this was without its satirical cutting edge, was the poems already mentioned on or about the Soviet Union, in which proletarian wisdom, the simple truths from simple people, seemingly coincided with systematic knowledge in the unified good sense of the good society. In the 'Tales of the Revolution' there is 'friendliness', and Bolsheviks, Party officials and people work in concert. Here too there is a 'consenting' Brecht. In the later poem 'The Moscow workers take possession of the great Metro on April 27 1935', the dream appears to have come true in a world of collective skill, pride and delight, all in a 'cheerful crush'. The workers are the owners of the product of their own labour. The poem ends:

> Where would it ever have happened that the fruits of labour
> Fell to those who had laboured? Where in all time
> Were the people who had put up a building
> Not always turned out of it?
> When we saw them riding in their trains
> The work of their own hands, we knew:
> This is the grand picture that once upon a time
> Rocked the classic writers who foresaw it. (P, p, 250)

It is worth pointing out that this is a poem about the Russian people, however, and not their leaders, and worth taking note of its title. Brecht's attitude towards the Soviet regime, towards Stalin and Stalinism, was consistently reserved and two-handed. In the present context Benjamin was one of those who knew of Brecht's ambiguous private dissent, from conversation, and from the poem 'The peasant's address to his ox' which Brecht presented to him as 'his Stalin poem'. Benjamin observes that this was 'in fact a poem in honour of Stalin, who in his opinion has immense merit', adding, in what is apparently a further paraphrase of Brecht's own views, that there was nevertheless cause for 'suspicion — a jusitifiable one — demanding a sceptical appraisal of Russian affairs.' (UB, p. 117) 'The peasant's address to his ox' itself, is, like many of Brecht's comments on Stalin, indirect and in parable form. Stalin is 'our godly puller of the plough', the 'dearest provider', 'o protector of the family'; but he is also in the poems last words, 'you dog'. The peasants labour and sleep in the damp, while the ox, their leader, sleeps in the dry. For now, at the time of ploughing, the main thing is that he pulls straight: he may however 'Peg out before the sowing' and let them down. (P, pp. 313–14)

This is indeed cautious, sceptical praise, much in line with the descriptions of Ni-en (Stalin) in *Me-Ti*, and a subtext almost for the later uninflected, public reference to Stalin as 'the Soviet people's great harvest-leader' in the long 'Die Erziehung der Hirse' of 1950.[12] In another instance, contemporary with 'The peasant's address to his ox', Brecht's scepticism was extended to workers and state, as well as to the figure of the leader. In 1938, the year of the above poem, he heard that Sergei Tretiakov had probably been shot as a spy. His resulting poem asks whether Tretiakov, 'my teacher', was not in fact innocent and the 'people's court' therefore fallible

> The sons of the people have found him guilty
> The factories and collective farms of the workers
> The world's most heroic institutions
> Have identified him as an enemy.
> No voice has been raised for him.
> Suppose he is innocent? (P, pp. 331–2)

If Russia was never entirely convincingly, or never yet, the promised land, capitalism's paradise, Los Angeles, to which Brecht repaired soon after the period of the above two poems, was all too plainly heaven for the rich and hell for the poor (cf. esp. P, pp. 367, 380). Brecht's reappraisal of America, from the early and distant hankerings of the 1920s to the direct experience of the 1940s, constituted, in fact, one of the most striking reversals in his thinking. As it turned out, however, the 'intrinsic contradictoriness' of the secular realm was as sharp in the city of Angels as elsewhere. For although no one would ever claim that Brecht 'approved' of Hollywood, he 'consented' all the same to its demands to 'deliver the goods', and joined the line with others selling 'lies' (P, pp. 378, 382). Yet here too in spite of everything, he found in Chaplin a model, and in Charles Laughton an actor for epic theatre. In Laughton's garden also, he detected an incomplete, 'enduring work of art', and along with the one gest of 'friendliness' already noted, he discovered another of generosity on the part of a 'democratic' Californian judge. (P, pp. 393, 405, 395, 385) There was neither in the event, therefore, an unqualified 'good', nor an unqualified 'evil' society, though in the unrelieved 'dark times', the second in Brecht's collocation of Hitler, Chicago gangsters and big business held the balance of power, in Europe and America.

Brecht's poems in the period of reconstruction after World War II, belonging to the years of his return to Europe and settlement in East Berlin, show a new simplicity and breadth of purview. They stretch back over the years of exile to his Augsburg youth and are more open, especially in the *Buckow Elegies*, to natural life and landscape. This is not to say, however, that Brecht saw this period as the coming at long last of the good times, for people or for poetry, nor that he greeted its arrival in the idiom and tones of conventional verse. In a poem of August 1951 he writes that he wishes his poetry to be remembered as having the claws *and* elegance of the lion in a Chinese carving:

The bad fear your claws.
The good enjoy your elegance.
This
I would like to hear said
Of my verse. (P. p. 431)

This is a familiar duality and Brecht's satirical claws still hook into the authorities in poems such as 'Unidentifiable errors of the Arts Commission', 'The office for literature' and 'The solution, (P, pp. 436, 440). The last poem, written in response to the riots of June 1953, accuses the SED of wishing to substitute a compliant for a dissenting people: 'the people/Had forfeited the confidence of the government'; wouldn't therefore the easiest solution be, Brecht asks, 'for the government/To dissolve the people/And elect another? (P, p. 440) There are other issues involved in this event and in Brecht's response to it, but the tone and tenor, indeed the politics of this poem, are little different from the much earlier 'Article One of the Weimar Constitution'.[13]

Brecht's priorities and the terms of his criticism had been announced in the 'Aufbaulied' of 1948, which, as Peter Whitaker writes, 'had insisted that political reconstruction should take the form of "sich-selbst-führen".' By the early 1950s, however, before the events of June 1953 and the *Buckow Elegies*, it was apparent, Whitaker continues, that the SED and the government of the DDR, 'had failed in one of their principal tasks: the effective promotion of proletarian self-government, of the democracy without which socialism is restricted to a matter of economic form.'[14] Brecht continued to make this demand, however, in the poems mentioned, and, unmistakably, in 'The bread of the people':

As daily bread is necessary
So is daily justice.
It is even necessary several times a day.
. . .
Like the other bread
The bread of justice must be baked
By the people. (P, p. 435)

Nor was Brecht's critique confined to these years or to the East German regime. The *Gesammelte Werke, Supplement 2* includes two poems, 'Die Neue Mundart' and 'Lebensmittel zum Zweck' belonging to the cycle of *Buckow Elegies* which are critical of the leader who has lost touch with the ways and needs and even the language of the people. Four other poems, also, from as late as February 1956, are trenchant in their assault on the 'cult of personality', and style Stalin first in mock homage as 'Honoured Murderer of the People', and then as 'Führer', and a 'putrid' God.[15]

Brecht continued therefore to speak with 'anger and bitterness' on behalf of socialist democracy. Elsewhere in the *Buckow Elegies*, he reflects that his voice is like an October storm (P, p. 432), and in another poem dreams that a storm brings down 'iron' scaffolding while that made of wood, a long-time symbol of flexibility for Brecht, survives the blast. To Helene Weigel also, in a poem on the first production of *Mutter Courage* in January 1949, Brecht advised a discriminating performance, both 'Full of patience, and at the same time relentless'. She should treat,

> What is foolish, with wisdom
> Hatred, with friendliness . . .
> But to the unteachable now show
> With some slight hope
> Your good face. (P, p. 415)

These are not the poems of a unified, freely consenting, entirely 'friendly' society, nor of a poet who, as some would have it, was deluded into seeing East Germany (and the Soviet Union) this way, or who had lapsed as poets should into pastoral and nostalgia. In fact the poems of Brecht's last years are full of principled discriminations and criticism, of tensions in public and personal life, of past echoes and promised changes, directly in society or signalled in nature. As the poem 'Looking for the old and new' puts it:

> . . . The hesitancy of the timid
> Proclaims the new time. Always
> Fix the 'still' and the 'already'.
> The struggles between the classes
> The struggles between new and old
> Rage also within each man. (P, p. 424)

The *Buckow Elegies* are especially marked, for all their simplicity, by a complicated over-lapping and separation of past and present. There are shadows 'still' of war-time occupations, such as the Nazi salute in a man's upraised hand as he tests for rain, and memories in the landscape which focus past and present, such as the copper fir trees, seen now 'With young eyes' as they were first seen 'half a century ago/Two world wars ago'. (P, p. 442) In a further poem, Brecht is impatient for a wheel to be changed although behind as in front of him there are places 'I do not like' (P, p. 439), and in another, the natural beauties of a celebrated silver poplar and lake seem wretched and cheap one 'nasty morning' as he awakes 'Conscience-stricken.' (P, p. 440)

Brecht, as these poems tell us, was unable in the words of the poem 'Antigone', to 'Emerge from the darkness' and so go forward, a 'Friendly one, with the light step of/Of total certainty'. (P, p. 414) Nor though it should be 'child's play' could he see 'a decent German nation' itself united, and united 'in friendship' with other lands, emerge from this same darkness without unsparing grace and labour, passion and intelligence. (P. p. 423) There are glimmers, nevertheless, of an alternative: poems in this late period, which suggest that anger and harshness can give way to friendliness, that labour and simple pleasures can unite with learning and dialectics, that youth and age, past and present can connect in a happy, everyday, coincidence. Thus in the poem 'Happy Encounter' written in 1951:

On Sundays in June among the saplings
Villagers looking for raspberries hear
Studious girls and women from the technical college
Pick out phrases from their textbooks
About dialectics and the care of children.

Looking up from their textbooks
The students see the villagers
Pick berries from the canes (P,p. 431)

In Brecht's German, 'picking' out phrases and 'picking' berries are both rendered by the verb 'lesen'. A pun of this kind which links activities is a significantly different device from the double voices of irony and satire which uncover the true meaning in the false. Finally, in '1954: first half' and the poem 'Pleasures' from the same year, Brecht finds in the form of the list, the simplest mode of all for connecting distinct items and areas of experience. Part diary entry, part announcement, part examplar, these poems build the typical and potential out of the personal, as Brecht becomes in his own person an historical gest, listing the entries, the earnest and props for a newly 'rounded' human type. He speaks in the poem 'Pleasures' good, common sense:

> The first look out of the window in the morning
> The old book found again
> Enthusiastic faces
> Snow, the change of the seasons
> The newspaper
> The dog
> Dialectics
> Taking showers, swimming
> Old music
> Comfortable shoes
> Taking things in
> New music
> Writing, planting
> Travelling
> Singing
> Being friendly. (P, p. 448)

Notes

1. Frederic Ewen sees the poem as an example of the period in Brecht's work when his 'aloof doctrinaire quality' was 'modified by a profound sympathy'. Brecht was on guard, he suggests, against 'a growing "harshness' within himself', *Bertolt Brecht. His Life, His Art, and His Times* (Citadel Press, New York, 1969), p. 325. Hannah Arendt says that the poem 'narrative in form and making no attempt at experimenting with either language or thought, is among the stillest and — strange to say — most consoling poems written in our century.' It teaches 'the lesson of non-violence and wisdom' and it became, spreading via Benjamin, 'like a rumor of good tidings . . . a source of consolation and patience and endurance', 'Bertolt Brecht' in *Men in Dark Times* (Jonathan Cape, London, 1970), pp. 244–5. Esslin's argument, similarly, is that Brecht 'the prophet of rational planning by violent methods' in this poem 'preaches the wisdom of non-violence', *Brecht. A Choice of Evils* (Eyre Methuen, London, 1959, revised 1980), p. 243. Willett refers to 'the idea of quiet subversion' in the poem, *Brecht in Context* (Methuen, London and New York, 1984), p. 207.

In a more vigorous reading of both poem and Benjamin's commentary than any of the above, Peter Whitaker suggests that the key stanza presents the sage's 'knowledge of the laws of conflict'. Its lesson is that, 'The weakest forces may ultimately triumph, if they combine in persistent action; again, Brecht illuminates the element of defiance which belongs to the dialectic.' *Brecht's Poetry. A Critical Study* (Clarendon Press, Oxford, 1985), pp. 128–9.

2. *Man equals Man*, in Bertolt Brecht, *Collected Plays, Vol. 2i*, John Willett and Ralph Manheim (eds) (Eyre Methuen, London, 1979), pp. 61–2.

3. Ibid., pp. 99–100.

4. Cf. the 'Five Epistles', especially 'The first letter to the halfbreeds', and also 'Everything new is better than everything old', *Poems*, pp. 79, 159.

5. *Poems*, pp. 5–8, 127, 155 and 156. Even so, there are quizzical and questioning notes in these chants to the USA. See also, in this respect, the poem, 'Of the crushing impact of cities', p. 108.

6. Antonio Gramsci, *The Modern Prince and Other Writings* (International Publishers, New York, 1957), p. 69.

7. *Gesammelte Werke*, 10 (Suhrkamp, Frankfurt am Main, 1967), p. 828. This translation appears in *Understanding Brecht*, p. xviii. For Brecht's second poem on Benjamin's suicide, see *Gesammelte Werke*, 10, pp. 828–9, and *Poems*, p. 363.

8. Antonio Gramsci, *Selections from the Prison Notebooks*, Quintin Hoare and Geoffrey Nowell-Smith (eds and trans.) (Lawrence and Wishart, London, 1971), pp. 330–1.

9. Marx, *On Dialectical Materialism* (Progress Publishers, Moscow, and Lawrence and Wishart, London, 1977), p. 30.

10. *Gesammelte Werke*, 8, p. 256. This dating is suggested by Willett, *Brecht in Context*, p. 133.

11. Gramsci, *Prison Notebooks*, p. 330.

12 'Die Erziehung der Hirse', *Gesammelte Werke*, 10, p. 948. See Willett's discussion of this and the references in *Me-Ti*, in *Brecht in Context*, pp. 211–18. Esslin discusses Brecht's criticisms of Stalin in *Me-Ti* in *Mediations. Essays on Brecht, Beckett and the Media* (Sphere Books, London, 1983), pp. 55–60.

13. In similar vein, Brecht wrote in *Me-Ti* of how 'Under Ni-en's leadership, industry in Su was built up without exploiters and agriculture collectively conducted and supplied with machinery. But the associations outside Su degenerated. It was no longer the members who elected the secretaries but the secretaries who elected the members.' *Gesammelte Werke*, 10, p. 539, trans. in Esslin *Mediations*, p. 59.

14. Whitaker, *Brecht's Poetry*, p. 199.

15. *Gesammelte Werke, Supplementband IV* (Suhrkamp, Frankfurt am Main, 1982), pp. 428, 437–8, and see *Anmerkungen 31* and *32*. Three of the late Stalin poems are given in Whitaker, pp. 259–60.

Part Three
Marxist Art and Critical Attitudes

8

'A Conceivable Aesthetic'

I

My argument in earlier chapters has been that Brecht consistently drew upon dialectical materialism in developing his political aesthetic. The distinction I believe we ought then to go on to make is not so much between the absence or presence of dialectics, as between the degrees of explicitness with which Brecht conceived of parts or the whole of his theory in terms of it. The early 'Dialectical drama' brings the theatre and a politicised audience face to face with the economy which then, or so this essay implies, would itself need to change in order for a fully dialectical theatre to come into being. In which case we can understand why in the hostile years of Nazi Germany and world war the term dialectics as a comprehensive and *explicit* description of theatre receded behind the actually more esoteric, if dialectically conceived, vocabularly of 'epic' and *Gestus* and *Verfremdungseffekt*. Prior to the fall of Hitler dialectics was not surprisingly drawn into the shadows of the 'dark times'.

There is at the same time a very positive aspect to Brecht's change of vocabulary and emphasis. Outside of the educated but bourgeois taste in art shown by Marx and Engels, the scattered discussions within their writings of 'classic realism', and writings by Lenin, Trotsky and Plekhanov (if indeed Brecht knew these), there was nothing in dialectical materialism itself which provided for a 'dialectical' aesthetic; certainly not of the non-illusionist, anti-bourgeois and non-propagandist kind Brecht sought. Only Eisenstein's essays provided anything like a precedent. In fact it is easier to derive 'socialist realism' and Lukács's 'critical realism' from earlier Marxist aesthetics than it is to find a parentage for Brecht. The consequence was that in 'adapting' dialectical materialism Brecht had also to adopt, and invent, a set of working artistic concepts ('epic', *Gestus*, and *Verfremdung*) to describe his artistic practices and their desired effects. While it is unjust and inaccurate, as I have said, to describe these terms as if they were narrowly formalist, they did express an emphasis on the *artistic* means — the 'social' measures', or 'techniques' in Benjamin's use of this term — by which Brecht's theatre and poetry could fulfil the political task of dialecticising their audience and readers.

We might see all this as a necessary, internal investigation of the means and meaning of a political art. Or we might see it as a matter of expediency, an enforced retreat into the realm of aesthetic theory or formal experiment to accompany the personal journey into exile. Both views are of course broadly correct, in as much as Brecht's freedom of choice was regulated, but not railroaded, by social and historical conditions. His plans and actual work in this period were nevertheless severly circumscribed. The events which removed him from a German-speaking audience and culture were clearly not of his own choosing. Nor were the circumstances of his subsequent exile. These years literally restricted Brecht's thinking and achievements, in theory and practice — to the point even of forcing these apart. By the end of the 1930s, for example, with the exception of *The Mother* and *Round Heads and Pointed Heads*, no play since *Saint Joan* had been tried out on the stage.[1] After ten years of exile there were ten plays. They comprised, Brecht said, 'Not a bad repertory for a thoroughly beaten class'. Even so, his work was stonelike and 'only with difficulty transportable'; it was the work of a 'fugitive stonemason', prone to 'an unnatural non-utilization'.[2]

Yet the experience of exile did have its constructive and 'useful' side: 'Die beste Schul für Dialektik ist die Emigration' ('The best school for dialectics is emigration') Brecht wrote in 1941[3], and in a more mundane sense than he intended, the 1930s and 1940s were a period of schooling, of study, and development. 'What's necessary now', he had written to Tretiakov, 'is a patient, relentless, laborious job of enlightenment and study.'[4] The major problem confronting Brecht in these years was how a political art, seeking to change the world, could exercise this function in ways appropriate to the sphere of artistic production, and do this in a world which had demonstrably changed for the worse in spite of his art. If fascism were to be defeated, moreover, that world would need to change dramatically once more, in ways again far removed from artistic innovation and production.

Brecht's answer was to subordinate but not sacrifice art to politics; to in fact strategically claim back, transform and politicise the autonomous discourse of artistic forms and effects rather than surrender them to events or to an officially controlled aesthetic. Only, that is to say, by attending to what he was later to describe as art's 'own regulations' (BT, p. 267), in the face of external regulations and an independently moving political world, could Brecht's art demonstrate and prompt the 'critical attitude' which gave it its political function. We can, in these terms, better understand the distant, ambigious and self-protective attitude Brecht often took in relation to the world of contemporary *real politik*. His political effectiveness depended less on direct involvement than on his political art, just as this in turn depended less on direct commentary and topical relevance than the interventions and changes it could effect in the realm of ideology. It was to precisely this end, after all, that *Verfremdungseffekte* were 'designed to free socially-conditioned phenomena from that stamp of familiarity which protects them against our grasp today'. (BT, p. 192)

When John Willett writes, therefore, in *Brecht in Context*, that Brecht made his political commitment 'a part of everything he did', he offers a useful correction to other, aestheticising, interpretations (including his own elsewhere), but then goes too far in suggesting that Brecht was as a result, 'all of a piece, fusing political and aesthetic considerations on a whole series of different levels.'[5] Certainly, Brecht's art was 'infused' with political purpose, but the circumstances of exile, in particular, did not permit his political art to be 'all of a piece' in theory and practice. No more were his art and political opinions and statements 'all of a piece' at their 'different levels'. The politics of Brecht's art, that is to say, consisting, to put it simply, of the use of artistic means for ideological ends, were in an ambiguous and shifting, but only rarely 'fused' relationship with his political beliefs and statements as a citizen and supporter of communism. And these political beliefs themselves were ambiguous. Willett himself writes, for example, of the 'mixture of intellectual independence and outward conformity' characterising Brecht's attitude to the Communist Party from the late twenties onwards.[6] Brecht's attitude towards Soviet Russia also, Willett sums up, similarly, as 'Critical, but *for* it'.[7] The point is that Brecht's 'intellectual independence' and his integrity as a critical but committed artist depended on the kind of ambiguity these descriptions suggest; on the realms of art and politics being somewhat out of joint rather than 'all of a piece'.

This was a precarious position obviously, whose evident tensions and uncertainties became more fraught in the post-war period, after Brecht's decision to settle in East Berlin. I want to take up some of the questions in this 'tangle of factors', to borrow another phrase from John Willett, in a later chapter. Meanwhile there are grounds for considering Brecht's political aesthetic, as a theory of artistic practice and production, separately from his political views or statements, or his relation to the Communist Party. Aside from the considerations offered above, a major expression of his theory occurred in the *Short Organum* of 1948. Here, in what Willett calls Brecht's 'most important theoretical work', Brecht writes of setting out 'to define an *aesthetic* drawn from a particular kind of theatrical performance which has been worked out in practice over the past few decades.' (BT, p. 179, my italics) In his previous writings he says,

> aesthetics have only been touched on casually and with comparative lack of interest . . . Aesthetics, that heirloom of a by now depraved and parasitic class, was in such a lamentable state that a theatre would have gained both in reputation and in elbowroom if it had rechristened itself thaëter. And yet what we achieved in the way of theatre for a scientific age was not science but theatre, and the accumulated innovations worked out during the Nazi period and the war — when practical demonstration was impossible — compel some attempt to set this species of theatre in its aesthetic background, or anyhow to sketch for it the outlines of a conceivable aesthetic. (BT, pp. 179–80)

Brecht's willingness to re-enter the realm of aesthetics, to consolidate the artistic innovations of the war years in what proved to be a major theoretical statement, is a clear expression of new-found confidence. There is a sense also in which, in this mood, his artistic theory and political convictions did move in tandem. Though he viewed the situation in post-war Europe with evident circumspection and was careful to protect himself with an Austrian passport and West German publisher, he nevertheless greeted this moment of transition and the prospect of reconstruction with some real anticipation.

A sure sign of this was the reappearance of 'dialectics' on his political and artistic agenda. Thus from California, in a letter to Korsch, he had looked to 'the good old dialectic' which will have to take over the 'battle of the working classes' though it was presently obscured by the weakness of the proletarian movement.[8] In analogous fashion dialectics made its way once more into his aesthetic vocabularly; in the model books, in entries in the *Theaterarbeit*, in the *Short Organum* itself, and then more decisively in the *Appendices* to this work, and of course in 'Dialectics in the theatre'.[9] These texts cover the last eight years of Brecht's life and coincide, after the 'dark times', with the 'twilight' period of 'upheaval, fearful and fruitful', as Brecht saw it in the *Appendices to the Short Organum*; a time when 'the evenings of the doomed classes coincide with the dawns of those that are rising.' (BT, p. 277)

The general implication of Brecht's remarks and this set of essays is that before he talked openly once again of a dialectical aesthetic, rooted in dialectical materialism, he needed to feel that there was some prospect of dialectics (and the working class) being roused from the atrophy they had fallen into under Hitler and Stalin.[10] Dialectics reappeared, once more in Berlin but on the other side of exile, less as a matter of urgency than as now an artistic and political possibility, heralding the birth of the new from the old.

I do not wish to claim on this evidence that Brecht's theory remained unaltered, or that it was in fact, if not in name, the same dialectical theory throughout the period 1929–56. Nor am I suggesting that the late 1940s and early 1950s saw the return from exile of the young Brecht, *circa* 1929–30. If his political aesthetic and political affiliations seem more 'of a piece', say, in 1929 and 1949 than at other times, his aesthetic had nevertheless altered in the interim, just as the conditions determining a connection between art and political action in the public sphere had themselves altered. As far as his debt to dialectical materialism is concerned we can say that after the 1931 essay which was as much a postponement as an announcement of a dialectical drama, Brecht worked upon the translation of dialectical materialist principles into a set of artistic techniques which he then theorised as 'a conceivable aesthetic', and came progressively to regard as the formal prerequisites for a fully transformed theatre in a transformed society. If there is any question of the 'fusion' of art and politics, it appeared more as a projected than a present fusion, a 'perfect example' for the future, and as such was an expression of Brecht's post-war optimism. It was in this mood that he spoke, for example, of the 'great independent task' a 'genuinely realistic art' could perform, making 'visible at the first stage of its evolution', the republic's progressive cultural policy; giving voice to the hope of the artists who were helping thousands 'to understand past and present and recognise the future.' (BT, p. 223)

As we shall see there were ways in which Brecht was sometimes betrayed into giving this future a premature reality and into setting art in a synchronous, and undialectical, relationship with economic and political movements. A socialist economy and culture did not arrive, simultaneously, in East Berlin, even officially. In the exceptional circumstances of the immediate post-war years, however, and most obviously on the artistic front, one can see that there were significant grounds for optimism. Brecht's heretofore 'non-utilised' drama acquired a stage and company enabling him to work alongside sympathetic actors, artists and technicians tutored in a collaborative ethos. Here there was provision for unhurried rehearsal time and the prospect of a new theatre building and independent theatre. After the nadirs of Hollywood, Brecht was granted personal security and artistic status. What is more, he could actively contribute, in ways he could never have done outside Germany, to the understanding of the past and present and the 'recognition' of a future, officially committed to communism.

For all the setbacks and signs to the contrary, Brecht was able to sustain this general political optimism, and, perhaps more impressively, in spite of opposition and indifference, sustain his renewed aesthetic theory in a more relaxed and reciprocal relationship with artistic practice. This theory was strengthened by the addition to Brecht's Marxist canon of Mao's *On Contradiction* and in different ways revised and broadened; in Brecht's attitude towards past literature and the emotional aspect of aesthetic experience, for example, and, most importantly, in the central place he now came to accord to pleasure. This new note enters in the *Short Organum* and sounds many times elsewhere. Brecht's thinking amounts in my view to an extension rather than to a recapitulation of his earlier theory, and, at the same time, to an important extension of Marxist aesthetics.

This is not, however, the way Brecht's theory, or since it has consequences for this also, the last phase of his life and the resulting shape of his career, are usually seen. I want therefore to elaborate on some aspects of this aesthetic, and respond to some of the views taken of it in what follows.

II

John Willett talks of Brecht as arriving after the years of exile at 'the theoretical compromise of the "Short Organum".' (BT, p. 135) From the time of the 1939 essay 'On experimental theatre', he feels, 'Brecht wanted to strike a balance between didacticism and entertainment. Ever since the *Lehrstücke*, his theoretical writing had been consistently on the side of the former'. (ibid.) Now it seems Brecht was prepared to recognise the place of amusement and entertainment, and to admit the existence of 'Aristotelian' theatre, even in his own productions. 'It was the period', Willett adds, 'of his greatest plays' — of *Galileo, Mother Courage* and *The Good Person of Szechwan*.

Other comments by Willett in *Brecht on Theatre* as well as interpretations by Esslin, Gray and a number of other writers, support the general picture of Brecht's development which these remarks already give. After the 'theoretical compromise' of the *Short Organum* Willett sees the practical emphasis of the *Theaterarbeit* as 'part of the apparent "mellowing" of his last years.' (BT, p. 246) The production and notes to *Katzgraben* (1952–3) he views as 'evidence of a considerable effort on Brecht's part to meet the requirement of the official aesthetic policy of the day', and the passage titled 'Emotions' in these notes as constituting 'a still further modification of Brecht's theory'. (BT, p. 251) Brecht's later comments on Stanislavsky, too, in contrast with earlier more aggressive attacks, 'seem like an effort to take as favourable a view as possible, though there is still a sting in the tail.' (BT, p. 237)

From another perspective but with similar results, Esslin refers to the 'fog' of the young Brecht's theories and his later attempts to dissipate this. He talks of 'the dogmatic and didactic tone of his earlier pronouncements' and of his theory as having 'changed, developed, and finally mellowed in accordance with the changes in his styles of writing and stage production'.[11] 'In the beginning', writes Esslin, 'Brecht proclaimed his conviction that the theatre had to be strictly didactic . . . By 1948 [i.e. by the date of his stated intention in the *Short Organum* 'to treat the theatre as a place of entertainment'] he had mellowed to the extent of openly repudiating much of this severity of approach.'[12] Elsewhere, in characteristically psychologistic fashion. Esslin associates 'this mellowing of Brecht's attitude, the re-integration of his violently divided personality' with the appearance of the 'mother-image' in his writing: 'the emotional side', he concludes, 'appeared in an increasingly sympathetic light.'[13]

Astonishingly enough, Esslin's remarks would set this process of mellowing and re-integration as beginning as early as 1932 with the production of *The Mother*. For Ronald Gray this play is associated more feasibly with Brecht's 'purely "class-conscious" theory of drama'.[14] The *Short Organum* he then sees very firmly as marking a significant reversal, since here Brecht 'announced a complete change of front . . . he deliberately recalls his earlier writings only in order to reject them'. Thenceforth Brecht's theatre was to be 'neither moralising nor didactic'; 'change is welcomed for its own sake and the highest pleasure is the morally-unmoved witnessing of such change.' This 'aesthetic attitude' receives 'much the greater emphasis' in Brecht's later theory and is unreconciled with the political purpose and 'merely ostensible Communist solution' that remains.[15]

There are differences in these judgements clearly, and this is in itself revealing. For one thing we realise that there never has been nor will be 'the one true Brecht', but only the 'Brechts' produced through the rhetoric of differing critical discourses. In this case, however, these discourses prove more complementary than competing, and contribute in their broad similarities to the common view that the later Brecht was more tolerant, more accommodating, more practically minded, more artist and producer than theorist, and when theorist, more romantic than dogmatically Marxist. There are four connected ways, in this view, in which Brecht appears to have 'compromised' or 'mellowed'. There is his attitude towards socialist realism and Stanislavsky; his attitude towards other forms of theatre and past works; and then his views on the emotional aspect of drama and on the theatre as a place of entertainment.

The first of these can be dealt with most easily. As Willett concedes there is a 'sting in the tail' of Brecht's 'Some of the things that can be learnt from Stanislavsky' of 1952. This sting lies in the comment that,

> The Moscow Arts Theatre never rested on its laurels. S. [Stanislavsky] invented new artistic methods for every production. From his theatre came such important artists as Vakhtangov, who in turn developed their teacher's art further in complete freedom. (BT, p. 237)

Brecht had seen Vakhtangov as a 'meeting point' between Stanislavsky and Meyerhold, and his comment here, as Willett recognises, 'is clearly an appeal not to stick with Stanislavsky'. (BT, p. 238) Also, as Willett goes on to point out, the virtues Brecht finds in Stanislavsky amount to similarities with his own theatre. The difference between them was anyway very plain to the Party organisers at a Stanislavsky conference held in April 1953. The underestimation of Stanislavsky, the crimes of 'formalism and its twin-brother schematism' stood in the way of a breakthrough to socialist realism, of 'the most highly developed' Soviet form. Even if there were points of similarity between Stanislavsky and 'epic theatre', *Neues Deutschland* insisted that

> in so far as the Berliner Ensemble tries to put into practice Brecht's theoretical views embodied in *Kleines Organum fuer das Theater* and his other writings, it is undeniably in opposition to everything the name Stanislavsky stands for.[16]

Obviously Brecht did not comply sufficiently with the approved methods of socialist realism; and this verdict was only confirmed by the official carping and hostility towards *The Mother, Lucullus* and *Urfaust*.[17]

Meanwhile, Brecht's own definition of socialist realism remained consistent with the critique he had directed at Lukács and *International Literature* in the late 1930s. Willett say that Brecht came to terms with socialist realist doctrines 'in his own way', describing Brecht's definition as a 'heterodox adaptation' of the official aesthetic. (BT, pp. 251, 269) In fact it would be more accurate to describe Brecht's definition as a revision, or correction, of orthodox tenets. A note of 1954 sums up Brecht's position very succinctly. Here in five points he expresses an unequivocal commitment to the working class and to socialism; he gives socialist realism a specifically instructional and specifically dialectical materialist character, and emphasises as firmly as ever the role of the 'artistic means', or 'new means of representation'.

> 1. Socialist Realism means realistically reproducing men's life together by artistic means from a socialist point of view. It is reproduced in such a way as to promote insight into society's mechanisms and stimulate socialist impulses. In the case of Socialist Realism a large part of the pleasure which all art must provoke is pleasure at the possibility of society's mastering man's fate.
> 2. A Socialist Realist work of art lays bare the dialectical

> laws of movement of the social mechanism, whose revelation makes the mastering of man's fate easier. It provokes pleasure in their recognition and observation.
> 3. A Socialist Realist work of art shows characters and events as historical and alterable, and as contradictory. This entails a great change; a serious effort has to be made to find new means of representation.
> 4. A Socialist Realist work of art is based on a working-class viewpoint and appeals to all men of good will. It shows them the aims and outlook of the working class, which is trying to raise human productivity to an undreamt-of extent by transforming society and abolishing exploitation.
> 5. The Socialist Realist performance of old classical works is based on the view that mankind has preserved those works which gave artistic expression to advances towards a continually stronger, bolder and more delicate humanity. Such performance accordingly emphasises those works' progressive ideas. (BT, p. 269)

This is an important note, especially in the present context, for its reference to 'pleasure' and the positive attitude Brecht suggests should be taken towards past works — two of the main counts on which he is thought to have 'mellowed'. Within the terms of Brecht's overall definition of socialist realism these points do indeed contribute to a significant change, or to be precise, sum up changes announced from the period of the *Short Organum*. The question is how such changes are to be accounted for, if *not* in terms of compromise.

To take the issue of Brecht's attitude to other theatres and past works. Willett quotes Brecht's diary entry of 12 January 1941 as a sign of his changed attitude, but Brecht's statement here that '*non-aristotelian theatre* is only *one* form of theatre; if furthers specific social aims and has no claims to monopoly as far as the theatre in general is concerned' (BT, p. 135), is in itself an unremarkable statement of fact. The concession which then follows that 'I myself can use both aristotelian and non-aristotelian theatre in certain productions' is admittedly a different matter, and best dealt with separately.

First, however, the question of other theatres and dramatic forms. What Brecht says in the essay of 1939, *On Experimental Theatre*, to which Willett's note is attached, is that the epic style is the result of one continuing experimental route; 'only *one* of the conceivable solutions to the problem' of how the theatre could 'be both instructive and entertaining', and thus help 'the unfree, ignorant man of our century', the 'changeable and world-changing man . . . to master the world and himself.' (BT, p. 135) Epic theatre, employing V-Effekte, is therefore one kind of answer, occurring as Brecht's remarks also suggest, in one, diverse tradition:

> the theatre of past periods also, technically speaking, achieved results with alienation effects — for instance the Chinese Theatre, the Spanish classical theatre, the popular theatre of Brueghel's day and the Elizabethan theatre. (BT, pp. 134–5)

Of the epic style developed at the Schiffbauerdamm Theatre, Brecht says, 'From the start the *classical repertoire* supplied the basis of many of these experiments'. (BT, p. 134) This reference to the 'classical repertoire' in relation to his own theatre is surprising (one thinks of John Gay and *The Beggars Opera*, Marlowe, and Brecht's *Edward II*, and perhaps his adaptation of Gorky in *The Mother*), but what one also notices is that this statement of account is set in the past tense. Unless therefore Brecht is being ingenuous or deliberately misleading, *On Experimental Theatre* is a description of *early* work in Berlin, not of a *changed* position, or a changed perspective upon those early years.

Brecht's early writings bear this out. In 1926 he praised Shaw for his fun and naivety and 'his delight in dislocating our stock associations' (BT, p. 11); he found an example of rough textured 'gestic' verse in Christopher Marlowe and of epic narrative in Shakespeare.[18] and he made use in theatre and poetry of Rimbaud, Villon, Kipling, Upton Sinclair, Dreiser, Goethe and Luther. In the realm of theatre alone he noted the similarities and differences between his own epic style and agit-prop (BT, pp. 61–2); he repeatedly acknowledged the influence on subject-matter and technical innovations of Piscator, and referred with respect and admiration to the work of Tretiakov, Meyerhold and Chaplin (BT, p. 65). To take two examples, in a note of 1929 Brecht referred to Piscator, to the new subject-matter introduced by Bruckner, Lampel and Theodore Dreiser and to the production of *Oedipus Rex* and *Oedipus at Kolonnos* at the Staatstheater. This last he saw as the sum of the theatre's recent development (in a season including his own *Threepenny Opera*) (BT, pp. 24, 25, cf, also p. 65). Secondly, in 1934, at a time when he spoke unambiguously of the theatre of Ibsen and Strindberg and the traditional form of naturalistic acting as having outlived their usefulness, he says

> . . . I do feel that one shouldn't be satisfied with just one way of writing plays. There should be several different sorts for different purposes.
>
> All this demands a new and special technique, and I'm not the only writer to have tried to create it.

He then goes on to refer to Georg Kaiser, O'Neill, Paul Claudel (helping to pioneer technique though 'a severe and reactionary writer') and Chaplin. (BT, p. 68, cf. also pp. 69, 77)

There is nothing new then in Brecht's later acknowledgement of 'other theatres'. The real question concerned his attitude towards past works, especially in post-war East Germany when the Party saw fit to protect the 'classical heritage' against subjective and formalistic distortion. As in other matters, this is a question of interpretations of socialist realism. Willett sees Brecht as 'coming to terms with the Party's anti-formalist compaign' in the *Katzgraben* notes. Brecht says there that we must learn from the old plays how their playwrights 'would give shape to something that was new for their age . . . The old must teach us how to make something new'; he then goes on to distinguish between 'real innovations' and false 'purely formalistic efforts' which disguise an 'unchanging reactionary social content by wild changes of fashion in external form.' (BT, pp. 250–1) But, once again, this line of thinking was not new, although the context and artistic circumstances of Brecht's remarks had changed. As early as the *Mahagonny* notes we find him making a distinction between formalistic innovations which dress up an opera for 'an evening's entertainment' and real innovations 'which threaten to change its function'. (BT, p. 34) Then in the 1938 essay, 'The popular and the realistic', while calling characteristically for new techniques and new means of representation appropriate to a changing reality, Brecht warns against 'a wholly formalistic procedure' as regards both realism and the question of popularity. (BT, p. 112) 'Nothing arises from nothing', he says in the same essay, 'the new springs from the old, but that is what makes it new.' (BT, p. 110) As these essays suggest, Brecht was concerned throughout with new techniques for new purposes, with what there was in the old, and the new, which could contribute to genuine artistic and social progress.

Finally in the late essay 'Classical status as an inhibiting factor', in a manner entirely consistent with these earlier writings, Brecht rejected both 'a traditional style of performance which is automatically counted as part of our cultural heritage' and the spicing up of the old with 'new and hitherto unknown sensational effects, which are however of a purely formalist kind'. (BT, p. 272) He sees both as damaging 'the true heritage' and the classic status which consists in the work's 'original freshness, the element of surprise (in terms of their period), of newness, of productive stimulus that is the hallmark of such works.' (ibid.) Brecht was therefore, and without question, anti-formalist. But this meant that he was opposed equally to superficial titivation, and to the uncritical reverence, the 'false, hypocritical, lip-serving' respect officially paid to the classics. (BT, p. 273) The second, as he had shown in his reply to Lukács in the 1930s, resulted in 'formalism' just as much as the first. He did not comply therefore with the official attitude theoretically, nor in the Berliner Ensemble's own productions of plays from the German heritage such as *The Private Tutor, The Broken Jug* and *Urfaust*. Neither did he toe the Party line in the production or planning of other past works not strictly in the national canon, such as *Antigone, Coriolanus* (without Shakespeare, said Brecht, 'a national theatre is almost impossible' BT, p. 229), *Don Juan* and *The Recruiting Officer*.[19] Brecht's castigation in 'Classical status as an inhibiting factor' of 'a fake, superficial, decadent, petty-bourgeois idea of what constitutes a classic', (BT, p. 273) is in fact his reply to the official aesthetic; his answer, specifically, to the criticism of the Ensemble's production of *Urfaust* in *Neues Deutschland*, the Party newspaper, as expressing an attitude 'directed against Germany's cultural heritage, against Germany's national culture.'[20]

The second main issue Willett and others raise concerns Brecht's attitude towards emotion in art and in aesthetic experience. The most common view is that 'epic' theory and theatre were un- or anti-emotional, especially in their early forms. Ronald Gray takes a particularly straightforward view of this. Commenting on Brecht's notes to *Mahagonny*, he writes that Brecht 'gave the impression at the time, a justified one in view of his propagandist plays, that he discountenanced all emotion, and was obliged to correct this explicitly at a later stage.'[21] As I have pointed out above, Brecht distinguished between his own 'pedagogic' theatre and forms of 'committed' or 'propagandist' theatre, naturalistic or otherwise. Leaving this aside, however, Gray's opinion is exactly the kind of misrepresentation Brecht noted in his 'Short list of the most frequent, common and boring misconceptions about the epic theatre'. Of five points, Brecht lists as number three:

> The epic theatre is against all emotions. But reason and emotion can't be divided.

Brecht's answer then follows:

> (The epic theatre isn't against the emotions; it tries to examine them, and is not satisfied just to stimulate them. It is the orthodox theatre which sins by dividing reason and emotion, in that it virtually rules out the former. As soon as one makes the slightest move to introduce a modicum of reason into theatrical practice its protagonists scream that one is trying to abolish the emotions.) (BT, pp. 162–3)

The explicit correction 'at a later stage' Gray says Brecht was 'obliged' to make is presumably his comment in the *Theaterarbeit*, dating from an interview in 1949. Here Brecht says:

> It is not true, though it is sometimes suggested, that epic theatre . . . proclaims the slogan: 'Reason this side, Emotion (feeling) that.' It by no means renounces emotion, least of all the sense of justice, the urge to freedom, and righteous anger; it is so far from renouncing these that it does not even assume their presence but tries to arouse or to reinforce them. The 'attitude of criticism' which it tries to awaken in its audience cannot be passionate enough for it. (BT, p. 227)

A similar statement about the need for 'new passions' ('the passion for extracting more fruits from the earth, or the passion for moulding men together into working collectives') appears in Brecht's notes to *Katzgraben*. (BT, p. 249) It is the passage 'Emotions' in these notes which Willett directs our attention to as evidence of a 'still further modification of Brecht's theory'. (BT, p. 251) The point Brecht makes in this section is that whereas actors in 'other theatres' are likely to overplay emotions, actors playing epic theatre can err in the opposite direction:

> Aiming to avoid artificial heat, we fall short in natural warmth. We make no attempt to share the emotions of the characters we portray, but these emotions must none the less be fully and movingly represented, nor must they be treated with coldness, but likewise with an emotion of some force: thus, the character's despair with genuine anger on our part,

> or his anger with genuine despair. (BT, pp. 248–9)

In what ways this constitutes a 'further modification' is simply unclear: Brecht is still distinguishing in this passage between acting in other theatres and in his own, between the 'grand passions' of the old theatre and the 'new passions (as well as old)', and still recommending, in these lines, a form of acting which discourages identification while it demonstrates and contradicts a presented dramatic emotion.

Willett, and Gray, might say that *any* talk of emotions was new in Brecht. But this is simply not the case. In a letter to Max Gorelik, for example, dated June 1944, and roughly contemporary with the 'Short list' referred to above, Brecht wrote:

> It is only the opponents of the new drama, the champions of the 'eternal laws of the theatre', who suppose that in renouncing the empathy process the modern theatre is renouncing the emotions. All the modern theatre is doing is to discard an outworn, decrepit, subjective sphere of the emotions and pave the way for the new, manifold, socially productive emotions of a new age. (BT, p. 161)

An earlier essay, 'Short description of a new technique of acting' (written in 1940), makes Brecht's position and thinking even clearer:

> The rejection of empathy is not the result of a rejection of the emotions, nor does it lead to such. The crude aesthetic thesis that emotions can only be stimulated by means of empathy is wrong. None the less a non-aristotelian dramaturgy has to apply a cautious criticism to the emotions which it aims at and incorporates . . . Fascism's grotesque emphasizing of the emotions, together perhaps with the no less important threat to the rational element in Marxist aesthetics, led us to lay particular stress on the rational. Nevertheless there are many contemporary works of art where one can speak of a decline in emotional effectiveness due to their isolation from reason, or its revival thanks to a stronger rationalist message. This will surprise no one who has not got a completely conventional idea of the emotions.
>
> The emotions always have a quite definite class basis; the form they take at any time is historical, restricted and limited in specific ways. The emotions are in no sense universally human and timeless. (BT, p. 145)

Earlier in the same essay, in describing the V-Effekt (designed 'to make the spectator adopt an attitude of enquiry and criticism' as opposed to empathy), Brecht writes of the actor that 'in his efforts to reproduce particular characters and show their behaviour he need not renounce the means of empathy entirely. He uses these means just as any normal person with no particular acting talent would use them if he wanted to portray someone else, i.e. show how he behaves.' (BT, p. 136) 'As for the emotions', he ends the essay, 'the experimental use of the V-Effekt in the epic theatre's German productions indicated that this way of acting too can stimulate them. though possibly a different class of emotion is involved from those of the orthodox theatre.' (BT, p. 140)

Statements such as these plainly contradict at every turn any idea that 'towards the end of his life' Brecht 'modified' or reversed his earlier rejection of the emotions. Even if these statements from the early 1940s are themselves identified as marking the point of modification or compromise (with what? one still asks, since Brecht's view of the emotions remains thoroughly materialist in these essays) they are prepared for by earlier comments. For example, Brecht's account of Helene Weigel's acting in *The Mother* (from notes published in 1933). Here Brecht writes:

> The Mother has to discuss her revolutionary work with her son under the enemy's nose: she deceives the prison warder by displaying what seems to him the moving, harmless attitude of the average mother. She encourages his own harmless sympathy. So this example of a quite new and active kind of mother-love is herself exploiting her knowledge of the old familiar out-of-date kind. The actress showed that the Mother is quite aware of the humour of the situation . . . (BT, p. 59)

In this account the actress demonstrates a character and an emotion (rather than repressing it) which requires a degree of empathy (this process is also shown), but as far as the spectator is concerned forestalls this so as to encourage instead a critical response, which can set 'a quite new and active kind of mother-love' (a new, politicised passion) against the old. In this light the later statements appear as elaborations, or reiterations, of a style of playing first worked out in practice, and often then — mistakenly, as it turns out — taken for granted.

One other thing these statements suggest, though this too has been a source of confusion, is Brecht's concern to distinguish between emotion in general and in its new positive forms, and empathy. The first was to be demonstrated, historicised, criticised, transformed or encouraged; the second was to be utilised where it was of assistance to this first function, but in the main checked and frustrated because of the way empathy, in Brecht's view, reinforced an organicist aesthetic, a conception of an eternal human nature, and the *status quo*. In his later writings he talks of 'demonstration' and 'empathy', or as he also puts it, 'acting' and 'experience', being contradictorily joined, as 'two mutually hostile processes which fuse in the actor's work'. (BT, pp. 277–8) It is fair to read this as a significant change, since empathy is now included rather than excluded; but what in fact Brecht's description of this contradictory fusion amounts to is the transposition, now to a style of acting, of the dialectical principle of the unity of opposites. As such it is hardly the kind of theoretical reversal Willett and others have in mind.

To discover in the terms of these critics an opposition between emotion and reason, which has the force of dogmatically *excluding* the first rather than of incorporating it, or of joining empathy with criticism in a contradictory unity, one has to go back to the notes to *Mahagonny* and *The Threepenny Opera*. In the first, 'feeling' is tabled against 'reason' as one in a series of distinctions between dramatic and epic theatre (distinctions representing 'certain changes of emphasis', BT, p. 37) while in the second Brecht talks of 'The epic drama, with its materialistic standpoint and its lack of interest in any investment of its spectators' emotions'. (BT, p. 45) Even so, prior to both essays, in 1927, when Brecht conceived of epic theatre as appealing 'less to the feelings than to the spectator's reason', he was still careful to add that, 'At the same time it would be quite wrong to try and deny emotions to this kind of theatre. It would be much the same thing as trying to deny emotion to modern science.' (BT, p. 23)

The change we can identify in Brecht's thinking amounts therefore to a clearer distinction over the years between types and forms of emotion, an appreciation of the dialectical co-existence of empathy (as one of those forms) with demonstration or criticism, and the identification and encouragement of new, productive passions. We can see this change at the same time as related to Brecht's awareness of the fascist manipulation of mass emotion. What it appears Brecht attempted to do, primarily through the art of the theatre, was first to frustrate the narcotic aspect of art which would, as it were, hypnotise both art and its audience into serving a reactionary ideology; then later, in the face of Nazi consolidation and eventual defeat, to oppose and supplant the collective passivity it had induced with new active passions appropriate to a time of social reconstruction. Brecht's political purpose was clear throughout, but took a fuller dialectical shape according to changed historical and political circumstances. The consoling and grotesque mass emotions which he feared could be built on empathetic identification, and which negated the exercise of reasoned, critical thought, would be itself negated (subsumed and overcome) by the discovery of new, collectively inspired, productive emotions. One could talk of a 'qualitative' change to describe this process, but not of a modification, or compromise, or reversal, or mellowing.

From a theoretical and political point of view, the most important 'new emotions' Brecht is concerned with are those connected with amusement and pleasure. In anticipating the 'theoretical compromise' of his entry into the realm of aesthetic entertainment in the *Short Organum*, John Willett refers us to the essay 'Theatre for pleasure or theatre for instruction' (dating from 1935 or 1936) as a contrasting illustration of Brecht's early didacticism. (BT, p. 135) In fact Brecht argues in this essay that the distinction between learning and amusement (as between knowledge and art) is a generally accepted, but not therefore unalterable one; nor one that epic theatre need adopt.

> Generally there is felt to be a very sharp distinction between learning and amusing oneself. The first may be useful, but only the second is pleasant. So we have to defend the epic theatre against the suspicion that it is a highly disagreeable, humourless, indeed strenuous affair.
>
> Well: all that can be said is that the contrast between learning and amusing oneself is not laid down by divine rule; it is not one that has always been and must continue to be. (BT, p. 72)

He talks then of different attitudes towards knowledge and the conditions which foster these, and concludes:

> Thus the pleasure of learning depends on all sorts of things; but none the less there is such a thing as pleasurable learning, cheerful and militant learning.
>
> If there were not such amusement to be had from learning the theatre's whole structure would unfit it for teaching.
>
> Theatre remains theatre even when it is instructive theatre,

> and in so far as it is good theatre it will amuse. (BT, p. 73)

Even earlier, at a time when Brecht's theory and practice might be thought to be if anything more severely didactic, he attacks this distinction, in his notes on *The Mother*, as the product of bourgeois criticism. His remarks stand even now as a reply to Willett, Gray and others:

> One of the chief objections made by bourgeois criticism to non-aristotelian plays like *Die Mutter* is based on an equally bourgeois distinction between the concepts 'entertaining' and 'instructive'. In this view *Die Mutter* is possibly instructive (if only for a small section of the potential audience, the argument goes) but definitely not entertaining (not even for this small section). There is a certain pleasure to be got out of looking more closely at this distinction. Surprising as it may seem, the object is to discredit learning by presenting it as not enjoyable. But in fact of course it is enjoyment that is being discredited by this deliberate suggestion that one learns nothing from it. (BT, p. 60)

In the 'Prologue' to the *Short Organum* Brecht says that he is now prepared to 'treat the theatre as a place of entertainment, as is proper in an aesthetic discussion'. He has in the past, he says, vacated 'the realm of the merely enjoyable' and viewed aesthetics as the 'heirloom of a by now depraved and parasitic class'. (BT, pp. 180, 179) These words have no doubt played their part in encouraging the view that while the early Brecht was excessively didactic, the later Brecht was ready to accommodate himself to bourgeois aesthetics. But this serves only to misrepresent both Brechts. In his earlier statements he was concerned, as we can see, to deny bourgeois categories and to *integrate* artistic pleasure and learning. In the *Appendices to the Short Organum* he returns to this problem in very similar terms.

> It is not just a matter of art presenting what needs to be learned in an enjoyable form. The contradiction between learning and enjoyment must be clearly grasped and its significance understood — in a period when knowledge is acquired in order to be resold for the highest possible price, and even a high price does not prevent further exploitation by those who pay it. Only once productivity has been set free

> can learning be transformed into enjoyment and vice versa. (BT, p. 276)

The difference is that, at this point, Brecht sees how the integration of enjoyment and learning, or the transformation of one into the other, depends on social and economic changes ('only once productivity has been set free'). His part, as the *Short Organum*, the *Appendices* and other writings suggest, is to show and encourage that productivity in and through the aesthetic realm. Added to which it becomes the principal aim of the theatre, in fulfilling this function, to amuse, to give pleasure and so 'win the public over' as Brecht puts it. (BT, p. 200) Obviously this does not imply a capitulation to 'bourgeois criticism'. Brecht is not talking about idle, 'useless' pleasure, but the 'cheerful, militant' pleasure he had described earlier, and which he associates throughout his later writings with the perception that man and the world are changing and changeable. This is not the pleasure in mere flux, the 'all accepting, amoral delight' in change 'for its own sake' which Gray associates with the aesthetic attitude.[22] Indeed Gray's interpretation only perpetuates the conventional divisions Brecht had been determined from an early date to question (the distinction between art and knowledge becomes, of course, in one of its manifestations the view that aesthetics and Marxism are incompatible). In Gray's view 'the nature of the change scarcely seems to matter'.[23] In fact, of course, it is vital, humanly and aesthetically; for in Brecht's politicised aesthetic an understanding of the laws of dialectical materialism and the possibilities of change and freedom this affords, becomes, in itself, a source of pleasure. Thus as Brecht writes in the *Organum*, and in other notes quoted above:

> . . . each step forward, every emancipation from nature that is scored in the field of production and leads to a transformation of society . . . lead us to take pleasure in the possibilities of change in all things. (BT, p. 202)

> Like the transformation of nature, that of society is a liberating act; and it is the joys of liberation which the theatre of a scientific age has got to convey. (BT, p. 196)

> The theatre of the scientific age is in a position to make dialectics into a source of enjoyment. (BT, p. 277)

> A Socialist Realist work of art lays bare the dialectical laws of movement of the social mechanism, whose revelation makes the mastering of man's fate easier. It provokes pleasure in their recognition and observation. (BT, p. 269)

> Epic theatre is a prerequisite for these contributions [made by a 'dialectical theatre'], but it does not of itself imply that productivity and mutability of society from which they derive their main element of pleasure. (BT, p. 282)

The attribution of pleasure to the demonstration of dialectics 'by artistic means', and therefore to the grasping of the possibilities of change and self-determination, becomes the keynote of Brecht's theory from the period of the *Short Organum* and his return to post-war Europe. To see this as some dismissal of his earlier thinking and as a belated acceptance of the conventional notion of artistic entertainment amounts to a serious distortion. Brecht's theory remained purposefully open and provisional, but it acquired here a new coherence, a new centre of gravity, which altered its general tone and the appeal and function attributed to art. Other aspects of his theory — the place of the emotions, the value and treatment accorded past works — had themselves developed in a consistent way; the new emerging from the old, according to changed needs and possibilities, but they too took on a different character under the informing principle of a newly defined, joyous and manifold productivity. In giving his theory this new emphasis Brecht did not so much compromise with bourgeois aesthetics as expropriate and politicise its central tenet. The result was a remarkable and original contribution to the Marxist theory of art, which, when it has not been entrapped by bourgeois categories, has tended to fall into petrified dogma at the very mention of aesthetic pleasure.

I would like to argue this point finally here in the form of a reply to comments on Brecht by Maynard Solomon.[24] Solomon accuses Brecht of ignoring the humanising 'radical aspect' of Aristotelian catharsis, of tending (mistakenly) to equate art with religion in his view of the 'artistic function' and of 'traditional art' as a narcotic. He sees Brecht as taking 'a partial view of the socio-psychological function of art', as warding off 'the aesthetic emotion itself', of being 'one-sided' and 'pessimistic'. (pp. 355–60, 424) He notes all the same, in what is almost a summation of the views we have met in Willett and others, that 'Brecht did not insist that his "epic theatre" was the only form which could create revolutionary art. And he recognised (especially in his later years) that pleasure and entertainment properly defined were a necessary complement to the instructive-didactic aspects of theatre'. (p. 360)

Solomon deploys the arguments of the German Marxist art historian and philosopher Max Raphael in this discussion as an indirect counter to Brecht. (Raphael was born in Schönlanke in 1889, lived and taught in Berlin from 1920 to 1932, and then in 1940 emigrated from France to the USA where he lived until his death in 1952. There is good reason therefore to compare him with Brecht.) At one point in his *The Demands of Art* Raphael refers to Marx's well-known comments on Greek art in his *A Contribution to the Critique of Political Economy*. Marx asks here why Greek art and epos 'still constitute with us a source of aesthetic enjoyment and in certain respects prevail as the standard and model beyond attainment'. In thus raising the question of the transcendent but historically delimited character of art, Marx formulates, says Raphael, 'the main, but still unsolved problem of his own — and every — theory of art'. (p. 451) Marx's answer to this problem, that Greek art exerts 'an eternal charm as an age that will never return', Raphael dismisses as 'petty-bourgeois', and as having 'nothing whatever to do either with historical materialism or with Communism as a guide for changing the world.' (ibid.) The reason Marx could not rise above this answer, he adds, was because historical materialism was the product of a transitional epoch and a specific, capitalist, economic order:

> we find that historical materialism itself is only an ideological superstructure of a specific economic order — the capitalistic order in which all productive forces are concentrated in the economic sector. A transitional epoch always implies uncertainty: Marx's struggle to understand his own epoch testifies to this. In such a period two attitudes are possible. One is to take advantage of the emergent forces of the new order with a view to undermining it, to affirm it in order to drive it beyond itself: this is the active, militant, revolutionary attitude. The other clings to the past, is retrospective and romantic, bewails or acknowledges the decline, asserts that the will to live is gone — in short, it is the passive attitude. Where economic, social, and political questions were at stake Marx took the first attitude; in questions of art he took neither. He reflected the actual changes of his time, which is to say that he made economics the foundations of thought which it had become in fact. He did not lose sight of the further

> problem, but as he could not see the solution, he left it unsolved. Had he been able to show that an active attitude toward art also exists, he would have brought the understanding of art up to the level of his revolutionary position. (p. 452)

Brecht, as we have seen, did take this active, militant, attitude towards art. 'Dialectics', said Marx, 'is essentially critical and revolutionary', and Brecht, having defined artistic appreciation as 'critical, contradictory, detached,' goes on:

> To introduce this critical attitude into art, the negative element which it doubtless includes must be shown from its positive side: this criticism of the world is active, practical, positive. Criticizing the course of a river means improving it, correcting it. Criticism of society is ultimately revolution; there you have criticism taken to its logical conclusion and playing an active part. A critical attitude of this type is an operative factor of productivity; it is deeply enjoyable as such, and if we commonly use the term 'arts' for enterprises that improve people's lives why should art proper remain aloof from arts of this sort? (BT, p. 146–7)

Dialectics, the critical attitude, social progress, productivity and aesthetic pleasure are linked for Brecht; in the present, as a future prospect, and as a perspective upon the past and therefore upon past art. He addresses this last item in the *Short Organum*, but more directly in an earlier passage in 'A short description of a new technique of acting', where it is possible he had Marx's comments on Greek art also in mind. Referring to Rimbaud's 'Bateau ivre' and Kipling's 'Ballad of east and west' as expressions at one level of different forms of colonialism, Brecht comments:

> It is less easy to explain the effect that such poems have on ourselves, as Marx already noticed. Apparently emotions accompanying social progress will long survive in the human mind as emotions linked with interests, and in the case of works of art will do so more strongly than might have been expected, given that in the meantime contrary interests will have made themselves felt. Every step forward means the end of the previous step forward, because that is where it starts and goes on from. At the same time it makes use of this previous step, which in a sense survives in men's consciousness

> as a step forward, just as it survives in its effects in real life . . . . Whenever the works of art handed down to us allow us to share the emotions of other men, of men of a bygone period, different social classes, etc., we have to conclude that we are partaking in interests which really were universally human. These men now dead represented the interests of classes that gave a lead to progress. (BT, p. 146)

Section 36 of the *Short Organum*, and a later appendix, confirm Brecht's view of the enduring, 'transcendent', but now specifically pleasurable, dimension of art as an expression not of the 'universally human', which would pull past and present together *via* the 'timeless' work of art, or at best set them in an evolutionary continuum, but as a factor of art's 'use value'. Art transcends time, that is to say, and continues to give pleasure and value so long as it remains appropriate and relevant, so long as it is 'timely' rather than 'timeless'. And this depends on a view of history to which the estrangement accruing from the *Verfremdungseffekt* is essential:

> The field has to be defined in historically relative terms. In other words we must drop our habit of taking the different social structures of past periods, then stripping them of everything that makes them different; so that they all look more or less like our own, which then acquires from this process a certain air of having been there all along, in other words of permanence pure and simple. Instead we must leave them their distinguishing marks and keep their impermanence always before our eyes, so that our period can be seen to be impermanent too. (BT, p. 190)
>
> Our enjoyment of old plays becomes greater, the more we can give ourselves up to the new kind of pleasures better suited to our time. To that end we need to develop the historical sense (needed also for the appreciation of new plays) into a real sensual delight. When our theatres perform plays of other periods they like to annihilate distance, fill in the gap, gloss over the differences. But what comes then of our delight in comparisons, in distance, in dissimilarity — which is at the same time a delight in what is close and proper to ourselves? (BT, p. 276)

The production of *Antigone* (appropriately a Greek classic), would seem to have borne out what Brecht is saying here, at least in intention. There was no question, he said, of using the old play as a 'pretext' for ''conjuring up the spirit of antiquity'' ', but nor was its apparent topicality, the analogy between the resister in the play and the German resistance figures, to provide the main subject of the new production. Only the person who realises this, writes Brecht,

> will be able to summon the measure of strangeness needed if the really remarkable element in this Antigone play — the role of force in the collapse of the head of state — is to be observed with profit . . . This possibility of objectively presenting a major state operation was due precisely to the fact (fatal in another respect) that the old play was historically so remote as to tempt nobody to identify himself with its principal figure. (BT, p. 210)

It is perhaps no accident that *Antigone* marked the first use also of the 'Model books' — 'by definition incomplete' and the expression of 'a collective creative process' in which the original production existed with subsequent versions in 'a continuum of a dialectical sort'. (BT, p. 211, 210)

Brecht's answers to the problem of 'transcendent' artistic value and pleasure bear comparison with two solutions indicated by Solomon. First, Solomon points to a moment in the *Grundrisse* where Marx returns to the problems raised in relation to Greek art, and provides on this occasion a materialist answer. Marx proposes that whereas in the ancient world man appears as the aim of production, under capitalism 'production is the aim of man and wealth the aim of production'. With progress therefore and the development of capitalist forces of production human productivity has been diminished; consequently, as Solomon reports, the 'childlike world of the ancients appears to be superior'. (p. 423) Brecht does not refer to past ages as a 'childlike world', or to past art as an ideal, but there is some affinity, surely, between Marx's view and his own that the contradiction between learning and enjoyment (as of science and art, and the productive forces and a productive aesthetic) is a characteristic of bourgeois society and waits for its resolution upon the transforming moment when 'productivity has been set free'. The reproduction of 'progressive' if not 'superior', past works helps, Brecht is saying, to realise this goal.

The second solution Solomon finds in Raphael's own thinking.

He glosses this as the belief that 'The art of the ancient Greeks . . . might be seen as an as-yet-unresolved stage in the liberation of humanity, stemming from a specific organisation of social relations, awaiting release by renewed contact with a revolutionary audience.' (p. 424) Brecht's sense of history and of relations between the past and present is more dynamic, active and critical than a phrase such as 'awaiting release' allows. Also the idea of 'renewed contact' implies, in Brecht's case, both a respect for a classic work's 'original freshness', and the need to renovate or 'refunction' it. Raphael's position is reminiscent nevertheless of Brecht's criterion for socialist realism quoted earlier:

> The Socialist Realist performance of old classical works is based on the view that mankind has preserved those works which gave artistic expression to advances towards a continually stronger, bolder and more delicate humanity. Such performance accordingly emphasises those works' progressive ideas. (BT, p. 269)

Perhaps this is no more a 'final' solution to the question of artistic transcendence than the remarks of Marx or Raphael. It is a significant contribution to a Marxist understanding of this problem none the less, not least because of the combined aesthetic and political *pleasure* with which Brecht invests the dialectical process of artistic appropriation in the advance towards a new humanity.

Notes

1. Klaus Völker, *Brecht. A Biography* (Marion Boyars, London and Boston, 1979), p. 263.
2. Quoted in Frederic Ewen, *Bertolt Brecht. His Life, His Art, and His Times* (Citadel Press, New York, 1969) pp. 407–8.
3. Brecht, *Flüchtlingsgespräche* in *Gesammelte Werke*, 14 (Suhrkamp, Frankfurt am Main, 1975) p. 1462.
4. Quoted in John Willett, *Brecht in Context* (Methuen, London and New York, 1984), p. 185.
5. Ibid., p. 179.
6. Ibid., p. 182
7. Ibid., p. 193. The phrase derives from an entry in Brecht's *Arbeitsjournal*, in which he concludes that the logical position for Marxists outside the Soviet Union 'is roughly that adopted by Marx towards German social democracy. Critical, but in favour', *Arbeitsjournal*, vol. 1, 1938–43, Werner

Hecht (ed.) (Suhrkamp, Frankfurt am Main, 1973), p. 36. Willett translates the relevant passage in *Brecht in Context*, p. 189.

8. Brecht, quoted and paraphrased in Ewen, *Bertolt Brecht*, p. 392.

9. Cf. in addition to the *Short Organum* and associated pieces, the references in the *Antigonemodell* and in *Theaterarbeit* in *Brecht on Theatre*, pp. 211–12, 225, 240.

10. In a late note, chiefly attacking the 'cult of personality', Brecht wrote,

> Eine der schlimmen Folgen des Stalinismus ist die Verkümmerung der Dialektik. Ohne Kenntnis der Dialektik sind solche Übergänge wie die von Stalin als Motor zu Stalin als Bremse nicht verstehbar. Auch nicht die Negierung der Partei durch den Apparat. Auch nicht die Verwandlung von Meinungskämpfen in Machtkämpfe. Noch das Mittel der Idealisierung und Legendisierung einer führenden Person zur Gewinnung der großen rückständigen Massen in eine Ursache der Distanzierung und Lahmlegung dieser Massen. (One of the serious consequences of Stalinism is the atrophy of the dialectic. Without knowledge of the dialectic transitions such as that of Stalin as driving force to Stalin as brake are unintelligible. No more is the negation of the party by its apparatus. Nor the transformation of conflicts of opinion into power struggles. Nor the way in which the idealisation and making into a legend of a leading figure so as to win over the large backward masses [turned into] a cause of these masses being distanced and paralysed.)

Gesammelte Werke, 20, p. 326.

11. Martin Esslin, *Brecht, A Choice of Evils* (Eyre Methuen, London, 1959, revised 1980), pp. 110–11.

12. Ibid., pp. 116–17.

13. Ibid., pp. 231, 232.

14. Ronald Gray, *Brecht. The Dramatist* (Cambridge University Press, 1976), p. 85.

15. Ibid., pp. 86–8.

16. Quoted Esslin, *Brecht*, pp. 167, 168.

17. For a discussion of this episode, see Esslin, ibid., pp. 159–67.

18. Cf. Brecht's comments in 'On rhymeless verse with irregular rhythms', *Poems, pp. 464–5; his 'Notizen über Shakespeare' in Gesammelte Werke*, 15, pp. 332–6; and the discussion in Ewen, *Bertolt Brecht*, p. 162.

19. Cf. Willett on Brecht's response to criticism of *The Private Tutor* as 'negative'. *Brecht on Theatre*, p. 230, and also Esslin, *Brecht*, p. 166. Perhaps the most revealing example of Brecht's relation to official criticism arose over *The Trial of Lucullus*, a revival of a radio play of 1939. The opera was changed in response to official pressure but printed in *Versuche 11* in its original form with the revisions included as an appendix, and also performed, again in its unrevised form, in Western Germany with Brecht's permission. See Esslin's account, *Brecht*, p. 164.

20. Quoted Esslin, *Brecht*, p. 166.

21. Gray, *Brecht. The Dramatist*, p. 72.

22. Ibid., pp. 83, 87.

23. Ibid., p. 87.

24. Maynard Solomon, (ed.), *Marxism and Art. Essays Classic and Contemporary* (Harvester Press, Brighton, Sussex, 1979). In the following discussion page references are given in the text.

9

A Choice of Critics

The effect of the conventional critical response to Brecht's theory is to reconcile it with bourgeois aesthetics (the language of 'modification', 'mellowing', 'balance'; of emotion and entertainment 'complementing' reason or didacticism, is of course very revealing in this respect). Brecht is compromised with an aesthetics of compromise whose roots stretch deep into romanticism and liberal humanism. Instead of conflict, contradictions and impermanence, there is harmony, consistency, completion and organic wholeness. Instead of dialectics there is the discovery of a personal evolution from youthful excess to even-handed maturity.

This view, essentially that Brecht learned his lesson and relaxed the stringent principles of his youth, has ramifications naturally beyond the sphere of aesthetic theory. Given the artistic and ideological issues involved it could not be otherwise. These surface particularly in the views critics have taken of Brecht's dramatic development, and in their response to his political beliefs. Alongside the broad agreements which emerge here there are some genuine differences and changes, or inconsistencies — critics as it turns out being no more 'all of a piece' than creative writers — but also some unexpected alliances. For example, what might be termed the 'embourgeoisement' of Brecht's aesthetic theory, consorts at one level with an apparently quite opposite view that far from 'mellowing', Brecht sold his soul to communism and joined in Stalinist hagiography to the eternal detriment of his art.

The notable example of this second interpretation is Hannah Arendt's 'profile' of Brecht in the *New Yorker* of 1966, reprinted in *Men In Dark Times* (1970).[1] Arendt bases her opinion on Brecht's decision to return to and then settle in East rather than West Berlin, his acceptance of a state subsidy and official positions, his written commitment to the Ulbricht government, but above all on his apparent public praise of Stalin. Some of these points it will be best to take up later, in the context of Brecht's position in East Berlin. The short answer to Arendt's argument, however, is that Brecht preferred an imperfect socialist system to Western capitalism. This is the burden of his response to Stalin, as documented by Völker, and by both Esslin and Willett.[2] Brecht's remarks on Stalin were restricted, Willett argues in a direct reply to Arendt, to three references: one in the *Herrnberg Report* (where Mao and Stalin express admiration of the new generation), a second in the poem 'The cultivation of millet' where Stalin is described as the 'useful one', and thirdly a non-committal note on the event of Stalin's death. There are then a series of more indirect references in the posthumously published prose work *Me-Ti*, and in the 'Stalin poems' previously mentioned.

The note on Stalin's death speaks of the loss which must have been felt by 'The oppressed of all five continents, those who have already freed themselves, and all those who fight for world peace' for whom Stalin was 'the embodiment of their hopes'. It ends 'But the spiritual ['geistigen'] and material weapons he made exist, and so does the doctrine to make new ones.'[3] This is a decidedly cool response, amounting as Völker says to no more than a 'factual description' of people's feelings.[4] In *Me-Ti* Stalin is 'Ni-en' (ie 'nein' = 'no') and is cast as a despot (perhaps in contrast with the 'little man', such as Schweik or Galy Gay, 'who cannot say no'). Ni-en built up the 'great machinery' (i.e. heavy industry) but degraded the 'great method' (i.e. Marxism) and failed wholly to implement the 'great order' (i.e. socialism). This forms the basis of Brecht's verdict on Stalin's 'usefulness', but even this description, as Willett says, 'seems double or triple-edged':

> Me-Ti [i.e. Brecht] suggested that Ni-en should always be called the Great, but the Useful one. But the time was not yet ripe for this type of praise. Useful people had been for too long without any reputation, so that saying a man was useful no longer inspired confidence in his ability to lead. Leaders had always been identified by their knowledge of how to be useful to themselves.[5]

Arendt had felt that Brecht's 'praise' of Stalin as the 'useful one' 'refers to the well-known old Communist theory that Stalin's crimes were necessary and useful for the development of socialism in

Russia as well as by implication, the world revolution.'[6] Willett's reply is that Brecht's 'paradoxical half-camouflaged musings . . . add up to nothing so straightforward as any "well-known old Communist theory", let alone a fulsome tribute to Stalin.'[7] On Russian communism, as Willett appreciates, Brecht's attitude, in *Me-Ti*, as elsewhere, was ambiguous; this 'new system' was 'the most advanced in the history of the world' but 'is being forced into existence . . . there is force everywhere and no real popular rule . . . many basic elements of *die Grosse Ordnung* still have to be realised and developed.'[8]

Willett's conclusion is that Brecht's attitude towards Soviet communism was 'Critical, but *for* it'; and that Brecht had himself indicated as much in an entry in the *Arbeitsjournal* in 1939; 'the logical position for Marxists outside', wrote Brecht, 'is roughly that adopted by Marx towards German social-democracy; critical, but in favour.'[9] If we accept this description of Brecht's attitude towards Stalinist Russia, however, it does not resolve the question of his response to *Stalinism* in *its* relation to Marxist-Leninism, or necessarily describe his position in post-war East Germany; since here Brecht was a Marxist *inside*, rather than 'outside' the regime.

These questions will run through my own subsequent discussion. In the meantime it is easy to agree with Völker and Esslin and Willett. Together they expose Arendt's position as uninformed and untenable. Yet for all their differences there are some revealing similarities here too. Firstly there is the commonly held belief, of which Esslin, Willett and Arendt are only some of the most prominent examples, that Brecht's work and/or politics can be seen, once again, as a matter of compromise. Either he compromised with bourgeois aesthetics as we have seen (the implication being that this is to his credit), or he compromised, or was in danger of compromising himself and his art in submitting to communism. Arendt talks thus of Brecht's 'sin' in praising Stalin and of his poetic faculty as having 'dried up' in East Berlin.[10] In the same vein Esslin, for all the contrary evidence he supplies on Brecht's attitude to Stalin, conceives of the political decisions confronting Brecht as a 'choice of evils', and also writes of his late sterility. In fact Esslin, unlike Völker and Willett, sees Brecht as having compromised in both respects, in the realms of art *and* politics. It thus becomes the critic's task to damn communism and Marxism, as in one breath; and so explain Brecht's compliance and rescue his art.[11] Accordingly, Esslin recovers the instinctual artist from beneath the hard surface 'of conscious Marxist dogma'. One could say that Arendt's remarks reveal something of the same self-righteous and salvationist attitude, and her sinful and ruined poet is in the end the same Brecht whom Esslin offers to regenerate and make whole. Both critics are anti-communist (and anti-Marxist), and aside from this fundamental difference from Brecht himself, they also assume, as he did not, that art and communism are incompatible. Both deplore this particular form of the meeting of art and politics, and therefore strive to separate them.

There is another judgement closely related to the above which critics of different persuasions share, though again not with Brecht. It appears in the very common contrast between what is seen as the Marxist schematism of the early *Lehrstücke* and the mature humanism of the plays principally of Brecht's middle period. The plays generally awarded the highest esteem are *Galileo, Mother Courage, The Good Person of Szechwan* and the slightly later *Caucasian Chalk Circle.* Willett as we have seen suggests a coincidence between the 'theoretical compromise' of the *Short Organum* and 'the period of his greatest plays' (*Galileo, Mother Courage* and *The Good Person of Szechwan*). Esslin describes *Galileo* as 'Brecht's masterpiece' and *The Caucasian Chalk Circle* as 'one of Brecht's greatest plays'; together they are 'Brecht's two most mature works'.[12] Ronald Gray, as ever, provides a categorical version of this in itself humanist judgement. Quoting Brecht's note on the play *The Mother* where Brecht had written that the Aristotelian drama creates a temporary 'collective entity' of the audience while the non-Aristotelian drama divides it, Gray comments 'Brecht could hardly have gone further than that in opposing common humanity to the standpoint of the Communist Party.'[13] Gray fails therefore to appreciate that Brecht's remarks are part of his argument against empathy and illusionism, and that Brecht is opposing, precisely, the forms and effects of bourgeois humanism in the theatre to a Marxist class analysis. For Gray, as for Esslin, there is little to no distinction between Marxism and communism and the Communist Party. Gray comes therefore to read the later plays in predictable fashion. Of *Galileo, Mother Courage, The Good Person of Szechwan, Herr Puntila* and *The Caucasian Chalk Circle*, he says,

> It is possible, though not logically necessary, to read out of them the corollary that only Communism can cure the ills they represent. Their general sphere of interest and concern is not, however, directly political, but rather one of general humanity . . . there is an in many ways humane theatre, tolerant,

> offering comprehension rather than persuasion . . . It is the 'human comedy' that Brecht seems most of all bent on showing in these works, and the Communist implications are at most a side-issue. (p. 109)

'All that Brecht gives' says Gray of *Mother Courage*, — as in all the maturer plays — is the intolerable awareness of how things are, not a Marxist or any other solution.' (p. 136)

Of other critics Frederic Ewen also characterises Brecht's *Lehrstücke* as 'abstract' and 'rigid'.[14] Echoing the position discussed previously, he writes of the earlier period, 'At this time Brecht did divorce feeling and reason mechanically, just as he tended to separate "pleasure" and "instruction" in his discussion of the Lehrstück. Both positions he was in time to modify radically.' (p. 254) 'It was in exile', Ewen adds later, 'that his most mature and his greatest works came to fruition', *Galileo* representing 'the peak of Brecht's achievement.' (pp. 294, 345) Commenting on the change in the works of the late thirties and forties, Ewen writes that, 'A certain aloof, doctrinaire quality that ran like a leitmotif through his earlier works even such a one as *Mother*, is now modified by a profound sympathy . . . the human and humane element becomes dominant.' (p. 325) The description Ewen gives to this new attitude is 'Marxist humanism' which he at the same time associates with both the several plays ('among the best he was ever to produce') from *Mother Courage* to *The Caucasian Chalk Circle* and the theoretical 'clarification of his dramatic ideas, culminating in the *Brief Organon*.' (pp. 419, 420)

Ewen substitutes 'Marxist' for 'liberal' humanism as a description of Brecht's 'mature' work and thinking, but much else, in the scheme allotted to Brecht's career, and in Ewen's terms of praise and opprobrium remains the same. A more explicitly Marxist critic such as Darko Suvin who sees Brecht as moving towards a 'dialectical' method and vision, also reinforces the accepted view of Brecht's development. Thus Brecht passed from a first, 'anarchist phase . . . marked by a tendency towards absolute *non-consenting* or a self-indulgent nihilism' through a second 'rationalist phase — from *Man is Man* to *The Mother* . . . marked by a tendency towards *absolute consenting* or a self-indulgent didacticism' to a third phase — 'The final, mature vision of the sequence from *The Good Woman of Szechwan* to *Life of Galileo*'. In spite of Suvin's recognition of 'the open-ended' character of Brecht's 'mature aesthetic' he sees the final stage as one of fusion (of 'plebeian anarchy', the view from below, with 'lay clericism' or rationalism, the view from above); Brecht here reaching a 'dynamic and utopian convergence point'.[15]

The critical map of Brecht's development therefore follows very similar outlines and the urge to see it as moving towards a point of mature synthesis (characteristically of emotion with reason — Suvin's analysis being only a more sophisticated version of this) proves irresistible.[16] It is on these grounds, obviously, that Brecht is deemed worthy of critical acclaim. The great artist 'matures' to meet the definition of the great artist as great humanist, reaffirming in himself (*sic*) the bourgeois concept of the unified individual rather than, for example, Marx's alternative perception of 'associated humanity'.[17]

A rare exception to the discovery of this scheme and accompanying scheme of values in Brecht's career is offered by David Roberts who argues that,

> The only continuity which marks Brecht's theatre from its very beginnings is the continuity of experiment. There is no 'organic' logic of development from *A Man's a Man* to *The Caucasian Chalk Circle*. In what sense can we speak of a progression of forms, in what way are the epic techniques of *The Chalk Circle* more 'advanced', more 'progressive' than those in *The Threepenny Opera*?[18]

Roberts therefore shifts discussion away from the problems of 'the alleged incompatibility of political commitment and artistic expression' which governs so much commentary on Brecht, to the dilemma, as he sees it, of a contradictory relationship between Brecht's modernist formal experiment and his didactic purpose, between the allegorical and distancing method of his political parables in the theatre and his announced aim to 'master' contemporary reality.

Roberts' argument raises questions in its own right, while, exception that it is, also proving the rule. There is a further factor, however, which ought to give us pause and which at one point applies also to Roberts' discussion. This is that the dominant view of Brecht's career, as well as the different problems this is seen to entail, corresponds less to Brecht's own opinions than to Georg Lukács's opinions on Brecht. Thus Lukács, like so many critics, sees a 'greater depth, range and intensity' in the period of Brecht's exile; 'a partial return to despised Aristotelian aesthetics' in *Senora*

Carrar and *Galileo*, and a concern with 'problems of humanity' in 'multi-dimensional' characters who are 'living human beings' in *Mother Courage, The Caucasian Chalk Circle* and *The Good Person of Szechwan*. The 'over-simplified scheme' of a play such as *The Measures Taken* gives way 'to a complex dialectic of good and evil . . . The mature Brecht, by overcoming his earlier one-sided theories, had evolved into the greatest realistic playwright of his age.'[19] The Marxist champion of 'critical realism' (whose theories Brecht associated with an official Soviet, one might almost say Stalinist, aesthetic) joins forces with an assortment of Marxist and bourgeois humanist critics generally opposed to Stalinism, who are agreed in setting the mature 'humanist' Brecht against Brecht the younger, dogmatic Marxist.

The affiliations here become quite bewildering, but the example of Lukács ought to make it quite clear that this set of consensual judgements on Brecht — or, in the first place, the aesthetic and ideological assumptions they derive from — differ profoundly from Brecht's own. This is true also in an important respect of David Roberts, whose view of the gulf between Brecht's epic 'realism' and contemporary reality is predicated on a very Lukácsian formulation of that theatre's project as 'the presentation of the totality of the social field of forces'.[20]

We have to say in response to the bulk of criticism in English that Brecht did not accept the concepts of an 'eternal human nature' or of a coherent ego, or coherent, fused, work of art; any more, one suspects, than he subscribed to the idea of a progressively cohering individual career, though these concepts are deployed in an unexamined and honorific way in much of the commentary upon him. No more did Brecht aim to create 'living human beings' in the manner of an illusionist realism, nor, in answer to Roberts, conceive of the ideological struggle in which his own formal experiment was involved as separated from 'the *real contradictions* of the time'.[21]

As to the question of the 'mature' plays and judgements of artistic quality, Brecht's own opinion was that *Frau Carrar* and *Galileo* were 'opportunist' and less than epic. 'Technically', he said, '*Galileo* is a big step backward'.[22] Both plays were written in Denmark where, as Völker reports, Brecht was faced with suspicion, a scandal over the performance of *Round Heads and Pointed Heads* and *The Seven Deadly Sins*, and a general reluctance to produce his work. The choice before him, as he put it, was to 'choose either a reactionary content or a reactionary form', adding that 'both together would be too much of a good thing'.[23] In the event he chose in these two works a 'reactionary' Aristotelian form; 'compromising' his principles as a matter of expediency; though he judged the result still as producing less than the epic theatre he desired. Brecht's later opinion that *Herr Puntila* (still within the range of his 'mature' works for Ewen) was 'only epic to the extent this can be accepted (and offered) today',[24] was very much in the same vein.

Nor is there much sign of Brecht's agreeing with the critical view, official communist or bourgeois, on *Mother Courage*. The communist playwright, Frederich Wolf, for example, put it to Brecht in an interview of 1949, firstly, that the audience's reactions 'showed the story's points of maximum emotion to be the highlights of the performance (dumb Kattrin's signal on the drum, and the whole of that scene; the death of the eldest son, the mother's scene where she curses the war, etc.)', and secondly, that the play 'would have been even *more* effective if at the end the mother had given her curse on the war some visible expression in the action (as Kattrin did) and drawn the logical conclusions from her change of mind.' (BT, pp. 228–9) Brecht's answer on this occasion, as on others, was that Mother Courage was not a positive character, that she 'has learnt nothing from the disasters that befall her' but that even so 'at least the audience can . . . learn something by observing her.' (BT, p. 229)[25] On the emotional aspect of the play Brecht was dismayed by the first Zurich production of 1941 which 'gave the bourgeois press occasion to talk about a Niobe-tragedy and about the moving endurance of the female animal'.[26] He accordingly made some revisions for the play's performance later in Berlin. The same public and critical reaction, however, apparently persisted to the extent that Brecht, writing in the *Theaterarbeit* in 1952, conceded that 'Members of the audience may identify themselves with dumb Kattrin in this scene; they may get into her skin by empathy and enjoy feeling that they themselves have the same latent strength. But they will not have experienced empathy throughout the whole play . . .' (BT, p. 221) Another note reiterates Brecht's familiar position:

> In order that the play's realistic attitude may be of advantage to the audience — so that the audience, in fact, may learn something — our theatres must establish a way of acting which does not aim at the audience's identification with the main character (the heroine). (BT, p. 221)

As far as possible, then, Brecht resisted both the demands of conventional socialist realism and the 'deeply ingrained habit' as he called it, which induced petty bourgeois audiences and critics to seek emotional identification with leading characters. So deeply ingrained and unexamined is this habit in fact that critics contrive to argue that Brecht's practice, in his 'best work', simply belies his intentions. This is Esslin's argument on *Mother Courage* and is perfectly in keeping with his discovery of a divided Brecht in whom the true poet (and instinctive humanist) triumphs over the theorising Marxist. Frederic Ewen, similarly, aware of Brecht's reservations on *Galileo*, feels that it is 'one of those fortunate misfortunes' that the play contradicted Brecht's epic theory.[27] Lukács' critical strategy is essentially the same. In each case Brecht is appropriated, made familiar one might say, by a critical discourse at odds with his own.

I do not wish to suggest by this that Brecht has himself sole authority over the meaning of his texts, or that there is no contradiction between his theory and practice. Nor that I or any other critic with some supposed direct line to Brecht can discount all other readings as misreadings. Critics will obviously read Brecht according to announced or unannounced aesthetic and ideological preferences. In which case we should realise that it is these principles and beliefs, though they usually operate at the silent depths of criticism, which are most often at issue. In studies of Brecht, however, where there are the evident discrepancies of the kind I have shown between the aesthetic and broadly political attitudes of many critics and Brecht himself, more is involved than polite fisticuffs between rival interpretations or even critical ideologies. The contradictions, conflicts and developments many critics perceive tend more than usually to be of their own self-reflective ideological making. Meanings and values are assigned, with an equally revealing complacency or contrivance and perversity, which contradict not only other emphases and critical perspectives, but Brecht's own announced ideas, intentions or understanding of his work and situation. There is some cause therefore for trying to look at these afresh.

My own first concern is with the Marxist provenance of Brecht's ideas and with how developments in his thinking relate to his changing situation as a Marxist artist. I want, in pursuing these questions, and in response to the conventional scheme given to Brecht's career, to examine two plays at either end of his years as a conscious Marxist playwright: firstly the *Lehrstück, The Measures Taken* ('an important play', says Hannah Arendt, for her argument that 'a poet's real sins are avenged by the gods of poetry'[28]), and, then, finally, following a discussion in the next section of Brecht's situation in post-war Berlin, the late play, *Days of the Commune.*

Notes

1. Hannah Arendt, *Men in Dark Times* (Jonathan Cape, London, 1970), pp. 207–49.

2. Klaus Völker, *Brecht. A Biography* (Marion Boyars, London and Boston, 1979) pp. 3563–4; Martin Esslin, *Brecht. A Choice of Evils* (Eyre Methuen, London, 1959, revised 1980), pp. 156–7, also two essays from *Encounter* from 1966 and 1977, collected in Martin Esslin, *Mediations* (Sphere Books, London, 1983). Esslin feels that Völker's 'new left puritanism' induces him to 'play . . . down' the facts of Stalin and Stalinism, 'even at the cost of distorting Brecht's reaction to them.' pp. 37–8, cf. also pp. 44, 55–60. John Willett's reply to Hannah Arendt appears in *Brecht in Context* (Methuen, London and New York, 984), pp. 211–18, cf. also pp. 178–211. On this theme, see also the useful information and discussion in Helmut Dahmer, 'Bertolt Brecht and Stalinism', *Telos*, 22 (Winter 1974–5), pp. 96–105.

3. *Gesammelte Werke* (Suhrkamp, Frankfurt am Main, 1967), 20, p. 325, trans. Esslin, *Brecht*, p. 168.

4. Völker, *Brecht* p. 354.

5. *Gesammelte Werke*, 12, p. 467; trans. Willett, *Brecht in Context*, p. 215. Esslin offers useful documentation from *Me-Ti* of the 'twists and turns' in Brecht's attitudes towards Stalinism in *Mediations*, pp. 55–60.

6. In a written reply to Willett, quoted, *Brecht in Context*, p. 213.

7. Ibid., p. 215.

8. *Gesammelte Werke*, 12, p. 535; quoted Willett, ibid., p. 192.

9. *Arbeitsjournal*, Vol. I, 1938–43, Werner Hecht (ed.) (Suhrkamp, Frankfurt am Main, 1973), p. 36. Quoted Willett, *Brecht in Context*, p. 189, and cf. p. 193.

10. Arendt, *Men in Dark Times*, pp. 242, 246, 247.

11. From Esslin's positon there seems, in fact, to be not only little difference between political theories in the Marxist tradition, or between these and political systems (whether Bolshevik or State Socialist, for example), but a fundamental similarity between communism whatever its forms, and fascism. A striking example appears in his comment on a note of Brecht's of July 1943 in which Brecht suggests how the German petty bourgeoisie in its creation of 'state capitalism' borrows institutions and ideology from Russian 'state socialism'. Brecht comments, 'In fascism, socialism sees its distorted mirror-image, with none of its virtues, but all its vices.' Esslin introduces this statement with a description of Brecht's 'keen political grasp' of 'the close similarities between totalitarian systems' (when Brecht is pointing to similarities and differences), and as proof that he 'saw the *Leninist* origins of Hitlerism' (my italics), *Mediations*, pp. 44–5.

12. Esslin, *Brecht*, pp. 273, 279, 233.

13. Gray, *Brecht. The Dramatist*, (Cambridge University Press, 1976) p. 85. In the following paragraph page references are given in the text.

14. Frederic Ewen, *Bertolt Brecht. His Life, His Art, and His Times* (Citadel Press, New York, 1969), pp. 243–4. In the following paragraph page references are given in the text.

15. Darko Suvin, *To Brecht and Beyond. Soundings in Modern Dramaturgy* (Harvester Press, Brighton, Sussex, 1984). pp. 125–9. Cf. also Suvin's later self-critical comment on this schema, ibid., p. 268.

16. The hegemonic influence of this 'aesthetic' judgement is indicated by the passing comments of two critics who are otherwise very judicious in their discussion of Brecht's theoretical and political ideas. T.W.H. Metscher, for example, while affirming the importance of Brecht's theoretical and political writings between 1926 and 1939, writes, parenthetically, that this later date and the composition of *Galileo*, 'marks the beginning of the period of his most accomplished dramatic activity', 'Brecht and Marxist dialectics', *Oxford German Studies*, 6 (1971–2), p. 135. In a similar way, Eugen Lunn writes that, 'it may be that Brecht was able to produce his finest work free from official discipline in the late 1930s and early 1940s, and from the sorry spectacle of an actually functioning Stalinist society, an independence which he lost in adopting East Germany in 1948.' I am not suggesting that we need demur from this view of Stalinism, but that judgements on Brecht's 'independence' or loss of it (Lunn footnotes Hannah Arendt's essay at this point), do not synchronise automatically either with this view or with judgements on the artistic quality of his work. In this case, the 'finest work' Lunn is thinking of is described, routinely I believe, as 'those plays and poems whose connection with politics was indirect (*Galileo, The Caucasian Chalk Circle*, etc.)', *Marxism and Modernism. Lukács, Brecht, Benjamin, Adorno* (University of California Press, 1982; Verso, London, 1985), pp. 135–6.

17. Marx, 'Theses on Feuerbach', *On Dialectical Materialism* (Progress Publishers, Moscow, and Lawrence and Wishart, London, 1977), p. 31.

18. David Roberts, 'Brecht, epic form and realism: a reconsideration', *Thesis Eleven*, 5/6 (Philip Institute of Sociology, Victoria, Australia, 1982), pp. 42–3.

19. George Lukács, *The Meaning of Contemporary Realism* (Merlin Press, London, 1962), pp. 88, 89.

20. Roberts, 'Brecht, epic form and realism', p. 45.

21. Roberts writes, 'For Brecht did not show the contemporary world in his work but its ideological reflection in the distorting light of tradition', and of how the plays 'carefully keep their distance from the *real contradictions* of the time.' (ibid., pp. 52, 55) Thus while Roberts recognises that 'Brecht's sphere of investigation is not the material infrastructure but the ideological superstructure' (ibid., p. 51), he persists in a reflectionist view of art and ideology, and a separated rather than materialist view of 'reality' which are of his own rather than of Brecht's making.

22. Quoted Völker, *Brecht*, p. 243.

23. Quoted ibid., p. 226.

24. Quoted ibid., p. 336.

25. Cf. also *Brecht on Theatre*, p. 221, and Esslin, *Brecht*, pp. 211–13. Esslin sees Brecht's arguments, perversely, as 'nothing but the rational-

isations of instinctive responses'; 'his poetic instinct' would not allow him to change the character of Mother Courage, which audiences, says Esslin, have continued to find moving, despite Brecht's intentions.

26. Quoted Esslin, *Brecht*, p. 212.
27. Ewen, *Bertolt Brecht*, p. 345.
28. Arendt, *Men in Dark Times*, p. 242.

10

Lenin and/or Stalin: 'The Measures Mistaken'

The Measures Taken has been regularly discussed as a prominent example, even as the culmination, of the early phase of Brecht's 'rigid' and 'indulgent' didacticism. Since at the same time it represents the kind of theatre Brecht is deemed to have rejected, or in some way modified, it is an important reference for any assessment of subsequent changes in his aesthetic or political ideas.

Critics have rightly seen the play as a product of Brecht's early association with the Communist Party, and as an attempt to politicise the form and function of drama following a reading of Marx and Marxist texts in the late 1920s. On the first question, Klaus Völker promptly rejects Esslin's opinion that Brecht aligned himself with communism simply because he 'felt a desire or need to be identified with something' and that Brecht's text was a 'premature key-play to the Moscow trials.'[1] He also makes the very useful point that in this play, and *The Mother*, Brecht was translating to the theatre and in the process commenting upon Lenin's *What is to be Done?* and *One Step Forward, Two Steps Back.*[2] To party representatives who felt that *The Measures Taken* was too abstract and unhistorical, Brecht retorted, he says, that 'One did not become a party worker . . . through a passionate belief in the working class but by acquiring political knowledge and assimilating the teachings of the Marxist classics.'[3] This view accorded with Lenin's insistence on the indispensable role of revolutionary theory and was consistent too with Karl Kautsky's claim that 'socialist consciousness' depended on 'profound scientific knowledge', introduced 'into the proletarian class struggle from without' through the agency of advanced party workers and bourgeois intellectuals. Lenin had quoted Kautsky's argument approvingly in *What is to be Done?* in making his own case for the superior revolutionary effectiveness of a trained party cadre as against the unreliable and limited effects of spontaneous political action.[4]

In *The Measures Taken* itself, a young comrade who acts according to political instinct, and out of pity rather than calculation, endangers the revolutionary work of three undercover communist agitators who enlist his aid. He learns that he is wrong and consents to his own death at their hands. This is the 'measure' taken; it safeguards the revolutionary cause (the play opens with the message that their 'work has been successful' and that 'The revolution marches forward even in that country').[5] Brecht's play can therefore be seen as presenting Lenin's argument against spontaneity, and on the necessary subordination of the individual to the Party, in parable form.

The play has provoked a good deal of dogma, ironically, and doubt, amongst critics of various ideological persuasions. In general terms it is agreed, however, that, like other of Brecht's 'didactic' plays and a play such as *Man equals Man, The Measures Taken* is concerned with the theme of 'Einverstandnis'; of consent or acquiescence in the group or mass, involving a consequent loss of individuality. It is probably the fact that the collectivity in the case of *The Measures Taken* is the Communist 'Party' rather than the working class or the people, or community more vaguely defined, which has given rise to most of the controversy and criticism of the play, from communists and non-communists alike. As it is, Brecht's apparent later accommodation of the individual (and therefore of feeling and humanity) has prompted the accounts of his 'mature' work discussed above.

But if we are to see Brecht as developing from the learning plays and a rigidly doctrinal Marxism to a more conventional, less than epic drama, and liberal or 'Marxist humanist' outlook, we would expect Lenin and the didactic use of the parable form to decline in favour. In fact there is a variety of interesting if piecemeal evidence tending, on the contrary, to confirm Hanns Eisler's view that Brecht remained more the 'pupil of Lenin' than critics have wanted to accept.[6] For example, as both Völker and Willett report, in planning a play with Eisler in late 1953 on Hans Garbe, the East German working-class activist, Brecht turned again to the examples of *The Measures Taken* and *The Mother*.[7] Also, very shortly before his death, in conversation with Manfred Wekwerth, Brecht named *The Measures Taken* as representing the theatre of the future.[8] Earlier conversations with Wekwerth and Ernst Schumacher make the association between the parable form and Lenin quite clear.

Thus, ' "Lenin used parables not as an idealist but as a materialist" ' and for the playwright the parable was 'the best of all forms', offering 'the advantage of simplicity and easy assimilation'; it was ' "concrete in abstraction making essentials clearly visible" '.[9] Similarly, to Wekwerth, Brecht recommended 'liveliness' and 'naivety': 'the dialectical solution' he said 'is always more lively, more diverse, more naive'; 'dialectic was the chance to show an event in a living way', and 'Brecht', says Wekwerth, 'prized liveliness just as highly as Lenin did in his last writings on dialectic'.[10] ' "The naive" ', said Brecht, in the same conversation, ' "is an aesthetic category," ' citing Lenin's parable of climbing mountains, 'As a classical example of naive presentation in political literature'. The production of the *Commune* which he was considering with Wekwerth and others at the time ' "must have something of this naivety".'[11]

In another remark to Schumacher, Brecht showed that the issues raised in *The Measures Taken* were still present and still controlled his political analysis and artistic decisions. Confessing to the difficulty of writing a play about Rosa Luxemburg, since ' "a truthful study would only deepen the conflict in the working class movement" ', Brecht added that,

> the struggle between Rosa and Lenin about the better type of party, about the spontaneity theory, was not yet forgotten. In a sort of way I would have to have argued against the Party. But I have no intention of chopping off my foot just to prove that I am handy with an axe.[12]

Beyond this we know that the Berliner Ensemble was instructed in dialectics and was familiar with Lenin's 'On the question of dialectics' as well as Mao's *On Contradiction*.[13] A debt to Lenin can also be detected in certain plays. Thus Darko Suvin, describing the presentation of the Roman plebeian democracy in *Coriolan* as charged with Brecht's 'Marxian Utopianism', traces this to Lenin's writings on the theme of State and revolution,[14] and Keith A. Dickson sees *The Caucasian Chalk Circle* as including a utopian projection which echoes Lenin's vision of a communist future 'without force, without compulsion, without subordination, without that special apparatus for compulsion which is called the state.'[15]

Lenin and the didactic play do not therefore disappear from Brecht's thinking. Once again, however, we should understand their appearance, and their collocation with dialectics and the ideal of collective and co-operative work either end of Brecht's career, as a set of continuities in changed circumstances rather than as a circular return. The same is true of the dramatic theme of the individual and the social collective, which works its way through both earlier and later periods (*Coriolan* we might say treats of the expendable leader as *The Measures Taken* does of the young comrade). But this theme cannot be discussed, any more than it was produced, in abstract separation from a changing artistic and political milieu. The positions described as 'doctrinaire' or 'Marxist humanist' were arrived at under determinate, but shifting, and in different respects, constraining and enabling conditions. If a set of guiding principles for understanding such change exists, it is to be found in dialectical materialism, or as Brecht formulated it for the human actor in *He Who Says No*, 'the Custom of rethinking every new situation.'[16] Following this custom it is possible and necessary sometimes to say yes, sometimes no, and sometimes, true to the dialectical unity of opposites, both yes and no. This is in principle the reverse of dogma, though it may lapse into it, or into opportunism or expediency if it is not controlled by a sense of intellectual and political responsibility. It involves one might say a tactical calculation of the greater good.

Interestingly, Lenin provides an example of just this principle in action, in his views of the relation of the party to the working class. The position he takes in *What is to be Done?* that the working class is limited to a trade-union consciousness and will never proceed to revolution without the spur of a trained revolutionary vanguard, emerged as less of a law than a tactic, relevant to the pre-revolutionary situation of 1901–2 in which it was conceived. After 1917 he wished in fact to withdraw it from publication. It was Stalin, as David McLellan reports, who thought otherwise, and is responsible for the text's being canonised.[17] Tony Cliff's remarks on *What is to be Done?* in his biography of Lenin tend in a similar direction. He writes that Lenin's distinction in this text between spontaneity and consciousness, and thus between economic and political struggles, was 'mechanical and non-dialectical' and, as such, contradicted by earlier and later writings, but was 'nevertheless, quite useful operationally.'[18] In *What is to be Done?* Lenin had consciously 'bent the stick', in his own phrase, to correct the extreme emphasis on working-class spontaneity. Within a matter of months, however, in the document *Letter to a Comrade on Our Organisational Tasks* he had formulated the more dialectical concept of 'democratic centralism' on which the Party should be founded.[19] Stalin's concept of the Party, on the other hand, even in his earlier pronouncements, lacked this double aspect of what Cliff calls 'a real interventionist, centralist leadership, and the widest possible spread of responsibility and initiative amongst the membership as a whole.'[20] In his essays titled *Foundations of Leninism* published in 1924, Stalin spoke of the Party as absorbing 'the best elements' of the proletariat, of 'their selfless devotion to the cause of the proletariat' of the 'iron discipline' of the Party, presupposing 'conscious and voluntary submission.'[21] John Molyneux describes these essays as 'a rigid schematic codification of Lenin's principles.'[22] By 1930, however, the date of the first performance of *The Measures Taken*, the religion of the Party which Stalin set forth, and the centralised state which characterised his rule, were securely in place.

This means that if Brecht, in Völker's words, was attempting 'to translate essential points in Lenin's ideas to the stage' in *The Measures Taken*, he ought to have attempted some translation of Lenin's theoretical and practical flexibility, his sense of his own criticism even in *What is to be Done*? of 'the worship of spontaneity' as being a dissatisfaction with what 'exists "at the present moment." '[23] Otherwise Brecht was in danger of translating an early 'mechanical and non-dialectical' Lenin, or was in effect translating not Lenin but Stalin. It is possible, of course, given that Brecht was after all aware in 1929 of debates *within* Marxism, and of Karl Korsch's criticism of Kautsky and the undialectical 'orthodoxy' of the Second International, that he was translating both, and therefore inviting debate in his play. This would suggest that Brecht perceived a distinction between the mechanical materialist (and potentially Stalinist) aspects, or moments, of Lenin's thought and its later dialectical materialist character. Korsch himself did not admit to this distinction even though he was acquainted with the section 'A few words on dialectics' at the close of *One Step Forward, Two Steps Back* and with the impeccably dialectical *Philosophical Notebooks*.[24] In fact it is likely that Brecht's disagreement with Korsch on Lenin amounted to a defence of what they both saw, in Korsch's words in 1930, as a concern on Lenin's part less 'with the *theoretical problem* of whether the materialist philsophy he propounds is true or untrue' (a matter of concern to Korsch) than 'with the practical question of its use for the revolutionary struggle of the proletariat.'[25] This 'practical question' was uppermost, one is inclined to think, for Brecht also.

At the close of the same 'anti-critique' to his *Marxism and Philosophy* Korsch revises his thoughts on what he had called an 'ideological dictatorship', distinguishing it

> from the *system of intellectual oppression* established in Russia today in the name of the 'dictatorship of the proletariat'. First of all, it [an 'ideological dictatorship'] is a dictatorship *of* the proletariat and not *over* the proletariat. Secondly, it is a dictatorship of a class and not of a party or party leadership. Thirdly, and most importantly, as a revolutionary dictatorship it is one element only of that radical process of social overthrow which by suppressing classes and class contradictions creates the preconditions for a 'withering away of the State.'[26]

It is difficult to see how, thinking along these lines, Korsch could have received *The Measures Taken* as anything other than a defence of 'Russian orthodoxy' and of the Party's 'dictatorsip *over* the proletariat'. That Brecht was prepared to defend just such a regime is borne out by the later comment recorded in August 1934 by Walter Benjamin:

> In Russia there is a dictatorship *over* the proletariat. We should avoid dissociating ourselves from this dictatorship for as long as it still does useful work for the proletariat.(UB, p. 121)

The idea of the dictatorship *of* the proletariat does not revive in Brecht's thinking until he presents forms of plebeian and participatory democracy in *The Caucasian Chalk Circle, Coriolanus* and *Days of the Commune*. But then these ideas, as suggested earlier, can also be traced to Lenin. The implication is that changes in Brecht's political thinking, specifically on questions of the relation of the State and the Party and proletariat, and thus on the general nature of communism, can be mapped through his *different* understanding, or reading and use of Lenin. His early interpretation, derived from a more Stalinist reading of *What is to be Done*?, was mechanical and undialectical. The result was the 'Marxist dogma' of *The Measures Taken* and Brecht's ambiguous 'critical support' for a Russian 'dictatorship *over* the proletariat'. His later understanding and use of Lenin was however more dialectical and more in line with the principle of democratic centralism. There were, as we shall see, other models than Lenin in Brecht's later political thinking; notably Mao, which drew it away from Lenin's concept of the relation of the Party and the working class. The fact remains, however, that both early and late Brecht can be described as Leninist. Even though, once said, this requires elaboration and qualification, it provides a more accurate description than the term 'Marxist' with the conventional tags this acquires in Brecht criticism, of ideologue or humanist.

To describe Brecht as 'Leninist' does not mean that his thinking did not change, therefore. It presents us rather with the question of under what conditions and with what effects this occurred. I suggest that the major determining events either side of the war were the obvious ones; namely, the rise of Hitler and the death of Stalin. It was the first of these and Brecht's response to it which produced his early 'Leninism' and its expression in *The Measures Taken*. Even here, however, the result was not simply a didactic play, but a contradiction between the play's political content and the purpose Brecht ascribed generally to the *Lehrstücke*. Ernst Schumacher warned that the parable-play 'carries with it the danger of being undialectic',[27] and this, as we have seen, is the problem with *The Measures Taken*, as it is with Lenin's *What is to be Done*? Yet Brecht talked of the *Lehrstüke's* purpose as being 'lernend zu lehren' ('in learning, to teach'), and as not to be undertaken 'ohne Kenntnis des Abc des dialektischen Materialismus' (without a knowledge of the ABC of dialectical materialism').[28] The plays were open to discussion, he said, by an audience deemed 'capable of thinking and reasoning, of making judgements even in the theatre'; they were seen and enjoyed and discussed by 'plain people' and philosophers — ('such philosophers as wished not just to explain the world but also to change it'). (BT, pp. 79–80, 72) But the text of *The Measures Taken* itself, though it might provoke controversy and has sent criticism into enough of a dialectical spin to turn the play into its opposite, i.e. into an attack on communism,[29] is in fundamental ways closed to revision or criticism — of the kind Korsch might have offered for example, in the name of Marxism, or the criticism that might be offered in the name of an earlier or later, or de-Stalinised, Lenin. The play's views on revolutionary tactics, on the role of the Party and the Central Committee (in the form of 'the Control Chorus') are set as in statute. In terms of the theme of 'Einverständnis', *The Measures Taken* drives to an extreme of self-sacrifice Lenin's stress on the need for Party organisation and discipline, taking literally Stalin's 'selfless devotion' and 'conscious and voluntary submission'. Behind this there no doubt lies the firm materialist tenet that 'the essence of man . . . is the ensemble of the social relations.'[30] But the argument of *The Measures Taken* does not express the full dialectic of Lenin's 'democratic centralism' nor the general Marxist belief that 'Man . . . can develop into an individual only in society'.[31] To accommodate this would have required a second play in the manner of Brecht's addition, after criticism, of *He Who Says No* to *He Who Says Yes*. In such a play, we might speculate, the outside agitators and Control Chorus who educate and judge in the original would themselves be judged and educated, after another of Marx's famous dicta. As it was the play was censored and withdrawn, though Brecht's comment that he had refused to permit further performances, 'as only the actor of the young comrade can learn from it', does perhaps acknowledge its weakness as a 'learning' play.[32]

We can perhaps blame Hitler for the play's hard-line message and the contradiction between this and Brecht's dialectical purpose. *The Measures Taken* was a product, that is to say, of an historical moment when the left, on the verge of defeat, looked still and somewhat desperately, for an answer to a right-wing extremism in the ascendant. The play's meaning, therefore, lay, in a real sense, in the last-ditch battle for the political destiny of Germany. Some of Brecht's own later and contemporary remarks in fact bear this out. There was his reply, for example, to the House UnAmerican Activities Committee in 1947, when, in answer to the question of whether *The Measures Taken* was pro- or anti-communist, or neutral (which is basically the question that has vexed so much criticism), Brecht said it was an attempt 'to express the feelings and the ideas of the German workers who then fought against Hitler.'[33] Nor was this necessarily the Schweikian evasion on Brecht's part it has been taken for. A related comment appeared in the again retrospective remark referred to earlier that he was concerned in the play *Man equals Man* to distinguish between what he called the 'false, bad collectivity' of 'Hitler and his backers' and the genuinely social 'collectivity of the workers.'[34] These remarks help make political sense of Brecht's criticism of the collective idea informing the experimental Baden-Baden music play (the Baden-Baden music festival had provided the forum for Brecht's first *Lehrstücke* and thus a basis for *The Measures Taken*):

> It is obvious that the didactic value of this sort of musical exercise, based on a 'thoughtful' text, 'which appeals to the imagination of the student', would be much too small. Even if one expected that the individual would 'adjust to something in the process' or that the musical basis would produce

> certain formal intellectual congruences, a shallow, artificial harmony of this sort would never be able to counter-balance even for minutes the widely based collective organisations that exercise a disintegrating effect on the people of our time, by using power of a very different kind.[35]

We can assume that the *Lehrstücke* were an attempt to find a more politically engaged collective form to help counterbalance the false and disintegrating collective ideology that was summoning the German petty bourgeoisie and working class to National Socialism. Given the defeat of the German Revolution of 1919 and the defeat, as it might well have seemed, of the 'spontaneity theory' of Rosa Luxemburg, plus the subsequent clashes between police and workers in May 1929 and the evident bankruptcy and villainy of Social Democratic leaders, it is not surprising that Brecht accepted the answers to Lenin's *What is to be Done?* The revolutionary party, along Bolshevik lines, now tried and tested in Russian theory and practice, no doubt looked like the only and the best 'genuine collectivity of the workers' to set against Hitler's false one. In the turbulence of the late 1920s and early 1930s in Germany, distinctions between Lenin and Stalin, or between what Korsch termed 'genuine proletarian dictatorship' and 'every false imitation of it',[36] may well have seemed academic.

Notes

1. Klaus Völker, *Brecht. A Biography* (Marion Boyars, London and Boston, 1979), pp. 149, 147.
2. Ibid., pp. 147, 165. In his notes to the play, Brecht also directly cites a passage from Lenin's 'Talk to the third Russian Congress of the Russian Young Communist League, October 2, 1920', *Gesammelte Werke*, 17 (Suhrkamp, Frankfurt am Main, 1967), p. 1033. As translated in Lenin's *Collected Works*, the passage runs as follows: 'It does not reply to the principal and most essential questions: what to learn, and how to learn? And the whole point here is that, with the transformation of the old, capitalist society, the upbringing, training and education of the new generations that will create the communist society cannot be conducted on the old lines.' (*Collected Works*, 31, Progress Publishers, Moscow; Lawrence and Wishart, London, 1966, pp. 283–4).
3. Völker, *Brecht* p. 147.
4. Lenin, *What is to be Done?* in *Collected Works*, vol. 5 (1964), pp. 347–530.
5. *The Measures Taken and other Lehrstücke* (Eyre Methuen, London, 1977), p. 9.

6. Hanns Eisler, 'Gespräche', *Sinn und Form. Sonderheft Hanns Eisler* (Rütten and Loening, Berlin, 1964), p. 292.

7. Cf. Völker, *Brecht*, p. 352–3, and Willett, *Brecht in Context* (Methuen, London and New York, 1984), p. 202.

8. Völker, *Brecht* p. 253.

9. Ernst Schumacher, 'He will remain' in Hubert Witt (ed.) and John Peet (trans.), *Brecht As They Knew Him* (Seven Seas Books, Berlin; International Publishers, New York, 1974, 1977; Lawrence and Wishart, London, 1974, 1980), pp. 223–5.

10. Manfred Wekwerth, 'Discovering an aesthetic category', in Witt and Peet, ibid., pp. 145, 147, 148.

11. Ibid., p. 149. Lenin's 'On climbing high mountains', which Eisler also says Brecht considered to be a 'masterwork of world literature', is included in Lenin, *Collected Works*, vol. 33 (1966), pp. 204–5.

12. Schumacher, in Witt and Peet, *Brecht As They Knew Him*, p. 221.

13. Cf. Frederic Ewen, *Bertolt Brecht. His Life, His Art, and His Times* (Citadel Press, New York, 1969), p. 460; *Gesammelte Werke*, 16, 'Anmerkung 13'.

14. Darko Suvin, *To Brecht and Beyond. Soundings in Modern Dramaturgy* (Harvester Press, Brighton, Sussex, 1984), pp. 177–9.

15. Lenin, quoted in Keith A. Dickson, *Towards Utopia. A Study of Brecht* (Clarendon Press, 1978), p. 154.

16. *The Measures Taken and other Lehrstücke*, p. 79.

17. David Mclellan, *Marxism After Marx. An Introduction* (Macmillan, London, 1979), p. 88.

18. Tony Cliff, *Lenin*, 4 vols (Pluto Press, London, 1975–9), vol. 1, pp. 80–2.

19. Cf. Chris Harman, *Party and Class* (Socialists Unlimited, London, 1983), pp. 11–13, on the apparent contradiction between Lenin's emphasis on revolutionary theory and the role of the Party vanguard on the one hand and on the revolutionary self-activity of the working class on the other. Harman's explanation is that, 'The real basis of his [Lenin's] argument is that the level of consciousness in the working class is never uniform.' See also John Molyneux, *Marxism and the Party* (Pluto Press, London, 1978), pp. 42–50, 59–60.

20. Tony Cliff, *Lenin*, pp. 91–2.

21. Joseph Stalin, *The Foundations of Leninism* in *Leninism* (Lawrence and Wishart, London, 1940) pp. 73, 81. Records of Brecht's library, held at the Brecht Archive in East Berlin, show that he possessed copies of Stalin's *The Foundations of Leninism* (1924), and *The Problems of Leninism* (1933).

22. John Molyneux, 'What is the real Marxist tradition?', in *International Socialism*, 20 (Summer, 1983), p. 29.

23. Lenin, quoted Molyneux, *Marxism and the Party*, p. 44.

24. Cf. Patrick Goode, *Karl Korsch. A Study in Western Marxism* (Macmillan, London, 1979), pp. 127–8.

25. Karl Korsch, *Marxism and Philosophy* (Monthly Review Press, New York, 1970), p. 113.

26. Ibid., p. 126.

27. Schumacher, in Witt and Peet, *Brecht As They Knew Him*, p. 224.

28. *Gesammelte Werke*, 17, pp. 1032, 1033.

29. Cf. Ronald Gray, *Brecht. The Dramatist* (Cambridge University Press, Cambridge, 1976), pp. 48–54.

30. Marx, 'Theses on Feuerbach', in *On Dialectical Materialism* (Progress Publishers, Moscow, and Lawrence and Wishart, London, 1977), pp. 30–1.

31. *Marx's Grundrisse*, David McLellean (ed.) (Granada Publishers, London, 1973), p. 27.

32. *Gesammelte Werke*, 17, p. 1035. Esslin dismisses Brecht's note as a piece of 'typically Brechtian irony and delight in mystification', *Brecht*, p. 145.

33. Quoted, Ewen, *Bertolt Brecht*, p. 502. Ewen presents the proceedings of the House Committee on Un-American Activities before which Brecht appeared on 30 October 1947, as an appendix to his book, pp. 497–509.

34. *Man equals Man*, John Willett and Ralph Manheim (eds), Gerhard Nellhouse (trans.) (Methuen, London, 1969), p. 108.

35. *Gesammelte Werke*, 17, p. 1028. This translation is given by Völker, *Brecht*, p. 142.

36. Korsch, *Marxism and Philosophy*, p. 126.

Part Four
The Marxist Artist in Socialist Berlin

11

He Who Says Yes and No

I

As far as Hitler was concerned Brecht's *What is to be Done?* in the parable form of *The Measures Taken* came too late and was frankly ineffectual. His 'changeable and world changing' drama was forced into exile, while on the world stage the candidature for a genuine collectivity and proletarian dictatorship passed, in the years of Hitler's defeat, from the dubious hands of Soviet Russia to its equally ambiguous post-war offspring in the Eastern bloc. For Brecht, once he had decided to settle in East Germany, the situation was immediately more complex than in the pre-war years. No longer could he simply italicise 'worker' against 'state' in the dialectical gesture with which he had assessed and held off Russia; most obviously because he had now to find a place for himself, not as worker, but as bourgeois-Marxist artist and intellectual within the East German regime. What followed between 1948 and 1956 is in the event by no means easy to describe, thanks in some measure to Brecht himself. Not only did he not comment on his situation or events very directly, or at any length, but some of his actions and statements, when he did commit himself, remain quite opaque. Moreover, there are occasions when what Brecht 'really' thought, or in fact said and wrote was not published, or not published in full in his lifetime.

Frequently Brecht's dealings with the authorities and the signs of censorship and self-censorship this entailed are interpreted as evidence of, on the one side, repressive political dogma, and on the other a lack of political courage, or a cunning instinct for self-preservation. We probably cannot avoid making, or responding to judgements of this kind, and no critic should pretend to disinterestedness, though many do of course in the very act of pronouncing a verdict. Judgements for or against Brecht or the GDR, however, do not so much settle the question of their relationship as reinforce the long-term ideological and political issues this involves. Brecht's elusiveness, what is more, though it is this which provokes the opinionated and reflex attitudes of critics, is the very thing that needs to be understood, as a product of the relations between artist and state, rather than dispelled. In the end, it is the enigma not the dogma which is revealing; the combination with its ambiguous and contradictory effects, of what Brecht did and did not do, or say, or write, or publish or produce, rather than one or the other of these, which is full of meaning.

In an earlier conversation in 1934 with Walter Benjamin, Brecht spoke of how he often imagined being interrogated by a tribunal. He was asked whether he was 'really in earnest' and would have to answer that he was not because he thought 'too much about artistic problems'. But then, he said, he would 'add something still more important: namely, that my attitude is, *permissible*'. (UB, pp. 106–7) Later, in the United States, and then the GDR, this imagined scene became more real and then more frequent, almost one might think perpetual, even if, outside the proceedings of the House UnAmerican Activities Committee before whom Brecht appeared in 1947, it did not assume the physical form of a trial. In effect the post-war period for Brecht comprised a series of negotiations with the authorities, spoken and unspoken, over what was 'permissible', politically and in the area of artistic work. There were broad areas of agreement in both respects and on Brecht's part a sustained belief in the basic compatibility of his Marxist art with a communist society. As disparities between them appeared, however, and communism was confirmed as more a prospective than established reality, Brecht's relation to the existing regime also acquired some distance. Real life, too, unlike the earlier imagined scene, brought relations of real power, in which Brecht's definitions of what it was to be 'really in earnest' and of 'artistic problems' and 'permissible' attitudes had to vie, on unequal terms, with official definitions. The general terms of reference, moreover, in Marxist thought and Communist Party policy were by no means held in common, though it could be assumed in the rhetoric of fraternal discussion that they were. There thus emerged on Brecht's part an ironic discourse which mixed principle with guile, calculation with reticence, outright with veiled criticism, and criticism with support and hope. He found ways of saying both yes and no;

and sometimes, frustratingly, of saying nothing.

Brecht's words to Walter Benjamin above remind us that his priorities were with artistic matters. I want in this chapter to give some description of Brecht's political views, but beyond this to ask how far he came to express and develop his own position as an artist in dialectical terms. Did he 'adapt' dialectical materialism, that is to say, not only internally, to the 'social devices' of his art, but to the social and political functions of the artist *vis-à-vis* the Party and his audience. If this question itself has a yes and no answer, as I believe it does, it also has the virtue of steering us past self-righteous name-calling towards what remains a quite central issue; namely, what kind of Marxist-Leninist artist Brecht was, or found it *permissible* to be, in a new German state itself claiming Marxist-Leninist credentials.

II

The question of Brecht's position in the new East German regime would seem at first sight of course to present no difficulties. The Marxist artist found a political home at last in the Marxist society. So at least many critics of different ideological persuasions have found it convenient to believe. And indeed there is something in this view, beyond the promptings of simple partisanship or wilful misreading. For it appears to have been Brecht's own first thought and main hope that socialist art and society would move forward hand in hand in the new period. The chief indication of this is his repeated use in essays from the late 1940s onwards of the terms 'production' and 'productivity' to refer to positive transformations in art and consciousness as well as in the economy. This thinking indeed lies at the base of Brecht's 'production aesthetic' and his idea of the politicised pleasure to be derived from art. In the full sweep of the analogy he talks in the *Short Organum* of the 'productive process' and developing scientific spirit (i.e. Marxism) amongst workers 'whose natural element is large-scale production', while referring at the same time to 'the critical approach, i.e. our great productive method', and announcing that 'a theatre which makes productivity its main source of entertainment has also to take it for its theme.' (BT, pp. 184–7) In sections 20 and 21 of the *Organum* Brecht writes:

> But science and art meet on this ground, that both are there

> to make men's life easier, the one setting out to maintain, the other to entertain us. In the age to come art will create entertainment from that new productivity which can so greatly improve our maintenance, and in itself, if only it is left unshackled, may prove to be the greatest pleasure of them all.
>
> If we want now to surrender ourselves to this great passion for producing, what ought our representations of men's life together to look like? What is that productive attitude in face of nature and of society which we children of a scientific age would like to take up pleasurably in our theatre? (BT, p. 185)

At the close of the *Organum* this collocation of social and artistic production is expressed in the appeal that people be allowed to 'produce their own lives in the simplest way; for the simplest way of living is in art.' (BT, p. 205) In the *Appendices* to this work, as we have seen, Brecht writes of how 'Only once productivity has been set free can learning be transformed into enjoyment and vice versa,' and then in connection with his view of Faust, that 'Spiritual and sensual activity are united in productive work for mankind; the production of life leads to satisfaction in life.' (BT, pp. 276, 280)

Statements such as these echo Marx's description of 'human sensuous activity, practice', and of ' "revolutionary" . . . practical-critical activity' in his *Theses on Feuerbach*, and carry the sense there is elsewhere in Marx, particularly at the close of the *Communist Manifesto*, that the fully realised individual of communist society will control rather than be controlled by economic production. Brecht is saying that society is founded on productivity, that its science, in its material and social aspect is Marxism, and that a Marxist art and theatre will enlist and treat this creative-critical productivity and imbue it with pleasure.

This thinking assists Brecht in the impressive extension of Marxist aesthetics discussed above. There is a suspicion, nevertheless, as one takes the full force and breadth of the analogy with economic production, that the connections Brecht is seeking are founded on *no more than* an analogy, and that in the end a bracketing of developments in art and the economy under the common concept of production does more to elide than elucidate their relationship. This is so because while the assumption of synchronous or parallel movements of 'productivity' might appear to be an advance on the belief that *separated* developments in art or the economy will precede and provide one for the other, the model of mutual enrichment Brecht discovers, can easily sirt the important problem of 'determination', or the agencies of social change. Like the models which attribute definitive causation respectively to a level of culture or to the economy, the coupling of spheres of productivity can tend in its own way, as they do, to an undialectical distortion of the relationship between culture and society, or in Marx's original terms between the ideological superstructure and the economic base. This is the point at which Brecht appears to have arrived with the *Short Organum*; laying culture and the economy down together in a dependent, but undialectical relationship.

At the same time, however, and shadowing this model, there is a familiar and 'orthodox' form of economic determinism, which Brecht does not shake off or successfully revise. The political lesson taught by both Marx and recent German history was that however vehemently intellectual and artistic culture had opposed Hitler, it had not prevented, nor could of itself impede a shift to the Right with its roots and reasons deep in the German economy. As a member of that blocked and frustrated culture Brecht appeared to accept the conclusion that the economy takes precedence over other developments. To a degree, in fact, that made him more of a materialist and less of a dialectician than Karl Korsch. His materialism came then to influence his view of Russian, and subsequently East German socialism, while it also helped to provide a language, as above, with which to describe a 'productive art'.

This gave rise to a series of problems and ambiguities. The first of these lies in the twist whereby a recognition of the determining role of the economy 'in the *last* instance' can render the economy a *first* priority, since if everything follows from movements at this level, even if only eventually, then this is what must be attended to above all else. If, moreover, the economy in question is 'socialist', i.e. 'productive', if only in intention, then a number of allowances can be made for the non-appearance of other 'slower-moving' features of the society. It was on grounds such as these that Brecht could accept and even admire Stalinist Russia, or at least withhold criticism of it. Thus, as Käthe Rülicke-Weiler has written, Brecht's understanding of communism, in his words, 'as primarily a theory with regard to production' led to his acceptance of 'how important it was for the Soviet Union to subordinate everything to the development of productive forces.'[1] The harsher implications of this are spelled out by Helmut Dahmer in a close study of Brecht's attitude to Stalin. Brecht, he writes,

> was satisfied with a partial (objectivist) truth, according to

> which the nationalised means of production are the basis for a new society and must be defended accordingly. Brecht, however, did not distinguish this 'basis' and the Soviet state, the proletariat and the Communist Party of the Soviet Union, or the Stalin-faction and the great organiser and butcher himself. He affirmed the 'basis' and simultaneously affirmed the 'top'.[2]

Inevitably this had further consequences. In a private note on the Moscow trials, for example, Brecht reasoned that 'it would be absolutely wrong when discussing them to adopt an attitude against the government of the Soviet Union which is organising them', since this would soon be 'directed against the Russian proletariat . . . and against its socialism which is in the course of construction.'[3] There was similarly, as Walter Benjamin records, Brecht's grotesque attempt to rationalise Stalin's 'personal rule' as a form of 'workers' monarchy', (UB, p. 121) and his notorious failure to speak out publicly on the disappearance of Russian and German emigré artists and friends.[4]

It was apparently a question of priorities. If the 'state served production' and this served the proletariat, or would do in the end, and Stalin could therefore be deemed 'useful', then Brecht was inclined to advise caution, or silence, to himself and others. Aside from the rights and wrongs of this as a political judgement, the economic determinism it invokes as justification, leads, in another direction, to the view that art and culture have a secondary, reflexive or reinforcing role, or that they are redundant to the making of socialism. To put the problem directly, if schematically, in relation to Brecht himself: if the object of his theatre and poetry was the creation of a classless, communist social order, it had to be acknowledged both on recent historical evidence (the rise of Nazism and World War II), as well as in Marxist theory, that this object could not be achieved by art alone and of itself, but only through fundamental social and economic changes in society. Art could nevertheless prepare the ground for this change by undermining existing ideology and by assuming a critical, transformative role. This was something like the anticipatory, pedagogic and 'dialecticising' function Brecht assigned to his art prior to his return to East Germany. It described, in short, the role of a Marxist art under capitalism. If, on the other hand, the society in question was already a 'socialist' one, or a 'socialist' society in the making, then the political function of Marxist art ought presumably to change. In one familiar set of answers the function of art in such a society is seen to be one of loyally maintaining the existing socialist regime, mirroring, or magnifying its best aspects. If that society is thought in any sense to be 'ideal', to be in all essentials 'correct', then the critical and pedagogic function of art is clearly re-defined if not eliminated.

This is a prescription we associate more readily with official socialist realism and party bureaucrats than with Brecht. Indeed, with the instigation in 1951 of the 'socialist cultural revolution' in East Germany, it was decreed by the Communist Party Central Committee that the new bureau for literature and publishing, along with the state commission for cultural affairs and the later state film and broadcasting committees, were to lead 'The struggle against formalism in art and literature, for a progressive German culture.' As Martin McCauley in his study of the post-war regime comments, 'Culture was seen by the party as a force of production which would help to raise labour productivity.'[5]

A 'production aesthetics' which takes its cue from, and aims to complement, an accepted process of economic growth can obviously bend to this 'official' model. Brecht's thinking is therefore not *inconsistent* with an economistic, undialectical and 'Stalinist' version of socialist realism. All the same, it can be understood and mobilised differently, so as to illustrate a benign, almost utopian, relationship between art and the economy in which the first enriches and reinforces while happily subserving the second. If, indeed, we look back at the statements quoted above from the *Short Organum* we see that Brecht's talk of the meeting-ground between science and art — the one maintaining, the other creating 'entertainment from that new productivity' — is offered more as a prospect for 'the age to come', than a description of present reality. Much depends then on the nature and direction of the economy, and whether the adjective 'socialist' alongside it, appears with or without its inverted commas. Brecht's tone often suggests that it should be so qualified, but also that the inverted commas be pencilled rather than permanently inked in, so as to indicate less a false than a transitional state. As a result his model of economic and artistic productivity tends to slide in its application between the past and the future, between the false and imperfect Russian precedent and the prospect of achieved socialism in East Germany. We might view this ambiguity as the product of Brecht's guile and irony, his caution or cynical self-interest, but I think there are other explanations. He was, for one thing, witness to a genuinely transitional, or twilight period, in which many hoped and believed that East Germany was going to outdistance the shadow of Russia. Secondly, Brecht tended himself to think of the period of socialist construction as proceeding along an evolutionary rather than a 'dialectical continuum', as if, with history in reverse, the Stalinism from which Europe was emerging would produce Leninism, and thus the socialism of the future. *Present* time as a result was held between the old and the new, in the unclassified suspension of quotation marks, with Brecht playing a waiting game.

This is not to say that Brecht at no time grasped the movement of his society or his place within it dialectically. His talk of 'never-ending labour' and a process of 'unceasing transformation' in respect of social and artistic production, at the close of the *Short Organum*, is clear evidence of this. Nevertheless, a tendency towards economistic or evolutionary determinism confused or frustrated this better understanding. A further illustration, which undercuts while it demonstrates this tendency, occurred in relation to his conception of the political function of his theatre as a Marxist theatre; a theatre, that is to say, which not only internalised and demonstrated dialectical materialism, but also produced dialectical materialists. The previously quoted *Arbeitsjournal* entry for late 1940, for example, while it is evidently conscious of the problems involved here, invites the conclusion that a 'dialectising theatre' in this sense was indeed possible:

> It is clear that a theatre of *Verfremdung* is a dialectical theatre. Yet I previously saw no possibility of explaining this theatre through the application of dialectical concepts: it would be easier for theatre people to understand dialectics from a *Verfremdungs* theatre than a *Verfremdungs* theatre from dialectics . . . since without recognising its dialectical nature reality is simply not open to control. The *V-Effekt* makes this dialectical nature apparent, that is its task.[6]

There are contrasting, and mostly later, statements, however, which imply that Brecht's theatre did not so much produce dialectical materalists as depend on them; his assumption being that only those who were already Marxists and socialists could appreciate its analyses and effects. Brecht's much quoted early comment that Marx would have been the best audience for his theatre is of this kind, as is his later complaint that an epic performance was 'quite impossible' since 'The actors would have to be Marxists and the audience as well. And where on earth do you get them?'[7] Again, in his notes on *Katzgraben* he says he feels unable to put the concept of *Verfremdung* in the *Short Organum* into effect since to do so 'Ich müßte die Schauspieler völlig umschulen und würde bei ihnen und beim Publikum einen ziemlich hohen Bewußtseinsstand benötigen, Verständnis für Dialektik und so weiter.' ('I would need to completely retrain the actors and require from them and the public a rather high level of consciousness, understanding of dialectics and so on.')[8]

Taken together these comments reveal two things. Firstly, the extent to which Brecht tended to conceive of the relation of his theatre to dialectics, and then of his dialecticising theatre to a Marxist audience, and of his Marxist art to a socialist society, in a relation of dependency; such that one or the other, the chicken or the egg, was thought to come first. Brecht the materialist and Brecht the dialectician pulled as it were in opposite directions, and in this contest, the materialist, aided by the strength and weight of economic priorities often won. But the victory of economic materialism without dialectics is, ironically, a counter-productive one for art. For Brecht it is an absurd conclusion, since to require Marxist actors and what is more a Marxist audience as conditions for an effective theatre is to put the end of the lesson before the pedagogy. It would reduce Brecht to a 'yes-man' and his theatre to a theatre for the converted of the most contemptible and useless 'socialist-realist' kind.

At the same time, however, Brecht's comments reveal that the major premise leading to this kind of artistic sycophancy is a mistaken one. When he asks in some desperation where the actors and audience with the right qualifications in dialectical materialism are to be found, one would have thought that the first place to look was a socialist society. But this answer does not apparently present itself to Brecht. The reason can only be either that this 'socialist society' is not a socialist society, and does, at best, deserve firm quotation marks, or that a socialist economy does not deliver a Marxist audience, or one attuned to Brecht's Marxist art. In which case the basic assumption of a dependent and consequential relationship between a 'productive' economy and a 'productive' art becomes suspect. One is led to conclude that the socialism of East Germany and Brecht's socialism were not identical, and that they did not guarantee each other.

In fact this is the general implication of Brecht's career in East Berlin. In Martin Esslin's words Brecht 'always considered himself a better Marxist than the Party pundits.'[9] But if Brecht believed this, or gave the impression that he did, his remarks can just as often be taken the other way. His superior Marxism did not lead him anyway to theorise the actually quite fraught relationship between art and society in the specific forms he experienced them, beyond the model of their mutual and reinforcing productivity — a model Party pundits could regard as quite acceptable. We can view this model more favourably, as I have suggested, as evidence of Brecht's early enthusiasm or as his hypothesis on the future. But even so, it was unequal to the more complicated relations he experienced with actors, audience, and the East German authorities in the last half dozen years of his life.

'The proof of the pudding', as Brecht was fond of saying, 'was in the eating'. What in the event he actually tasted in East Berlin after the poison of Nazi Germany and the indigestible flavours of the West, proved to be not so much acceptable or unacceptable, as underdone. If he did not fully theorise his position as it evolved in the GDR, he did, under the pressure of events — and to continue the culinary metaphor — advise on the preparation and cooking of the socialist dish in the belief that it could be improved. In the process he came quite firmly to reject the view that the role of art was to make a poor meal palatable. If we ask why he did not do more, or do more explicitly, we can find an indirect answer in one of the Herr Keuner stories. Herr Keuner compares Town 'A' with Town 'B': in Town 'A' he is loved, made use of and invited to the table, in Town 'B' people are friendly, they need him and he is invited into the kitchen.[10] Herr Keuner prefers Town 'B' as Brecht might have done. According to both Esslin and Willett, Brecht is in this way expressing a preference for East Berlin.[11] It does not occur to them that East Berlin is the Town 'A' rather than Town 'B' of the story, and that it therefore implies a criticism of official hospitality in that city where, esteemed artist though he was, Brecht was not as an artist 'permitted' into the socialist kitchen. The truth of his situation was that the strengths of the questioning, critical, and transformative role of his art, and the degree of optimism with which he viewed this, were dialectically bound up with broad political and economic movements in his society. As an artist, a Marxist and socialist of integrity, Brecht had a degree of ideological influence, but this gave him only licensed power. There were certain quarters, moreover, certain agencies and institutions of political and economic power, where Brecht and his art were simply impotent, unless invited in and listened to. The difficulty, then, on those occasions when artist and politicians were brought face to face over the political meaning of events, was which of the many ways of speaking the truth it would be best to adopt.[12]

Notes

1. Käthe Rülike-Weiler, 'Since then the world has hope', in Hubert Witt (ed.) and John Peet (trans.), *Brecht As They Knew Him* (Seven Seas Books, Berlin; International Publishers, New York, 1974, 1977; Lawrence and Wishart, London, 1974, 1980), p. 202. Stalin had defined 'the main task of socialism' as 'the organisation of socialist production' in *The Problems of Leninism* in Joseph Stalin, *Leninism* (Lawrence and Wishart, London, 1940), p. 173.

2. Helmut Dahmer, 'Bertolt Brecht and Stalinism', *Telos*, 22 (Winter, 1974–5), pp. 97–8.

3. Quoted, Rülike-Weiler in Witt and Peet, *Brecht As They Knew Him*, p. 202.

4. Cf. Helmut Dahmer, 'Bertolt Brecht and Stalinism', p. 101. On Brecht's attitude to the 'show trials', Dahmer writes that Brecht convinced himself . . . of the plausibility of the charges and the truth of the confessions', but that in *Me-Ti* he shows he 'nevertheless conceives of them as lacking evidence.' ibid., p. 100. In *Me-Ti*, Brecht writes, 'Ni-en may have benefited the people by removing his enemies from the association, but he has not proved his point. By conducting a trial without proofs he has harmed the people. He should have taught the people to demand proof, and in particular from himself, who in general has been of so much service.' Quoted in Martin Esslin, *Mediations* (Sphere Books, London 1983), p. 59. Esslin also cites Brecht's notoriously ambiguous response to Sidney Hook's reference to the mass arrests taking place under Stalin. 'The more innocent they are, the more they deserve to die,' said Brecht. Hook apparently promptly showed him the door, but as Esslin argues, Brecht is implying that those who are innocent of *resisting* Stalin deserve to die. ibid., p. 38. On these questions, see also the poem 'Is the people fallible?', *Poems 1913–1956*, John Willett and Ralph Manheim (eds) (Eyre Methuen, London, 1981), p. 331, and discussed above, p. 142.

5. Martin McCauley, *The German Democratic Republic Since 1945* (Macmillan, London, 1983), pp. 57–8.

6. Brecht, *Arbeitsjournal*, Vol. I, 1938–43, Werner Hecht (ed.) (Suhrkamp, Frankfurt am Main, 1973), p. 216.

7. Quoted, Ernst Schumacher in Witt and Peet, *Brecht As They Knew Him*, p. 227.

8. *Gesammelte Werke*, 16 (Suhrkamp, Frankfurt am Main, 1967), p. 798.

9. Martin Esslin, *Brecht. A Choice of Evils* (Eyre Methuen, London, 1959, revised 1980), p. 144.

10. 'Zwei Städte', *Gesammelte Werke*, 12, p. 389.

11. Esslin, *Brecht*, p. 82: Willett, *Brecht in Context*, p. 197.

12. Brecht had written 'Five difficulties in writing the truth' for

German underground propaganda in the middle 1930s, *Gesammelte Werke*, 18, p. 222. Whoever wishes to write the truth,

> muß den *Mut haben*, die Wahrheit zu schreiben, obwohl sie allenthalben unterdrückt wird; die *Klugheit*, sie zu erkennen, obwohl sie allenthalben verhüllt wird, die *Kunst*, sie handhabbar zu machen als eine Waffe; das *Urteil*, jene auszuwählen, in deren Händen sie wirksam wird; die *List*, sie unter diesen zu verbreiten. (must have the *courage*, to write the truth, although it is everywhere suppressed; the *shrewdness*, to recognise it, although it is everywhere veiled; the *art*, to make it available as a weapon; the *judgement*, to select those in whose hands it will be effective, and the *cunning*, to disseminate it among them.)

12

'The Travails of the Plains'

I

In the short poem 'Observation' written a few months after Brecht's return to Berlin, he writes of exchanging 'the travails of the mountains' for 'the travails of the plains' (P, p. 416); a description confirmed even in the early period of ruins and reconstruction by the continuing inequalities and disparities of wealth and privilege Brecht witnessed.[1] The new Germany, he said, gave him 'an eerie, sinister feeling'.[2] There followed his personal tussles with those who strove hamfistedly to apply the doctrines of socialist realism, and signs too of active discontent amongst workers in the face of a stiffening and uncomprehending state bureaucracy. 'In 1951', McCauley reports, 'it was commonplace for books to be pulped, plays to be banned and paintings to be defaced — all in the name of socialist realism.'[3] The officially adopted campaign against formalism in the arts had followed the launching of the first Five Year Plan in January of that year. This resulted in an increase in the production of pig iron, steel and chemicals, but only at the expense of light industry and living standards. The pulping of undesirable books was accompanied therefore by the continued rationing of butter, meat and sugar, and a limited supply of much desired consumer goods.[4] By 1953, in spite of the breath of liberalisation greeting Stalin's death, the general situation had worsened. Brecht saw the Berliner Ensemble ignored and its members grow disenchanted, and then in June felt the full shock to the pretensions of the new order, as Berlin workers took to the streets in protest against the imposition of new production norms.

These years were in obvious and profound ways a period of mounting division, leading in its most notorious aspect to the building of the Berlin wall five years after Brecht's death. We might say that Brecht anticipated this era of psychic and social division in the divided souls of *The Good Person of Szechwan* and *Herr Puntila* — the performance of which in November 1949 had marked the opening of the Berliner Ensemble, a month after the founding of the GDR. Works such as *Galileo, The Tutor, Faust* and *Turandot*, also explored the question, of great pertinence to Brecht himself, of the intellectual's divided loyalties, putting the case for and against defiance and acquiescence. At the same time, the drama of real events outside the theatre pointed up new divisions in the political and class composition of the new state, altering Brecht's sense of his position and tasks in relation to the Party and German people.

The important period in this development was between 1953 and 1956. Brecht moved in these years to a position summed up in a brief, late note of summer 1956. Stalinism he said then could only be liquidated 'durch eine gigantische Mobilisierung der Weisheit der Massen durch die Partei gelingen. Sie liegt auf der geraden Linie zum Kommunismus.' ('through a gigantic mobilisation of the wisdom of the masses by the Party. It lies on the direct path to communism.')[5] Brecht was as this confirms anti-Stalinist and broadly Marxist-Leninist. He had moved away from the strictures of *What is to be Done?*, but expressed a firm belief still in the revolutionary role of the Party in organising the good common sense ('the wisdom') of the masses. His vocabulary suggests a mixture of Lenin and Mao, and I shall return to this later. The main implication of his remarks, however, is that Stalinism had not yet been liquidated. It follows that either the (real) party in power, the SED (the Socialist Unity Party led by Walter Ulbricht), cannot be the (ideal) party Brecht has in mind, or that 'the wisdom of the masses' has not materialised, or been sufficiently mobilised. Or all three — the party is not sufficiently anti-Stalinist, the masses are not sufficiently revolutionary, and their relationship with the Party is not sufficiently dialectical. The net result being that East Germany is not a communist society. Nevertheless, Brecht's statement is an optimisic one, pointing the way to a communist future. I suggest that the combination of this implicit, and as it stands ambiguous criticism, on these different fronts, with Brecht's continuing optimism at the delayed prospect of communism, is characteristic of his political thinking in his last years. It only requires the above note to have been written but not published in Brecht's lifetime, as was indeed the case, for it to be typical.

It was the events of 1953 above all, I believe, which gave this enigmatic tone to Brecht's politics. The arbitrary raising of production quotas for Berlin building workers at a time when real wages were less than half their level in 1936, when consumer goods were in very short supply and living standards generally miserable, served only to demonstrate that the Stalinist 'dictatorship *over* the proletariat' had not been superseded with Stalin's death three months earlier. On June 16th, 10,000 workers marched in protest in Berlin and on the following day there were strikes involving 300,000 East German workers.[6] In Völker's words this 'spontaneous uprising of workers' confounded the government which 'could think of no other solution than to demonstrate its strength by calling out Russian tanks.'[7] Contemporary witnesses saw things in similar terms: 'The mass movement' said Heinz Brandt, Secretary of the SED organisation in Berlin, 'was absolutely spontaneous, without central leadership or organisation . . . The Party and State officials were overwhelmed by the events and increasingly paralysed . . . *the worker was rising against* the *worker-peasant state*. They were petrified'. It was, Brandt felt, 'like Lenin's dream come true only this mass action was directed against the totalitarian regime ruling in Lenin's name.'[8]

Brecht's response was not in line with these interpretations. In a sense the events of June were a repeat in history of the issues raised in *The Measures Taken* — only now real events and Brecht's attitudes were more complex than in his *Lehrstück*. He felt, as others did, that the rising was spontaneous, but viewed this as a danger rather than a positive gain, because without organisation the working class could be duped into supporting 'the re-emergent fascism of the fascist era'.[9] Brecht's thoughts ran then, as Lenin's had, on the need to 'combat' and 'divert' spontaneous working-class activity — with the important proviso that the early Lenin had associated 'spontaneity' with 'trade-unionist striving' whereas subsequent history had given it for Brecht an entirely different aspect. Brecht did not welcome the events of June therefore as a second Spartacist rising or as a Leninist revolution, because, firstly, he felt there was a lack of revolutionary organisation, and, secondly, because he feared a second 'National Socialist revolution' and consequently a Third World War; an outcome only prevented in his view by the 'swift and certain intervention of Soviet troops' which was 'in no way directed against the workers' demonstrations.' It was in these terms — 'when it had become clear that the workers' demonstrations were being misused for war-like purposes — that Brecht expressed his loyalty to the SED.[10]

Brecht's words on this occasion formed part of the second public response he made to June 17, after the Party newspaper *Neues Deutschland* had printed an edited version of a first statement. On the morning of the 17th he had written to Ulbricht, and in similar terms, apparently, to Otto Grotewohl, Minister-President of the GDR, and Vladimir Semenov, the Soviet High Commissioner. To Ulbricht he wrote, 'History will respect the revolutionary impatience of Germany's Socialist Unity Party. The great discussion with the masses on the tempo of socialist construction will lead to the socialist achievements being sorted out and safeguarded. I feel the need at this moment to express to you my loyal allegiance to the Socialist Unity Party.'[11] *Neues Deutschland* printed only the last sentence of this statement, thereby annulling the self-qualifying phrases of Brecht's opening, while provoking, ironically, the fuller response of his second letter. Elsewhere he had spoken of the Party as being out of touch with the people, as having, in the fiercely satirical (but unpublished) poem 'The solution' referred to earlier, reversed their proper relationship, so that the 'solution' to the problem of a dissenting public was for the Party to elect another. (P, p. 440) The rulers, having forgotten their beginnings once in power, had come, Brecht wrote, to adopt 'a new idiom, the jargon of their class, which is spoken with the threatening voice of the schoolmaster and fills the shops — but not with onions'.[12]

It cannot be said on this evidence that Brecht approved of 'the measures taken' by the Party. The workers had 'demonstrated because of justifiable grievances' and the Party while it was to be respected for its 'revolutionary impatience' had, beneath this polite formula, abused its power. The official explanation of the rising as expressed by Ulbricht was that it was an 'attempted coup d'état and fascist putsch'.[13] This, again, was quite different from Brecht's fear of the workers being misled by fascist infiltrators. He hoped now, as he wrote in his second letter to *Neues Deutschland*,

> daß die Provokateure isoliert und ihrer Verbindungsnetze zerstört werden, die Arbeiter aber, die in berechtiger Unzufriedenheit demonstriert haben, nicht mit den Provokateuren auf eine Stufe gestellt werden, damit nicht die so nötige große Aussprache über die allseitig gemachten Fehler von vornherein gestört wird.
> (that the provocateurs will be isolated and their networks destroyed, but that the workers who demonstrated out of justified dissatisfaction, will not be put on the same level as

the provocateurs, so that the very necessary major discussions of the mistakes made on all sides will not be obstructed at the outset.)[14]

Brecht's attitude to the Party in this episode was that of loyal critic, and the same may be said of his relation to the authorities as an artist. He had been prepared to revise *Lucullus* in 1951, to consider the application of Stanislavskian principles, and to debate his ideas. But he was adamantly opposed to 'administrative shackles' as he termed the work of the state commissions in his essay 'Cultural policy and academy of arts' in August 1953. 'Art has its own regulations', he insisted, and in similar vein later, 'Art has no competence to make works of art out of the artistic notions of some official department.' (BT, pp. 268, 267, 270) It followed that 'politically well-educated people' could be badly educated aesthetically and that the 'Marxist-Leninist Party' might mistake its job, tying to 'organise production of poems as on a poultry farm', when it should 'supply motive force' and a '*productive* influence on poetry and not just an administrative one.' (BT, p. 269) In like manner, in two poems, Brecht exposed the perfunctory self-criticism and deep-seated complacency and philistinism of the Commission for Art Affairs, and the Office for Literature. (P, pp. 436–7)

These poems, published in the *Berliner Zeitung* in July 1953, along with the article 'Cultural policy and academy of arts', followed soon after the events of June. They were not the works of a 'yes-man', who kow-towed to Party dictats. But nor were they written in outright opposition to the Party. Brecht took and gave criticism, as an *insider*, in two respects: firstly as someone with an inside knowledge of artistic practices and a developed conception of socialist realism who berated bureaucratic philistinism from a position of strength and confidence; and secondly as someone who had committed himself to the hope of a better future in East Germany. By 1955, Brecht no longer saw himself as caught between the two stools of East and West, but as sitting on one — 'And that one stands in the East.'[15] Thus, after his years of distant, 'sceptical' support of Stalinist Russia, Brecht assumed the role of artistic and sometime political conscience *within* the East German regime. His position was as double edged as one might expect of a Brechtian 'gest', but it was, all the same, freely chosen. 'I do not think as I do because I am here', he said, 'I am here because I think as I do.'[16]

Brecht had said of June 17 in *Neues Deutschland* that mistakes had been made on both sides. The theme of his response was accordingly the need for talks — the 'great discussion with the masses on the tempo of socialist construction'; his assumption being, in political, as in artistic matters, that the Party and people stood open to debate and correction, and would advance through a dialectical process of mutual criticism. It was this belief which encouraged him to see the uprising as more than 'in a merely negative light'.[17] In the contemporary poem, 'Reading a late Greek poet', Brecht finds a precedent for his optimism in the Trojans who 'when their fall was certain . . . adjusted small pieces, small pieces/In the triple wooden gates . . . And began to take courage, to hope.' (P, p. 445) In a second, more vigorously optimistic poem, 'The truth unites', he urges:

> Friends, I'd like you to know the truth and speak it.
> Not like tired, evasive Caesars: 'Tomorrow grain will come'
> But like Lenin: By tomorrow
> We'll be done for, unless . . .
> As the jingle has it:
>   'Brothers, my first obligation
>   Is to tell you outright:
>   We're in a tough situation
>   With no hope in sight.'
> Friends, wholehearted admission
> And a wholehearted UNLESS! (P, p. 441)

Völker says that Brecht sent this poem to Paul Wandel (Minister of Education from 1949 to 1952, and dismissed for 'insufficient hardness' as Secretary for Culture by Ulbricht in 1957) 'for internal consumption' ('zum inneren Gebräuche')[18] If so, it is a typically puzzling act on Brecht's part. For how does 'internal consumption' meet the 'first obligation' to speak the truth '*outright*'? Brecht was, as ever we might say, the cautious and calculating dialectician, attempting to draw a positive lesson from an incident which showed that the 'bad times' were not yet at an end.

It is difficult to escape the impression all the same that he was sometimes 'evasive' and was sometimes saying 'Tomorrow the grain will come . . . ' His hope, that is to say, well principled though it was, takes on at this juncture not only a cautious, but a weakly utopian, 'inevitablist' aspect; with few signs in this particular episode to warrant it. 'Things change' in the title of a later poem, and the dissolution of the Arts Commissions and the establishment of a new Ministry of Culture, in which Brecht played a significant part, would be one of the positive changes to point to as occurring after June 1953. But other developments in the political and economic realm took on a quite different tone and direction. In particular, after the imposition of martial law in Berlin in response to the uprising, 1,300 workers were brought to trial, four were sentenced to life imprisonment and six to death. At the most modest East German estimate, 19 people were killed by Russian troops (West German sources put the figure at 267).[19] The authorities did expedite certain economic reforms, raising the wages of the lowest paid workers, and making stockpiled food and clothing available for sale. But they ignored the workers' demands for free elections and, according to Harman, revoked many concessions, before eventually re-imposing the higher work norms.[20] Brecht, it has to be said, did not record any comment on *these* 'measures taken'.

Putting Brecht's silence to one side, there is still a sense in which this episode reveals that he, and not only the government or workers, had made a 'mistake'. For it was precisely his adopted theory of communism as 'a theory with regard to production', the belief, in the Party mind, that everything could be subordinated to the development of productive forces, which led to the uprising. In May, for example, the SED had called for 'a rigorous economic regime and thorough carrying out of all to do with the decrees of accumulation.' The increased work norms were necessary, it was said, because accumulation was only possible 'through the continual advance of labour productivity'.[21] The outcome could be put down to 'revolutionary impatience', a failure to properly address 'the tempo of socialist construction', but Brecht had been as guilty of this as others.

Martin Esslin states that as early as Brecht's return to East Berlin in 1948, 'he was well aware of the duality, the truly Hegelian contradiction between his own ideals of Communism and the realities of life in a Communist country,'[22] — that communist country being of course the Soviet Union. I think it is quite clear that Brecht wanted an end to Stalinism and the coming to power in East Germany of a Marxist-Leninist party in more than name; one which would be responsive to both the economy and to culture, to both workers and artists. Its role would be to generally exercise a '*productive influence*' rather than administer to the growth of communism. His criticisms of the regime's failures to meet this ideal recall Lenin's attack on 'bureaucratic misrule and wilfulness'.[23] And beneath this lies another more profound similarity. For while Lenin, for still debatable reasons, could not forestall the growth of Stalinism, so Brecht at the point of Stalinism's apparent demise, miscalculated its persistence, and in particular the economistic and philistine distortion to which Marxist-Leninist theory was subject.

June 1953, which 'showed the discontent of workers with a series of mistaken economic measures', in fact made this distortion clear to Brecht. In his second statement in *Neues Deutschland* he argued, for example, that the source of discontent for workers and artists was the same, that workers were pressed to raise production and artists to make this palatable.[24] The result was that production became a joyless means to an end. He ends the letter:

> Vom Standpunkt des Sozialismus aus müssen wir, meiner Meinung nach, diese Aufteilung, *Mittel* und *Zweck, Produzieren* und *Lebensstandard*, aufheben. Wir müssen das Produzieren zum eigentlichen Lebensinhalt machen und es so gestalten, es mit so viel Freiheit und Freiheiten ausstatten, daß es an sich verlockend ist.
>
> (From the standpoint of socialism we must, in my opinion, overcome this separation between *means* and *ends*, between *production* and *living standard*. We must make production into the proper content of life and so organise it, furnish it with such freedom and liberties, that it is attractive in itself.) [25]

The tone of this is more like Lenin's 'unless' in 'The truth unites', particularly in the light of Brecht's warning in the same letter of 'organised fascistic elements' and a threatened Third World War. He rejects here the division between economic and cultural production, as well as the view, which had been his own in the *Short Organum*, that their respective roles, in a separated but complementary way, were to maintain, and entertain us. A model such as this could not protect itself, as I have said, against the expediencies of a hard-faced economic determinism. Now, in 1953, however, Brecht argues that production must be made 'attractive' in itself, and cannot depend on artistic culture as a reinforcement or cosmetic: sweetening what is passed off as a necessarily bitter economic pill. This is a significant revision, and, to this extent, Brecht corrects his 'mistake', strengthening the criticism of his 'critical support' of official economic strategy. Nowhere, however, does this revision penetrate to a criticism of the economic or political order as such, or to those in political power. Nor is Brecht led to explicitly question his own earlier assumptions. A (self) critique and different perspective on cultural and economic development are glimpsed, but then closed off, Brecht's reaffirmed support for the Party, and for the actions of Russian troops, emerging finally, in the cumulative effect of the whole letter, to balance and blunt his sharpened criticism.

In the end his response is reminiscent of another of Lenin's later remarks on Bolshevik Russia, that 'we lack sufficient civilisation to enable us to pass straight on to socialism, although we have the political requisites.'[26] The problem with this thinking, once again, being that it compartmentalises 'civilisation' and 'politics', and conceives of history as an accumulative sequence in which, given time, talks, and the right tempo, civilisation can be added onto certain established prerequisites, and thus produce socialism as a joint grand total.

Brecht's hope and loyalty were therefore shaken by June 1953, but not rocked to their foundations. Its single main effect, one feels, was, in his view, to postpone the prospect of socialism, until Stalinism was liquidated. How this was to occur without an open and consistent critique of the economic reductionism and paranoia which were Stalin's heritage, Brecht does not say. Meanwhile, present 'communism' moved in a quite contrary direction: a joyless 'means' to what would have to be a different 'end'; its record indelibly tainted by the ill-treatment and execution of Berlin workers.

Nor were developments in artistic culture, in Brecht's experience, any more encouraging. There were signs even in early 1953 of official indifference to the productions of the Berliner Ensemble, and this was coupled with outright hostility towards Eisler's *Faust* and Brecht's *Urfaust*; condemned alike as offending against the 'cultural heritage' and, in Eisler's case, by no less than Ulbricht, as having 'formalistically defaced by caricaturing the great ideas of Goethe's *Faust*'.[27] The signs were, in fact, that the Party was responsive to neither workers nor artists 'from the standpoint of socialism', as Brecht understood it. Brecht did not, it is true, fully revise his views on how to achieve socialism in the face of the evident reluctance of Stalinism to liquidate itself, but no more did he compromise with what Esslin calls 'the realities of life in a Communist country'. Brecht's commitment to a socialist future and in his last years particularly to the cause of peace, appeared if anything more idealistic, with all the strengths and weaknesses this implies; precisely because it was maintained in spite of a reality which gave his 'ideals' the slimmest of chances. Some of the leading ingredients of this difficult situation — Brecht's idealism, his relation to the Party and, along with this, the misrepresentation of his views in the West — are well expressed in the poem, from 1953, 'Not what was meant'. It ends

Even the narrowest minds
In which peace is harboured
Are more welcome to the arts than the art lover
Who is also a lover of the art of war. (P, p. 438)

In the very last years of his life Brecht spoke 'outright' against the reintroduction of military conscription in both East and West; he warned against war and argued in favour of the eventual reunification of Germany.[28] The brute facts, however, are that the GDR, in immediate response to the FRG's joining Nato, entered a military agreement which brought the Warsaw Pact into existence on 14 May 1955, and led shortly after, in January 1956, to the formation of The National People's Army under the Warsaw Pact's commander-in-chief.[29] National service was introduced in January 1962, and over 30 years after Brecht's death the Berlin wall still stands. 'Socialism' apparently continues to lack 'sufficient civilisation', while all the time accumulating the needful military, economic and political 'prerequisites' which fail to produce it.

II

The political and cultural events of 1953 established, I suggest, both that the SED was not the party of Brecht's hopes, and that there was no other. The difficult relation with its 'narrowest minds' then ensued. At the same time, Brecht's situation and perspective were not exclusively governed by his relation to the Party. An additional factor in the making of East German communism, as June 1953 also revealed, was the working class. Brecht's perception of and relation to this class, as artist and intellectual, was obviously a further determining ingredient in his own 'Marxist-Leninism' and fidelity to dialectical materialism. I want therefore to turn now to this relationship.

June 1953 'alienated' existence Brecht said: it was like 'a blow with the fist' from the working class,[30] awakening himself and others who had subscribed to a fiction of that class to its reality. What Brecht perceived in this connection was the uneven and unsettled nature of working-class consciousness; its potential inclination to competing fascist and progressive or socialist ideologies. His view of the political role of the working class, indeed of the middle class, was therefore altered. 'The people' or 'mass' assumed a stronger place in his political vocabularly, and this change in turn affected the tasks he assigned his theatre, and the ways he thought of its audience.

This is not a change which can be attributed exclusively to June 1953, although this confrontation provided a focus for it. What we can say, first of all, is that prior to his return to Europe, Brecht had seen the German working class at a distance, in subjectively contradictory ways, but came once in Berlin to see working-class consciousness as composed of objective contradictions. In March 1945, for example, while at work on his versification of *The Communist Manifesto*, he received news from Germany with the words 'ruins, and not a sign from the working classes there'.[31] Fritz Kortner, similarly, remembered Brecht's complaint that the German people were 'lackey-souled'. And yet in an earlier exchange with Thomas Mann, in the midst of much talk of the 'good' and 'bad' Germany, Brecht had defended the war-time underground opposition to Hitler, and on another occasion, at the end of 1946, spoken confidently to Alfred Kantorowicz of progressive forces having arisen in Germany equal to the task of reconstruction.[32] After the workers' revolt of 1953, however, we find Brecht referring in 'Cultural policy and academy of arts' both to 'parts of the working class' with a 'completely capitalist way of looking at things', and to 'the revolutionary proletariat'. (BT, p. 268) Then in a note titled 'Contradiction in the proletariat' he talks, directly identifying this inner division, of the bulk of workers who in their fear of change and support for the status quo, join their exploiters, the bourgeoisie, in its struggle against other workers.[33] On the same theme, pointing to its reverse aspect, he writes in the *Appendices to the Short Organum* of how

> members of a given class are not immune to ideas from which their class cannot benefit. Just as the oppressed can succumb to the ideas of their oppressors, so members of the oppressor class can fall victim to those of the oppressed. In certain periods when the classes are fighting for the leadership of mankind any man who is not hopelessly corrupt may feel a strong urge to be counted among its pioneers and to press ahead. (BT, p. 278)

As an artist Brecht responded to these divisions and shifting class allegiances by seeing it as his task to address both proletarian and bourgeois elements in his society, or more particularly, that section of it which constituted his audience; some of whom were working class ('a bare 7%' Brecht wrote), some Party members and Party officials, but most of whom were middle class and from the West.[34] He spoke thus of artists

> producing for a public recruited from various classes. Its level of education and also its degree of demoralisation are very varied. Equally various are the needs that art must satisfy. The state is primarily interested in the workers; our best artists are primarily interested in them too. But at the same time there are other classes' tastes and needs that must be taken account of. All of this can only be accomplished by a highly qualified, highly differentiated art. (BT, p. 267)

In a note of September 1954, this is summed up in the description 'A Socialist Realist work of art is based on a working-class viewpoint and appeals to all men of good will.' (BT, p. 269) Brecht's concern to reach this broader audience accounts for his frustration, mentioned above, at the lack of ready-made dialectical materialists. It also appears to offer further grounds for the view that he 'compromised' in his last years. But 'compromise' is not the word for a sharpened sense of political reality and the complexities of class consciousness. Indeed the perception of the uneven nature of working-class consciousness is perfectly Leninist and a sign of Brecht's advance upon *The Measures Taken* and the one-sided view of Lenin, the Party and the working class, which that play and *What is to be Done?*, on its own, have given.[35] Brecht does not talk, moreover, of pandering to the 'capitalist way of looking at things' evident in certain sections of the working class, but of how 'In getting rid of this attitude the arts must do their bit.' (BT, p. 268) Nor does he at all abandon the principle of political organisation and discipline necessary to revolution. As he writes in 'Contradiction in the proletariat':

> Ein Umsturz ist mit großen Mühen, Gefahren, Änderungen aller Gewohnheiten und so weiter verknüpft. Vor allem müssen sich die Arbeiter, die ihn anstreben, in kriegerische Handlungen gegen die Bourgeoisie einlassen und sich unter eine strikte strenge Disziplin stellen, um den sehr harten

Kampf führen zu könen.

(A revolution is associated with great troubles, dangers, changes in all kinds of habits and so on. Above all the workers who aspire to it must engage in war-like actions against the bourgeoisie and put themselves under strict and rigorous discipline, in order to be able to continue the very bitter struggle.)[36]

All the same it cannot be said that Brecht's ideas in this period have their provenance entirely in Lenin. The concept of an interventionist art in which, as Brecht put it in relation to Strittmatter's *Katzgraben*, 'we must infect a working class audience with the urge to alter the world (and supply it with some of the relevant knowledge)', (BT, p. 247) would seem to confer on art a political role analogous to that of the Leninist party. Although in saying this we have to recognise that more was involved at this point than putting a Leninist thesis on stage, and that Brecht was *extending* Lenin's ideas into the realm of art in ways which have no direct precedent in Lenin himself. If, however, we agree to call this idea of art's function and relation to the working-class 'Leninist', other statements would appear to owe more to Marx, in whose writings the idea of 'the Party' is undeveloped, and to Marx's emphasis on working-class self-emancipation. Brecht's statement in the *Theaterarbeit*, for example, that 'Nothing but the advance of the workers and furthering the advance of the workers can lead to their [the arts'] own advance', (BT, p. 240) would seem to carry this Marxist echo, prioritising working-class over cultural activity, since the arts here 'contribute' to working-class advance, but do not politicise it in the external and politically avant-garde sense the language of 'infecting' and 'supplying' above suggests. Along the same lines, Brecht speaks in the *Short Organum* of a theatre for the suburbs 'at the disposal of those who live hard and produce much', where if they find it hard to pay and understand, the theatre will 'have to learn in many respects what they need and how they need it'. (BT, p. 186)

These statements, and others of a similar kind, were made prior to the events of June 1953, and though it would be wrong to suggest that either position (and Brecht's debt to Lenin and Marx) was abandoned after this date, they are joined in statements and poems from the middle 1950s with a belief in the 'wisdom of the masses' or the 'wisdom of the people' which give a new inflection to Brecht's thinking.[37] Völker is right to point in this connection to Brecht's enthusiasm for the Chinese Revolution and to suggest that these 'frequent references to the "wisdom of the people'' during the last years of his life reflected a political idea gleaned from the writings of Mao Tse Tung.'[38]

We should neither over- nor underestimate this change. Brecht referred to the 'people' and 'masses' much earlier, in the essay 'The popular and the realistic' of 1938 for example. In that essay, however, these terms appeared more or less interchangeably with others, such as 'the working people', 'the broad working mass', 'workers' and 'proletariat', and they were together employed in an argument which assumed at the outset that class conflict was stark and uncomplicated; a matter of 'open warfare' in which 'It has become easier to take sides.' (BT, p. 107) The difference between this and Brecht's later thinking was that, as already indicated, he came in the East Berlin of the 1950s, to see divisions within and across class lines, between latent reactionary elements, and new potentially progressive groupings, and saw these moreover in a 'workers state' in which the odds had lengthened considerably against the concept of popularity, meaning 'accessible to the people' ('Volkstümlichkeit') such as he had explored in the previous essay, in favour now of a presiding 'Funkstionärstümlichkeit' ('accessible to the official'). (BT, p. 269) The 'wisdom of the people' served in these changed circumstances, I suggest, as a broader category than the 'revolutionary proletariat' rather than as a substitute for it. It combined, as it were, 'a working-class viewpoint' with 'all men of good will', and derived as much as anything from the failures of the East German 'Marxist-Leninist' party, and the non-revolutionary consciousness of 'even the majority' of the working class.

This change in Brecht's political vocabulary can also be given a more intellectual derivation, however. The relevant essay here being of course Mao's *On Contradiction*, named by Brecht as having made the strongest impression on him of any book in 1954.[39] Brecht's comments elsewhere suggest that he valued Mao's text firstly for its distinction between principal and secondary contradictions, and as a means therefore of analysing the changing relation between class struggle and national conflict, and secondly, as an example of the continued life of dialectical thought after its elimination under Stalin.[40] Other texts by Mao, including a three-volume set of *Selected Writings* published in German translation in 1956, were in Brecht's library in Berlin, and though it is not possible to say what he read of these or when he read them, there are nevertheless quite striking similarities between Brecht's views in the period and, to take one instance, Mao's *Talks at the Yenam Forum on Literature and Art* (1942). This had become a central text in the formation of cultural and artistic policy in post-revolutionary China, and Brecht did possess a separate translation, published as a pamphlet in Berlin in 1952. Brecht's argument, for example, in the 1953 essay 'Cultural policy and academy of arts' that 'For a truly socialist art the question of quality is politically decisive' — by which he means to distinguish between a true and a false, unaesthetic, socialist realism (marked by 'the mere presence on the canvas of workers and peasants', BT, p. 267), recalls quite closely Mao's distinction between 'the political criterion' and 'the artistic criterion':

> We deny not only that there is an abstract and absolutely unchangeable political criterion, but also that there is an abstract and absolutely unchangeable artistic criterion . . . what we demand is the unity of politics and art, the unity of content and form, the unity of revolutionary political content and the highest possible perfection of artistic form. Works of art which lack artistic quality have no force, however progressive they are politically. Therefore, we oppose both the tendency to produce works of art with a wrong political viewpoint and the tendency towards the 'poster and slogan style' which is correct in political viewpoint but lacking in artistic power. On questions of literature and art we must carry on a struggle on two fronts.[41]

Brecht would have been very likely to agree with this, as with the ensuing emphasis, which indeed occurs in his own essay, on the need to raise both artistic and political standards of education. 'The people, too, have their shortcomings', writes Mao; 'Among the proletariat many retain petty-bourgeois ideas', and later, that these 'should be overcome by criticism and self-criticism within the people's own ranks, and such criticism and self-criticism is also one of the most important tasks of literature and art.'[42] Amongst several other points of similarity (the dialectic between popularisation and education, the need to learn dialectical materialism as opposed to 'Dogmatic "Marxism" ', the need for intellectuals to adopt a proletarian standpoint, the enlivening transformation of the literary heritage), one feels that Brecht would have welcomed the general concern in Mao's essay with what Dave Laing calls 'the relations of production of revolutionary art.' Mao 'is concerned', writes Laing, 'with clarifying the elements of the mode of production of revolutionary art, ensuring the productivity of revolutionary artists, rather than in regulating or legislating for, the precise forms of the finished products.'[43] This we remember was precisely Brecht's requirement of the SED. Finally, in a most Brechtian formulation, Mao writes of the revolutionary writer or artist, that 'only by speaking for the masses can he educate them and only by being their pupil can he be their teacher.'[44]

Beyond similarities such as these there is evidence of a diverse and sometimes perhaps trivial kind suggesting that China held a consistent attraction for Brecht. There were his own 'Chinese Poems', for example, including his version of Mao's 'Thoughts while flying over the Great Wall', his special admiration for the poet Po Chü-yi, his interest in the ancient dialectician Mo Tse and in Confucius, the essay 'V-effects in Chinese acting', the Chinese settings of many plays, poems and prose works, and even the simplicity of his personal tastes.[45] Though many of these habits and influences often of course predate the Chinese Revolution and any possible acquaintance with Mao's writing, they nevertheless indicate a predilection, which was then confirmed as a more precise interest in, and affinity with, aspects of Mao's thought. This is not to say that these features overtook more 'Western' characteristics in Brecht's work, any more than Mao's *On Contradiction* replaced his long debt to Marx and Lenin. The *Appendices to the Short Organum* refer typically, for example, to both Mao's essay and Lenin's 'On the question of dialectics' (BT, pp. 278, 279), and both texts, as we have seen, were said to be required reading for the participants in the *Coriolanus* dialogue.

The question of Brecht's Marxism becomes therefore a question of the compatibility of the three 'classics', Marx, Lenin and Mao. The argument has often been made that the emphasis in Maoism on the political role of the peasantry rather than the urban proletariat puts it outside the tradition of revolutionary Marxism.[46] In which case, to revert to an earlier theme, Brecht's Marxism can be said to be 'compromised' although this is hardly the compromise anti-communist and liberal humanist critics have in mind. On the other hand, references to the 'masses' or to 'the people' are not of themselves unMarxist (as Marx's analysis of the French Commune discussed below demonstrates). Brecht did not comment on such niceties, or on the revolutionary 'authenticity' of Maoism. We can put this down to his confusion, or indifference, or as my remarks have suggested, to a more pragmatic attempt to respond to the differentiated class structure and consciousness he witnessed in East Germany with a militantly populist and appropriately 'differentiated' art.

What, in addition, quite clearly impressed Brecht, and joined Mao with Marx and Lenin in his thinking was their common exploration of dialectical materialism: at once the enemy of party dogma and a tool for analysing complex class relations and the process of social change. Though Brecht talks therefore of the revolutionary proletariat, the progressive middle class, the people, the wisdom of the mass, and so on, his relationship to the mixed audience this vocabulary represents, was consistently conceived in dialectical terms, as between leader and led, teacher and pupil.

Thus in the essay, 'The popular and the realistic', once more, Brecht had defined 'popular' by way of a series of conditions which give the writer a role analogous to that of the revolutionary vanguard. (There is significantly, at this date, no mention of the complicating relationship with the Party as such.) Popular literature is described as being 'intelligible to the broad masses, taking over their own forms of expression and enriching them/adopting and consolidating their standpoint/representing the most progressive section of the people in such a way that it can take over the leadership: thus intelligible to other sections too'. (BT, p. 108) This is remarkably close to later statements for all that has been said about Brecht's changed perspective. The difference, I think, lies in the fact that in later writings, the writer does not only 'take over' or 'consolidate' or 'make intelligible' but more actively, criticises and educates. To Max Gorelik in 1944, for example, speaking of the artist's relation to the 'oppressed classes', Brecht says the artist 'needn't land up in an ivory tower so long as he is really concerned to take part in the struggles of the oppressed, to find out their interests and represent them and develop his art on their behalf.' But this is said in the context of a 'sharpening of the class struggle' which had engendered disabling 'conflicts of interest in our audience', and with the proviso that the artist cannot 'blindly admit the oppressed classes as a court of first instance, for their taste and their instincts are oppressed as well.' (BT, p. 160) The perception of 'conflicts of interest' again alters the function of Brecht's art; it becomes less 'blindly' the servant and representative of the oppressed class, and more discriminating (and less compromising) at the same time as its educative net is spread more widely. In this vein he writes in notes from the middle 1950s on the theme, firstly, of 'comprehensibility', that 'Not everything that the Russian working and peasant masses failed to grasp immediately in the Bolsheviks' statements was nonsense' (BT, p. 269) and, secondly, on 'intelligibility', that,

> style only comes into the matter in so far as the style needs to be as simple as possible, as intelligible as possible; the battle for socialism cannot be won by a handful of highly educated connoisseurs, a few people who know how to understand complicated charades. But I said as simple *as possible*. Certain complex processes which we need to understand cannot be *quite* simply portrayed. (BT, p. 270)

Finally on this theme, in a note commenting on the tangled, contradictory process of learning, Brecht concludes 'Die Weisheit des Volks muß in allem das letzte Wort sprechen *und doch* ist sie vermengt mit Aberglaube. Iregendwo müssen wir anfangen, nirgends dürfen wir aufhören.' ('The wisdom of the people must have the last word in everything *and yet* it is muddled with superstition. We must begin somewhere, nowhere may we cease.') (my italics)[47]

The 'travails of the plains' did not end therefore. As Brecht wrote in the poem 'Looking for the new and old':

> . . . For our time
> And the time of our children is the time of struggles
> Between the new and the old . . .
> The struggles between the classes
> The struggles between new and old
> Rage also within one man. (P, p. 424)

It was these intersecting processes of struggle; subjective, social and historical, as Brecht depicts them, which he himself experienced and illuminated. His eight years in East Berlin were marked by unresolved friction, conflict and differentiation; and altogether by a sense of incompletion and imperfection which Brecht persisted in meeting in the spirit of an openness to change, and a readiness for the new. The working class did not arrive on cue at a revolutionary consciousness, the state did not 'wither', communism was 'only hinted at, never put into practice';[48] but this did not mean that Brecht abandoned the hope of a communist future. The times were not yet right for a new production of *The Measures Taken;* he was not ready and nor, until late 1956, was East Germany ready for a performance of *Days of the Commune*, and meanwhile, a successful play such as *Herr Puntila* was 'only epic theatre to the extent this can be accepted (and offered) today'.[49] Yet the concept of epic theatre was subsumed in a more comprehensive and more overtly political dramatic theory. And this itself was incomplete: or in a better description, an expression *in* its very incompleteness, of Brecht's commitment to a process of revision and development. His artistic theory, his political beliefs and creative work were all held in tension with official definitions, present complacencies, and what 'can be accepted (and offered) today'.

This did not mean that Brecht was above contradiction and ambiguity — far from it, as the foregoing discussion attests. He did have to hand, however, the means to comprehend and negotiate the manifold aspects of struggle and contradiction. For if dialectics was slowed by Stalin, and soon removed from the official agenda of the GDR, it was advanced and reaffirmed on Brecht's own. To draw upon and recommend texts in the tradition of dialectical materialism, as he did, to call his theatre a 'dialectical theatre' was in a manner to express the critical distance there was between himself and — to do justice to Brecht's loyalties — an, *as yet,* unMarxist 'socialist' society. We can say the same of the term 'dialectics' in this context as Brecht said of *Verfremdung*: that its use 'announce(d) a contradiction.'[50]

Notes

1. And of which he was himself an example, cf. 'A new house', *Poems 1913-1956*, John Willett and Ralph Manheim (eds) (Eyre Methuen, London, 1979), p. 416.
2. Quoted, Klaus Völker, *Brecht: A Biography* (Marion Boyars, London and Boston, 1979), p. 337.
3. Martin McCauley, *The German Democratic Republic Since 1945* (Macmillan, London, 1983), p. 58, and cf. Völker, *Brecht*, p. 338.
4. McCauley, p. 55.
5. *Gesammelte Werke*, 20 (Suhrkamp, Frankfurt am Main, 1967), p. 326.
6. Chris Harman, *Bureaucracy and Revolution in Eastern Europe* (Pluto Press, London, 1974), pp. 70, 75. See also the account in McCauley, pp. 63-6.
7. Völker, *Brecht*, pp. 354-5.
8. Quoted, Harman, *Bureaucracy and Revolution*, p. 72.
9. Völker, *Brecht*, p. 355; and Brecht quoted p. 357.
10. *Gesammelte Werke*, 20, p. 327.
11. Quoted, Völker, *Brecht*, p. 356.
12. Ibid., p. 355.
13. Harman, *Bureaucracy and Revolution*, p. 79; and cf. McCauley, p. 211.
14. *Gesammelte Werke*, 20, p. 327.
15. Quoted, Ewen, *Bertolt Brecht. His Life, His Art, and His Times* (Citadel Press, New York, 1969), p. 458.

16. Quoted, Völker, *Brecht*, p. 339.
17. Quoted, ibid., p. 357.
18. *Poems 1913-1956*, p. 601.
19. Harman, *Bureaucracy and Revolution*, p. 78. McCauley says estimates of those dead ranged 'from 25 to over 300', p. 65.
20. Harman, *Bureaucracy and Revolution*, p. 79.
21. Ibid., p. 157.
22. Esslin, *Brecht. A Choice of Evils* (Eyre Methuen, London, 1959, revised 1980), p. 157.
23. Quoted, Robert Conquest, *Lenin* (Fontana, London, 1972), p. 113.
24. *Gesammelte Werke*, 20, p. 327.
25. Ibid., p. 328.
26. Quoted, Conquest, *Lenin*, p. 113.
27. Quoted, Völker, *Brecht*, p. 341; cf. also p. 342, and John Willett, *Brecht in Context* (Methuen, London and New York, 1984), p. 201.
28. *Gesammelte Werke*, 20, p. 348-9.
29. McCauley, pp. 74, 75, 116.
30. *Arbeitsjournal*, vol. 2, 1943-55, Werner Hecht (ed.) (Suhrkamp, Frankfurt am Main, 1973), p. 1009.
31. Quoted Ewen, *Bertolt Brecht*, p. 393.
32. Ibid., pp. 301-2.
33. *Gesammelte Werke*, 20, p. 337.
34. Cf. Völker, *Brecht*, p. 343, and Willett, *Brecht in Context*, p. 201.
35. On Lenin's view of uneven class consciousness, see Chris Harman, *Party and Class* (Socialist Unlimited, London, 1983), p. 13.
36. *Gesammelte Werke*, 20, p. 337.
37. See the references in ibid., pp. 326, 332, as well as the poems 'The bread of the people', 'The solution', and 'Great times wasted', *Poems*, pp. 435, 440.
38. Völker, *Brecht*, pp. 373-4.
39. *Gesammelte Werke*, 20, p. 343.
40. Cf. *Brecht on Theatre*, pp. 262, 278, and the above quoted passage on the fate of dialectics under Stalin, *Gesammelte Werke*, 20, p. 326.
41. *Selected Works of Mao Tse Tung*, vol. III (Foreign Language Press, Peking, 1967), pp. 89-90.
42. Ibid., pp. 71, 91.
43. Dave Laing, *The Marxist Theory of Art* (Harvester Press, Brighton, Sussex, 1978), pp. 74, 76.
44. Mao, *Selected Works*, vol. III, pp. 84-5.
45. For some discussion of this aspect of Brecht's thought and persona, see Antony Tatlow, *The Mask of Evil: Brecht's Response to the Poetry, Theatre and Thought of China and Japan — a Comparative and Critical Evaluation* (Lang, Berne, 1977), esp. p. 500-27, and also John Willett, *Brecht in Context*, pp. 206-8, and Martin Esslin's essay on *Me-Ti*, 'Brecht in Chinese Garb', in *Mediations* (Sphere Books, London, 1983), esp. p. 54.
46. Cf. John Molyneux, 'What is the real Marxist tradition?', *International Socialism*, 20 (Summer, 1983), pp. 38-46.
47. *Gesammelte Werke*, 20, p. 332.
48. Quoted, Ronald Gray, *Brecht. The Dramatist* (Cambridge University

Press, Cambridge, 1976), p. 153.

49. Quoted, Völker, *Brecht*, p. 336.

50. *Arbeitsjoural*, vol. I, p. 216.

13

Communist Ways and *Days of the Commune*

Brecht's last 'original' play, *Days of the Commune*, sums up much of what has been said about his Marxism, his conception of 'the people' and the working class, as well as his relationship to the East German authorities.

First of all, as Keith Dickson points out, Brecht avoids presenting a 'positive' hero or heroine in the play of the kind official socialist realism required. Potentially 'heroic' figures 'are passed over', Dickson writes, 'in favour of representatives of the anonymous masses such as "Papa", Coco and Jean, and the Commune's legendary heroines . . . are replaced by unprepossessing figures such as Madame Cabet, Geneviève Guéricault, and Babette.'[1] Brecht also scales down other historically authentic personages such as Charles Delescluze, Eugène Varlin and Gabriel Ranvier, and reduces the degree of alleged fanaticism and violence associated with the Commune, both in its general reputation and in connection with the figure Raoul Rigault.[2] As a consequence Dickson feels that 'The whole point of [Brecht's] interpretation of the Commune is that its unique strength lay in its being a spontaneous uprising without leaders of the traditional stamp.'[3] Brecht was concerned, he argues, to highlight the forms of participatory democracy the Commune introduced as an expression of the popular will; he wanted to dramatise 'this dawning of a new era' rather than 'the academic issue of the Commune's socialist orthodoxy or the lessons to be learned from its failure.'[4]

Politically this interpretation would make Brecht's play more 'Luxemburgist' or syndicalist than Marxist or specifically Leninist. It rests, however, on a partial and in the end misleading view. For while it is perfectly true, and in keeping with the tendency in Brecht's thinking discussed above, that the 'masses' or 'people' —

Langevin, the 'women of the 11th District', and many literally anonymous men and women, as well as those mentioned above — play an important part in Brecht's production, this cannot, of itself, be said to distinguish his view from a Marxist interpretation of the Commune.

We can point to differences between these interpretations certainly. Marx in his essay 'The civil war in France', for example — which Brecht consulted while working on the play — writes of the 'true secret' of the Commune as being that 'It was essentially a working-class government.'[5] Engels similarly, and if anything more forcefully, refers consistently in his 1891 Introduction to Marx's essay, to 'workers' and 'working men', concluding in a celebrated passage that the Commune was an historical demonstration of the 'dictatorship of the proletariat'.[6] Against this we might set Varlin's words in the play on the '*people* of Paris' moving to elect 'their own, free, self-governing Commune' (my italics)[7] or Rigault's description of the state as 'the self-governing *people* of Paris'. (p. 54, my italics)

So far the 'Marxist' interpretation appears to be 'proletarian' while Brecht's is more 'populist' or 'plebeian'. But one can quite easily turn this kind of textual evidence around. Thus Marx spoke not only of 'working-class government', but of the 'armed people' of the Commune replacing the standing army,[8] just as Rigault does in the play ('the regular mercenary army will be dissolved' he says, 'The army of the Commune is the army of the people', p. 55). Again, in a letter of April 1871, Marx wrote with the Commune in mind, that the smashing of the bourgeois state was 'the precondition for every real people's revolution on the Continent'.[9] But then, if we can find a plebeian reading in Marx we can find a proletarian one in Brecht, for in the text of his play Varlin refers to 'the working class' and 'the working people' taking their future into their own hands (in the same speech in which he refers to the 'people of Paris') and later describes the Commune as 'A republic . . . which will hand the means of production back to the workers'. (pp. 39, 54)

The difference between 'workers' and 'people' might seem to be a mere splitting of the hairs of orthodoxy. But it is not. Lenin comments that 'This idea of a "people's" revolution seems strange coming from Marx', and explains it as referring to a revolution in which the 'mass of the people, their vast majority, come out actively, independently, with their own economic and political demands'.[10] The designation 'people's revolution' was, moreover,

Lenin explains, historically accurate, for 'In Europe, in 1871, the proletariat did not constitute the majority of the people in any country on the Continent'. The 'people' was composed, he says, of the proletariat and peasantry together. Only in a common alliance could they make a ' "real people's revolution" ' and in speaking of this, Marx was taking 'strict account of the actual balance of class forces' in 1871. Lenin comments that 'the Paris Commune was actually working its way toward such an alliance'.[11] In line with this we find in *Days of the Commune*, precisely an appeal from 'The Speaker of the Commune' to the peasants in Thiers' army to join in 'the great struggle of the people against their oppressors' since 'You are workers as we are.' (p. 76)

The political vocabularly of Brecht's play, its reference to both people and workers, is therefore historically accurate and Marxist. More importantly, in the light of what has been said above of Brecht's perception of the working class and his audience, the play takes on a relevance to the 'actual balance of class forces' and uneven political consciousness he saw in post-war Berlin. Dickson sees only half the play's importance, therefore. He praises Brecht for not having 'falsified the record' in his 'impressive historical mosaic',[12] but fails to consider the influence the post-war situation in East Germany had upon Brecht's choice of material. From this perspective the mixed working-class and plebeian character given to the Commune in the play appears as not only true to past history but relevant also to history in the making. The Commune provided the means for both historical drama and contemporary parable; an opportunity in short for the 'differentiated art' needed to instruct and entertain the militant and reactionary workers, progressive bourgeois, and Marxist and non-Marxists in official positions, comprising Brecht's potential audience and the social potential of the new Germany.

The characters in the play are accordingly themselves differentiated. Thus, if the 'anonymous masses' are 'the people', they are also workers ('Papa' is a bricklayer, Jean an unemployed engine driver, Mme Cabet and Babette are seamstresses, Geneviève is a schoolteacher), who are then further distinguished one from the other by their political views. Philippe, the baker's assistant, for example, acts according to his conservative political instincts. He joins Thiers' army, is prepared almost to shoot his brother, runs off to Versailles after the retreating bourgeoisie, and then, in a double change of heart, first joins then deserts the barricades. Philippe's mind is 'all in a jumble', or as his brother, the steady and tolerant Communard François describes him, he 'hasn't learned to think straight'. (pp. 41, 78) Jean, François's companion, is, unlike his friend, an impatient militant for whom the National Guard are 'too far to the right.' (p. 21) He defends the execution of the two Generals Lecomte and Thomas, and is ready to fight Thiers' army of peasants and march on Versailles while other prevaricate. The figure 'Papa' expresses a revolutionary and utopian conscience throughout the play ('You're always ahead of us', says Langevin, the Commune delegate, p. 39), while of the women Geneviève is more of a political idealist than Babette, and both are set off from the more self-seeking and cautious Mme Cabet.

The Commune delegates are similarly differentiated: firstly on the issue of legality and the appropriation of necessary funds from the Bank of France — the majority opposing the respectful Beslay — and then on the need to march on Versailles and the use of violence. The moderate Delescluze and a group of other virtually 'anonymous' delegates (Valles, Arnaud, Billioray, Avrial, Champy, Dupont, Vermorel, Jourde and Theisz) oppose the arguments of Varlin, Rigault and Ranvier that they use 'terror to fight terror'. Initially, Langevin takes the same moderate attitude, until he too is persuaded that 'we have no freedom other than to fight our enemies', and that the struggle offers a choice only 'between blood-stained hands and severed hands.' (pp. 74, 81) There are further differences between the more militant figures. Rigault, for example, refers consistently to the 'people' while Varlin, as befits a real-life member of the International, talks of both the people and of workers, the working class and proletariat. His is a minority voice, however, and the revolutionary argument is defeated, in keeping with Marx's assessment that 'the majority of the Commune was in no way socialist, nor could it be.'[13]

The result of Brecht's presentation is that lessons can be drawn from the play, as they have been drawn in the Marxist tradition from the historical Commune, which are much more specific for what Dickson terms 'the would-be revolutionary' than, in his words, 'the callousness of history on its circuitous route to Utopia.'[14] This utopian aspect, first of all, and what Dickson sees as the main interest of the play, is itself endebted, at one significant moment, as Dickson recognises, to Marx's own account. In the play 'Papa' speaks of the evening before the opening session of the Commune as:

> . . . the first night in the history of Paris, when there will be no murder, no cheating, no attacks on women. This is the

> first time it is safe to walk the streets. We don't need the police. The bankers, swindlers, tax collectors, factory owners, priests, prostitutes and politicians have all run off to Versailles. At long last, Paris is a fit place to live in. (p. 50)

In Marx, the inspiration for Brecht's passage runs as follows:

> Wonderful, indeed, was the change the Commune had wrought in Paris! No longer any trace of the meretricious Paris of the Second Empire. No longer was Paris the rendezvous of British landlords, Irish absentees, American ex-slaveholders and shoddy men, Russian ex-serf-owners, and Wallachian boyards. No more corpses at the morgue, no nocturnal burglaries, scarcely any robberies; in fact, for the first time since the days of February, 1848, the streets of Paris were safe, and that without any police of any kind. 'We', said a member of the Commune, 'hear no longer of assassination, theft, and personal assault; it seems, indeed, as if the police had dragged along with it to Versailles all its conservative friends.' The *cocottes* had refound the scent of their protectors — the absconding men of family, religion, and, above all, of property. In their stead, the real women of Paris showed again at the surface — heroic, noble, and devoted, like the women of antiquity. Working, thinking, fighting, bleeding Paris — almost forgetful, in its incubation of a new society, of the cannibals at its gates — radiant in the enthusiasm of its historic initiative![15]

Lenin, it might be pointed out, in a passage in *The State and Revolution* where he expands on Marx's belief in the dictatorship of the proletariat 'as the necessary transition from capitalism to communism', writes in a similarly 'utopian' vein, of a future when it will be possible to speak of unqualified freedom and democracy:

> Only in communist society, when the resistance of the capitalists has been completely crushed, when the capitalists have disappeared, when there are no classes . . . *only* then 'the state . . . ceases to exist,' and '*it becomes possible to speak of freedom*'. Only then will a complete democracy become possible and be realised, a democracy without any exceptions whatever . . . people will gradually *become accustomed* to observing the elementary rules of social intercourse . . . without force,

> without coercion, without subordination, *without the special apparatus* for coercion called the state.[16]

One of the lessons of the Commune in the Marxist tradition, therefore, was that it opened up the prospect of 'utopia', along the specific and far from 'circuitous route' of the dictatorship of the proletariat. At the same time, said Lenin, 'We are not utopians'.[17] Marx, he says, did not attempt 'to make up a utopia' but treated future communism and the transition to it on the basis of its known origin in capitalism and the nature of historical change. 'Marx', as Lenin puts it, 'did not set out to *discover* the political *forms* of this future state', but with the rise of the revolutionary proletarian movement 'began to study the forms it had *discovered*.' Here lies the special importance of the Commune, for

> The Commune is the form 'at last discovered' by the proletarian revolution, under which the economic emancipation of labour can take place.
> The Commune is the first attempt by a proletarian revolution to *smash* the bourgeois state machine; and it is the political form 'at last discovered' by which the smashed state machine can and must be *replaced*.[18]

The Paris Commune therefore 'discovered' the political form of the transition from capitalism to communism. For Lenin a recognition of this extension of the class struggle to the transitional form of proletarian dictatorship is 'the touchstone' of a '*real* understanding and recognition of Marxism'; it 'constitutes the most profound distinction between the Marxist and the bourgeois.'[19] If we view Brecht's play in the light of these remarks, we therefore have a way of assessing, simultaneously, both its lessons and Brecht's relation to Marxism-Leninism.

In response to Russia Brecht, as I have said, identified but equivocated on the Stalinist form of a 'dictatorship *over* the proletariat'. Dickson's view of Brecht's presentation of the Paris Commune as an uprising 'without leaders of the traditional stamp', which dispensed with heroes, and obliterated 'the distinction between the rules and the ruled', leads him to conclude that Brecht has here 'dramatised the short-lived dictatorship of the proletariat.'[20] Unfortunately, it is not this easy. Certainly we can accept that here, eventually, Brecht went behind recent history to set in motion a discussion of the acknowledged first instance of proletarian dictatorship. We might think too that with this play he intended to greet the new German state with his rejection, which he hoped it would adopt, of previous and continuing Soviet distortions of the transition to full communism. There are problems, however, in suggesting that Brecht simply dramatised the dictatorship of the proletariat with some or all of this in mind. Firstly because proletarian dictatorship, as discussed by Marx, Engels and Lenin, cannot be identified *only* with proletarian or participatory democracy, as Dickson's reading suggests it can. And secondly, because while it would seem on the evidence of the play that Brecht 'recognised' this fact, to use Lenin's term, the text of *Days of the Commune* does not present the dictatorship of the proletariat in the same *tone* as the Marxist classics.

To elaborate on these points. Marx, once again, concluded in 'The civil war in France', that the Paris Commune showed how the bourgeois state cannot simply be taken over by the proletariat, but must be 'smashed'. Before this view was reiterated and confirmed by Engels and Lenin, it was incorporated by Marx and Engels in their preface to the 1872 edition of the *Communist Manifesto*, a text Brecht had been in the process of versifying, prior to embarking on *Days of the Commune*. Marx and Engels write that the programme of the *Manifesto* 'has in some details become antiquated' and go on,

> One thing especially was proved by the Commune, viz., that 'the working class cannot simply lay hold of the ready-made State machinery and wield it for its own purposes.'[21]

Lenin, noting this addition, concludes that 'The only "correction" Marx thought it necessary to make to the *Communist Manifesto* he made on the basis of the revolutionary experience of the Paris Communards.'[22] In *Days of the Commune* this obviously important tenet is represented by Varlin:

> This situation clearly proves that it is not sufficient simply to take over the machinery of the state. It was never intended to serve our purposes. Therefore we must break it up. The only way we can do that is violently. (p. 63)

So far we might say that Brecht's text is perfectly in line with revolutionary Marxism. Beyond this, the Commune, as I have said, is thought to have demonstrated that the specific political form to replace 'the ready-made state machine' was the dictatorship of the proletariat. Most importantly, in Lenin's view, the transitional period culminating in the '*abolition* of the bourgeoisie' would be 'a period of an unprecedently violent class struggle in unprecedently acute forms.' Consequently the new state 'must inevitably be a state that is democratic *in a new way* (for the proletariat and the propertyless in general) and dictatorial *in a new way* (against the bourgeoisie).'[23] Both Marx and Lenin were deeply impressed by the Commune's achievement in the first respect, described elsewhere as the 'winning of the battle for democracy'. This is where Dickson places the emphasis in his interpretation, and where he suggests Brecht's own emphasis lay. But the dictatorship of the proletariat required more than the replacement of 'the smashed state machine . . . by fuller democracy'. In Lenin's words:

> It is still necessary to suppress the bourgeoisie and crush their resistance. This was particularly necessary for the Commune; and one of the reasons for its defeat was that it did not do this with sufficient determination.[24]

Brecht did not avoid this question: 'This means a dictatorship' says Billioray in reply to Rigault's 'Terror against terror; oppress or you'll be oppressed. Crush or they will crush you.' (p. 74) In fact, the issue of the Commune's use of violence against Thiers' army and bourgeois power provokes the sharpest divisions in the play. The lessons of the Commune in its strengths (that it was 'democratic *in a new way*'), as in its weaknesses and defeat (because it was unsufficiently 'dictatorial *in a new way*'), are consequently equally present in Brecht's text. Against 'Papa's' glimpse of utopia, for example, there is the hesitant accusation of a lack of 'sufficient determination', from the 'women of the 11th District' who feel, 'that the weakness of some members of the Commune is jeopardising our plans for the future.' (p. 71) Varlin then warns, shortly after this, that if the slaughter of the Versailles army continues unopposed 'there will be no New Age. We will be defeated because of our meekness.' (p. 72) And later Langevin recognises that they 'should have marched on Versailles at once on March the 18th', and comments 'What mistakes we're still making.' (p. 80)

Historically and politically a further lesson to be drawn from the Commune's defeat was, in Lenin's terms, the necessity for 'a vanguard of the proletariat, capable of assuming power and *leading the whole people* to socialism, of directing and organising the new system, of being the teacher, the guide, the leader of all the working and exploited people.'[25] The idea of a vanguard party was of course at the heart of Lenin's solution to the vexed question of the relationship between revolutionary intellectuals, workers, and the whole people. In *Days of the Commune*, Varlin, Rigault, Ranvier, Langevin, 'Papa', Geneviève and Jean would be obvious candidates for a Party cadre. But although Brecht's play *allows* for this conclusion, in the sense that one could infer from the play that the lack of an organised vanguard contributed to the Commune's defeat, his text at no point explicitly draws this lesson. Perhaps for one thing because any reference to the Leninist party would have been plainly anachronistic. Perhaps again because it would have been extremely difficult in 1949 to invoke Lenin or the concept of the Party, without also invoking Stalin, when Brecht was more concerned to distance himself from recent forms of the Communist Party. A third and main reason, I believe, is that to have presented a Leninist play, *in the sense of offering an open rationale for the Leninist party*, would have contradicted the pedagogic function of Brecht's theatre. As a latter-day 'learning-play' *Days of the Commune* could encourage, and of course still can encourage, critical thought on the Commune's defeat, without internally endorsing the political judgements that have been made of it. In this way the play can fulfil its own function as an example of a non-propagandist, yet politicising Marxist art.

Nor should this pedagogic intention be any surprise in the context of Brecht's work, or indeed in the context of this play, where the dialectics of political education is a particularly strong motif. Practically every character in fact is involved in this process. The revolutionary Varlin, for example, appeals to the delegates to 'learn from our enemies' (p. 72); Rigault stresses the need to 'learn from' the people, to 'trust the power of the people' (p. 65); and Langevin is ready to learn from 'Papa', coming thus to appreciate the choice between 'bloodstained hands and severed hands.' This he then teaches to Geneviève, who, though from the start opposed to bloodshed, has to accept the necessary murder of her fiancé the traitor Guy. 'We're learning', says Geneviève to François on the barricades, even if it is 'how to go down fighting.' (p. 84) Lastly, in a scene, of which this pedagogic theme forms the intricate backbone, Geneviève, as Delegate for Education, is enjoined by Langevin to 'Learn, teacher' in an exchange with the 'public', represented by Babette and Philippe, who are themselves urged to take collective responsibility, and to think collectively of 'we' not 'you'. 'Next thing we know', jokes Langevin of Philippe, who in the same scene teaches Geneviève to pick a lock, 'he'll be learning the job of governing.' (p. 58)

Brecht's play therefore typically employs dialectics for pedagogic ends, and does this in a way which is thoroughly 'informed' by a Marxist interpretation of history. This is not the same as saying, however, that it is thoroughly Marxist-Leninist. If the test of this is Brecht's view of the 'dictatorship of the proletariat' then the play is more Leninist certainly than Dickson allows. The most significant difference concerns not Brecht's 'utopianism' or his reference to the 'people', or his lack of reference to 'the Party', but his treatment of the question of political violence. The characters listed above as members of a potential proletarian vanguard all see or come to see the need for violence. In contrast to the earlier *The Measures Taken*, however, this is not to be directed at comrades, guilty of ideological or tactical errors, but at 'our enemies': the Generals Lecomte and Thomas, the traitor Guy, and Thiers' army. The communards have to learn from their enemies and to be 'taught by murderers', as Ranvier says, 'In order to exterminate them'. 'We have', says Langevin, 'to wage war better.' (p. 72)

The specific acts of violence in the play, however — against the generals and against Guy — take place in the background, and have a reluctant air. Geneviève faints, for example, after having stoically determined on Guy's death (p. 83); 'Papa' first denies and later only skulkily admits to being present at the shooting of the Generals (pp. 37, 83); and Jean's remarks on the execution are at best off-hand (p. 33). At another level, Varlin sees, as suggested earlier, that the breaking up of the state can only be done 'violently'. (p. 63) But nowhere is there anything like, in Lenin's words, Marx and Engels' 'proud and open proclamation of the inevitability of a violent revolution'.[26] In fact the one textual echo of the Marxist classics here is of a statement by Engels on Dühring, subsequently quoted by Lenin. Engels writes of Dühring that

> it is only with sighs and groans that he admits the possibility that force will perhaps be necessary for the overthrow of an economy based on exploitation — unfortunately, because all use of force demoralises, he says, the person who uses it.[27]

In what looks, therefore, like a deliberate response to the 'panegyric' on violent revolution in Marx, Engels and Lenin, Brecht in his play gives Dühring's attitude to Rigault, immediately after this character has called for 'terror to fight terror'. 'Do you deny', asks Vermorel, 'that violence degrades the aggressor?' and Rigault replies simply, 'No, I do not deny that.' (pp. 74–5)

There is no reason of course for thinking that Rigault's opinion is Brecht's own. But neither is there any counter-statement in the play (from Varlin, or 'Papa', for example) which openly and proudly honours revolutionary violence. On this critical issue, therefore, at this point in the play, we can say there is a departure, or distancing, from the revolutionary Marxist tradition.

Lenin wrote of Marx and Engel's panegyric that 'The necessity of systematically imbuing the masses with *this* and precisely this view of violent revolution lies at the root of the *entire* theory of Marx and Engels.'[28] Brecht's play neither meets this condition, nor approximates to Marx and Engel's tone. Perhaps, after all, Brecht was doing no more than specify the lack of determination of the Commune itself, but if we believe this we cannot account in the same way for his 'playing down' of violence and fanaticism generally in the play. We cannot say that in dealing with aspects essentially of the same theme, Brecht was at one moment being historically accurate and at another moderating historical accounts so as to present his own interpretation and political views. I think he was doing the second, both in Rigault's speech and in his general treatment of violence, and that his treatment of this issue was at the same time perfectly in keeping with his commitment after the violence of World War II to the cause of peace. This commitment, with the form it takes in *Days of the Commune*, helps in its own way to further explain Brecht's continued support of the GDR. As long, that is, as he could believe that this new state had already initiated, or would initiate, a 'workers' state', the question of revolutionary violence needed to introduce it was no longer a priority. Moreover, even if the state's identity was doubtful, and even if it showed no signs of 'withering away', Brecht could give it his support as being still on the side of peace.

The difficulty in reading Brecht's attitudes and his Marxism from *Days of the Commune* as I have done is that a reading of this kind obviously extrapolates from the *internal* evidence of the text. Though it does nothing to solve the riddle of Brecht's position we might also do well, finally, to consider the material circumstance of the play's production; or rather its non-production.

Brecht wrote *Days of the Commune* in 1948–9 as a counter-play to Grieg's *The Defeat* and intended his production to officially open the Berliner Ensemble at the Schiffbauerdamm Theatre in the autumn of 1949. The play was not performed, however, until three months after Brecht's death. Dickson writes that it was 'banned' in 1951, whereas in other accounts it has been described as 'unfinished'.[29] Völker writes that the play 'demanded too much' communism, and was dropped in favour of the comedy *Herr Puntila and His Servant Matti* because it was 'too disruptive politically for the East Germans.' It was, he adds, 'untimely because it portrayed an assumption of power by the lower classes in which the party did not play a leading role.'[30]

My own reading would suggest that *Days of the Commune* does not so much defend lower-class power or oppose determined leadership (the Commune succeeds, but also fails, in the play as in history), as provoke discussion on the political and moral form of that power, on revolutionary method, and the question of leadership. It reiterates the need 'to smash the bourgeois-military state machine', and *redefines* the dictatorship of the proletariat so as to set up expectations of popular democracy, while moderating its 'necessary' but unwelcome and 'degrading' repression of its enemies through force. If this was embarrassing to the East Germans in 1949, it could only have been more so in 1951, or 1953. While it remained unperformed, however, Brecht's pedagogy could come to nothing. We are left to judge a regime which in the act of censoring the play proved itself to be 'unnecessarily' repressive and closed to Marxist debate, and left at the same time to judge Brecht's dealings with it. Did he substitute a comedy for criticism so as to encourage rather than deflate the new Republic? Was the play in his judgement 'untimely'? Was he over-cautious, cowardly, or calculating?

There can be no simple verdict on these matters because Brecht's situation was not a simple one. A materialist criticism which goes in search of the context of Brecht's play finds that the context was emptied of his text. But then this enigmatic speaking silence communicates the very uncertainties, hesitations and disparities at the heart of Brecht's position. There could be no better image of the relation between socialist artist and 'socialist' state than the unperformed text which tested, exposed and outlived the judgement on its 'impermissibility', while its author showed every sign of collaborating in this very censorship.

To suggest that Brecht was silent, however, is too simple. To the textual reality of his unperformed play we have to add his last conversations with Ernst Schumacher and Manfred Wekwerth. To Schumacher, Brecht spoke of the 'spontaneity theory' and the case for a strong Party as still a live issue,[31] while with Wekwerth he talked over, precisely, a number of questions preliminary to the first production of *Days of the Commune*, which Wekwerth then went on to direct in November 1956. In this same conversation he spoke of the instructive use of parable, of naivety as being necessary to the production of *Days of the Commune*, and of both as being exemplified by Lenin. According to Wekwerth, Brecht was also in the habit at this time of referring to his theatre as a 'dialectical theatre.'[32] There was renewed conviction along with caution therefore, simplicity combined with cunning. As to what lay 'behind' it all, Wekwerth reports Brecht as speaking 'with malice of the way in which people attempted to find the common denominator for the lively variety, the innumerable shades, the moving unrest of contradictions and disharmonies'.[33] The common denominator was dialectics: examining, as Wekwerth recalls in his essay, 'the not . . . but'.[34] Only sometimes was this balancing act an act of equivocation.

Notes

1. Keith A. Dickson, *Towards Utopia. A Study of Brecht* (Clarendon Press, Oxford, 1978), pp. 111–12.
2. Ibid. Dickson writes that in *The Defeat*, a play on the Commune by the Norwegian dramatist Nordahl Grieg and to which Brecht's play was a reply, Rigault is shown as 'an almost demonically inspired terrorist' who 'has been compared with Beria and Eichmann as a coolly professional killer,' p. 113.
3. Ibid.
4. Ibid., p. 119.
5. *Karl Marx. The Paris Commune 1871*, edited and introduced by Christopher Hitchens (Sidgwick and Jackson, London, 1971), p. 96. Lenin in quoting this description italicises the last phrase, Lenin, *Collected Works*, vol. 25 (Progress Publishers, Moscow; Lawrence and Wishart, London, 1964), p. 431.
6. Hitchens, *The Paris Commune*, p. 50.
7. Brecht, *The Days of the Commune*, Clive Barker and Arno Reinfrank (trans.) (Eyre Methuen, London, 1978), p. 40. Subsequent page references are given in the text.
8. Hitchens, *The Paris Commune*, p. 93.
9. Quoted, Lenin, *Collected Works*, vol. 25, p. 415.
10. Ibid., p. 416.
11. Ibid., p. 417.
12. Dickson, *Towards Utopia*, p. 111.
13. Marx in a letter to D. Nieuwenhuis, 22 February 1881, quoted in Dickson, ibid., p. 119.
14. Dickson, ibid., p. 123.

15. Hitchens, *The Paris Commune*, pp. 103–4.
16. Lenin, *Collected Works*, vol. 25, p. 462.
17. Ibid., p. 464.
18. Ibid., p. 432.
19. Ibid., p. 412.
20. Dickson, *Towards Utopia*, p. 113–15.
21. Marx and Engels, *Selected Works. In One Volume* (International Publishers, New York, 1968), pp. 31–2.
22. Lenin, *Collected Works*, vol. 25, p. 414.
23. Ibid., p. 412.
24. Ibid., p. 419.
25. Ibid., p. 404..
26. Ibid., p. 400.
27. Engels, quoted, ibid., p. 399.
28. Ibid., p. 400.
29. Dickson, *Towards Utopia*, p. 10; Darko Suvin, *To Brecht and Beyond. Soundings in Modern Dramaturgy* (Harvester Press, Brighton, Sussex, 1984), p. 128.
30. Klaus Völker, *Brecht: A Biography* (Marion Boyars, London and Boston, 1979), p. 335.
31. Ernst Schumacher, 'He will remain', in Hubert Witt (ed.) and John Peet (trans.), *Brecht As They Knew Him* (Seven Sea Books, Berlin; International Publishers, New York, 1974, 1977; Lawrence and Wishart, London, 1974, 1980), p. 221.
32. Manfred Wekwerth, 'Discovering an aesthetic category', in Witt and Peet, ibid., pp. 147, 148.
33. Ibid., p. 143.
34. Ibid., p. 145.

Index

Page references incorporating 'n' refer to notes